SACRED MARRIAGE ASTROLOGY

THE SOUL'S DESIRE FOR WHOLENESS

ADAM GAINSBURG

Cold Tree Press
Nashville, Tennessee

Published by Cold Tree Press
Nashville, Tennessee
www.coldtreepress.com

DEVOTION

This book is devoted to the ancestors, teachers, allies, mentors, friends and colleagues whose guidance has blessed the unfolding of this work with their grace, wisdom, embodiment, courage, laughter and love.

GRATITUDE

Much gratitude is held for those astrologers throughout millennia who have kindled the astrological flame of truth to enlighten the world. We can leap further because of you.

HONORING

The principles of Evolutionary Astrology founded by Jeffrey Wolf Green, Astroshamanism by Franco Santoro, and Shamanic Astrology by Daniel Giamario have been influential in the formation of Sacred Marriage Astrology, along with many other brilliant astrologers, mystics and fools.

ACKNOWLEDGEMENTS

Deep love and gratitude for Aleathe Morrill's intelligence and powerful spirit which guided several parts of the writing process. Annamarie White's invaluable editorial assistance and encouragement provided clarity and cohesiveness. Peter Honsberger's graphic skill and patience allowed the book design to emerge beautifully.

SACRED MARRIAGE ASTROLOGY

Sacred Marriage Astrology illuminates our personal path to life purpose and innate energetic balance. It utilizes proven techniques for interpreting our Soul pattern, identifying karmic tendencies within the pattern, and describing specifically how we are wired to actualize the pattern throughout our lives. It addresses the uniqueness of each individual, couple or group from the level of the Soul, beyond personal identity. Sacred Marriage Astrology is housed in a larger context than biology or psychology, and thus can interpret both from the level of Soul – from the unified space of timelessness, truth, and unconditionality. In addition to the specific techniques of "reading" a chart, it also teaches several non-linear methods for accessing information which are all rooted in a Soul-awareness. These require intuition, connection and trust. Sacred Marriage Astrology empowers our personal alchemy of Soul & Identity and Masculinity & Femininity.

TABLE OF CONTENTS

SACRED MARRIAGE ASTROLOGY

THE SOUL'S DESIRE FOR WHOLENESS

ADAM GAINSBURG

The astrology of the future won't take us further out. It will lead us deeper in.

WELCOME

Greetings! This book intends to introduce Sacred Marriage Astrology to the truth-seeker, the astrology enthusiast, and the Soul-full. It is not 'astrology for dummies' nor is it an exhaustive tome on the full cadre of astrological techniques in use today. It is part astrology book, part consciousness study, and part evocateur. It is a Soul-trigger. It seeks to find a home in your heart. *It can catalyze your Soul-force in the direction of its unique Destiny through the astrological mysteries.*

What is presented in this book may in fact be troublesome to some. It may challenge tried-and-true notions. It may leave things unresolved in the mind. You may discard it after a chapter or two or you may demand a sequel. You may not grasp some of it. Which is fine...wonderful, even. For there may be as much benefit for you *'in between' the words and concepts* as from their literal meaning. I invite you to absorb them on *both* levels. This book is a 'breath-friendly' book... breathing is encouraged and heartfully welcomed!

Many of the chapters were originally individual essays on various topics so there may be inconsistent tones in the writing. This seems appropriate as much of our experience as Earthlings is designed to uncover the deeper threads of unity amidst the cloaks of diversity.

You'll find information on the signs, planets, houses, angles, aspects, nodes, and special focus placed on the relationship of the Soul to Identity, the Moon, Pluto and Chiron symbolisms, and retrogradation. There is also a collection of essays on various topics useful to the study of astrology, a group of quick-reference sheets, and some surprises waiting to be discovered!

Thank you for your interest in Sacred Marriage Astrology. It is a path of unfolding deeply supportive of risk-taking and growth. Your deepest knowing is welcomed here. Should you desire to learn more about SMA, there is a list of in-person workshops, CDs, essays and phone courses at the back of the book.

Visit the web site at: www.SacredMarriageAstrology.com

May All Life receive great and lasting benefit from your overflowing happiness and rediscovery of your purpose.

Capitalization

Throughout this book, capitalized words are used in untraditional ways. Capitalization may be used for a SMA-specific term, such as *Self-Essence*; a non-traditional understanding of an otherwise standard word, such as *Angles*; or a specific context, such as a discussion of *Masculinity*. In addition, the topic of each chapter may appear capitalized, such as is the case in the chapters on Houses, Angles and Aspects. In no way does the use of capitalization in these ways suggest a higher level of importance than non-capitalized words.

CHAPTER 1

UNDERLYING & OVERARCHING PRINCIPLES OF SACRED MARRIAGE ASTROLOGY

THE SOUL-IDENTITY PARTNERSHIP

Sacred Marriage Astrology operates from the following truths:

❧ Our *Self-Essence* or Soul is our timeless, essential nature which is the only consistency throughout incarnations. It is the essential spark of God-light within all creation. The Soul evolves through its incarnational experiences and choices.

❧ Our *Self-Identity* is the self-reflexive structure of individual beingness within incarnational experience. The Identity requires the ego function for its protection and safety, the persona for its interaction socially, the body for its physical mobility and the psyche or body-mind as its means of sensing, processing and comprehending its experience.

❧ At the beginning of a life, the Soul inhabits the Identity, becoming surrounded and interwoven into a context of duality. This produces an abiding inner conflict, which becomes the source of the Identity's conflicting desires and impulses, such as that between the masculine and feminine impulses.

❧ The *Soul's Desire* is always for a greater encompassment of oneness and love in as yet unknown domains. The *Identity's Desire* is always for security and the familiar. These are two very different drives within us.

❧ According to the current instructions of human DNA, the first half of life is geared to introduce and stabilize one's Identity – within itself, its world, and with others. On a more subtle level, this period also sees the initial stabilization of Soul vibration within the Identity 'shell.' The latter period of life is oriented to support the infusion of the Soul-knowing into greater amounts of the Identity's domain. These transformations or shifts of contexts can only occur within incarnation, the dimensional 'home' of the Identity.

➤ Evolution requires change and change upsets the security so crucial to the Identity. Ironically, the evolutionary urges causing upheavals and transformation emanate out of the Soul itself. It is the Identity's need for security and understanding which resists these urges toward change. The transformations we experience are attempts to resolve the natural conflicts between our Soul's Desire and the specific definitions our Identity uses to know itself.

➤ The higher aspiration of all human effort is the *alchemical resolution* of the primal conflict between masculine/feminine, Identity/Essence, and known/unknown.

THE SOUL & ASTROLOGY

A Soul is not bound by time and space. It views incarnational experience and manifest creation only as it can: from its perspective. It will see the possibilities of incarnational experience from its own state of wholeness, as infinitely varied shades or possibilities of light, love, sound or shape. It will not see the distinctions between the sign energies of astrology, for example, because it has no vibrational need of doing so. It will see their differences instead as a variegated unity. To illustrate this idea, when was the last time you picked up a chocolate chip cookie ready to eat but instead of biting into it you carefully broke it apart and divided it into chocolate chips, walnuts, cookie dough, sprinkles, coconut shavings and chocolate frosting? The Soul has no vibrational need to create distinctions in similar ways between facets of consciousness or of cookie innards and then prioritize one over another; it only desires to experience the many distinctive, yet unified qualities of consciousness viscerally as itself (which it is!)

It is from this injunction that a Soul chooses its next incarnation. It is looking to experience itself in new ways which link with how it has previously experienced itself. In this way a picture of a progression of growth forms. SMA is one of a few astrological modalities in which the identification of the Soul's position along its growth track is an essential element of its practice. As the Soul enters a new incarnation, which in SMA is called Self-Identity, it will forget who it is and what it is doing there – its purpose. Gradually through its life, the Soul-infused or Soul-cloaking Identity (whichever you prefer) will experience an increasing amount of qualities of itself, which will emanate from its Soul, which it will receive through the reflections from others and one's environments. These qualities will be deeply meaningful for the Identity, as they represent its own deepest nature: Self-essence or Soul. These types of experiences are subconsciously created and positioned in life to trigger its awakening of its Soul nature at key junctures in life. This is quite similar to the Tibetan Buddhist notion of *termas*, or 'consciousness time-capsules' which were said to be seeded by 'the second Buddha' Padmasambhava, the Lotus Guru, in the 8th century.

In its purest form, astrology is but one tool for identifying the full range of consciousness available to the Soul in its incarnation journey. The working components of astrology, particularly the sign energies, are best utilized as identifiers for Soul uniqueness from within a deep understanding of unity. As equal divisions of our solar system's ecliptic[1], signs are tools to frame conspicuous consciousnesses within our dualistic, time-space reality. What the signs and their progression from Aries to Pisces imply are the higher tools or definers for the Soul's journey within and through incarnations. If each astrological sign is understood in this way – as reflections of total consciousness, or as one component of the universal cookie – then it is illogical to believe that a Soul must begin at Aries and linearly progress to Pisces. The traditional notion that astrology begins at Aries, moves through each sign to end at Pisces is simply the result of observing the heavens and human development from a dualistic paradigm. Understandably, this conception tries to order that which is un-orderable. After all, in our duality, there are such things as beginnings, midpoints and endings, *because there has to be*. Duality itself demands that this be true. But this should not be assumed to be true for other realities, such as the Soul's reality.

Because each human life is ultimately guided by Soul intelligence and its inescapable nature to evolve, the actual progression of a Soul's evolution simply cannot occur unidirectionally. Life indeed must support life. And *incarnational* life supports a Soul life by giving it opportunities to remember itself in ever-expanding and ever–blossoming ways.

"It seems, does it not, that the Great Beginning has once again begun...us."—AG

SMA

Sacred Marriage Astrology was formed as an alternative to mainstream astrology's dependence on Sun-sign, personality-driven interpretation and as a re-invigoration of the deep heart of the sky. Powerfully affirming our Soul-level of being drives its practice. It has been described as 'multi-dimensional,' 'endlessly affirming of the human potential,' 'deeply caring,' and a 'wake-up call to what I always knew, but forgot.' Its principles have been built and arranged not from tired astrological methods, but from an active fascination with every level of the human being itself. Its perspective is that we are the holders of vast mysteries beyond our psychology and behavior, in contrast to the energetic paradigm which current mainstream astrology blindly maintains. It suggests we are innately complete in our design – we are *de facto* 'wired' as our own *alpha* and *omega*.

What you hold in your hand is not a recipe book for relationship, a roadmap to the doorstep of your Soul mate, or a compendium of mytho-logical lovers. It is also not an exhaustive treatise on astrological practices. Far from it. Astrology can *only* change with time, as the recent discovery of two new intra-solar system planets proves without question. Their discovery will change astrology itself; the rate of change being determined by astrologers' levels of resistance to incorporating them into their practice. As humanity evolves, its astrology must follow suit. If it does not, it will devolve into yet another close-hearted system lacking vision and missing the truly beautiful.

For its philosophical and cosmological bases, Sacred Marriage Astrology harkens back to the ancient rites of *hieros gamos* and the origins of alchemy:

▸ That which is known as human has a deeper Essence – which we name Soul – which transcends both its human-ness and its identity bound by time and space;

▸ Within the human being already exists – biologically, electrically and spiritually – the latent potential for its complete transformation of its un-awakened nature;

▸ The Self's experience with an Other on any level reflects the Self's own nature in the deepest ways;

▸ Our destiny as a species is the evolution of both time and matter *through* our incarnational experience; and

▸ The first and only *marriage* ultimately is the unification of self with Self.

Sacred Marriage Astrology implores us to deeply acknowledge that we live in a dualistic reality and that fear, separation, and survival are the initial, direct results of this reality. It also urges the acceptance that all dualistic urges within and without can be resolved within the many layers of the Self's self. We find this modeled in indigenous wisdom traditions for thousands and thousands of years. We can also look to the ancient Hebrew conception of God and Shekhinah as a symbol of the duality-producing-resolution. Or to Shiva and Shakti, or the Mesoamerican Tezcatlipoca and Quetzalcoatl, the Sufi Beloved and Lover, and the Chinese *yin* and *yang*, or the Kabbalistic *Bahir*. We can look at many other dyadic pairs throughout history, including the entire tradition of alchemy. In alchemical understandings, a central idea is that out of the genetic, irrational and cosmic resolution of opposites or cellular conflicts is produced an entirely new, third thing. This 'third' might be described as that which began itself – its primordial beginning – now sitting in realization of its nature.

Sacred Marriage Astrology functions within the general framework of how celestial bodies such as stars, planets and people influence one another. (We may, finally, have reached the point when we have no other choice but to remember ourselves *as* the stars themselves.) It reaches deeper into the bio-electrical, spiritual nature of the human organism and returns with specific, accurate information and images of one's very Soul, that euphemistic level of being which many generalize but few pinpoint with precision. As a syntropic system, Sacred Marriage Astrology is architecturally sparse, with minimal rules dictating its practice. This spaciousness is the very quality which allows it to dream bigger than many others and bring to the client a deeper vision longed for by the Soul. It's the very thing within us inviting the Mystery to speak *to* and *through* us.

Is SMA then a 'system'? It does seem to offer contiguous, conceptual parameters for its practitioner to work from, rather than demanding strict interpretations and pre-approving certain areas of astrological inquiry. But perhaps it isn't. Perhaps it's an *energetic orientation* to Mystery through astrological interpretation. Maybe it's a higher form of *intuitive science*, taking its guidance directly from our divine, essential nature. Or it might be an *art form* of the future, a dynamic, interactive experience of the information itself which lasts and opens the heart to affirm the Soul. Perhaps Sacred Marriage Astrology isn't, in its essence, astrology as normally conceived. Maybe it is something else.

Sacred Marriage Astrology utilizes archetypes and myth in its interpretive work, but avoids over-emphasizing either. As a culture, we need not make the mistake – yet again – of deifying a system, only to later realize we've forfeited – yet again – our sovereign, intuitive power into the hands of that system. Clearly, this is a time of evolving the archetypes and re-empowering the myths themselves through our lives. For haven't we yet learned it is our beliefs that limit us and our open-heartedness that frees us?

"Hieros Gamos"

The phrase 'sacred marriage' derives from the Latin phrase *hieros gamos* mentioned earlier which itself arose from the ancient Greeks' observations of rituals in pre-existing cultures. These rituals saw the King and the Priestess ritually consummate the re-unioning of the Feminine and Masculine principles in creation. There were many expressions of this core idea throughout the animistic and archaic cultures.

In addition to the ritualistic associations, *hieros gamos* suggests that we each possess the ability and, some might say, the responsibility to re-animate creation itself through the way we live our lives. *Hieros gamos* is an act of re-unioning, which has effects not only in this world, but in Heaven as well. Pioneering psychologist and author James Hillman seems to imply this when he says 'Each time I connect to a planet with astrology, it keeps the gods alive.' Through *hieros gamos*, we humans are the creators, like gods, and our lives become our creation. We forge our life according to our preferences. Through *hieros gamos* and the ever-deepening, ever-expanding realization which it produces, we become increasingly aligned to our actual essence – Self-Essence – and decreasingly identified with our incarnational mask – Self-Identity. In the process, we come to ask 'what are we becoming?' Perhaps we need only to look up into a dark sky on a clear night for our answer... we may begin to sense we have more in common with the stars than we do with our human travails. With this knowing comes a re-vivification of our humanity, rather than a dissociated escapism into the sky. Rather than separating us, it congeals us as a star might be congealed: systemically balanced, active *and* receptive, creative, brilliant.

It may be that the pervasive astrology of the future will seek to catalyze *actual* changes of consciousness as its main intention while not excluding its other applications, such as predictive, electional, horary, etc. If this proves true, astrology will need to include a mastery of the mundane and the heavenly, both within and without. We can begin that future now, if we approach *both* our sacred acts and our profane acts with the same honesty, courage and intelligence. For both hold the key for our deeper alignment.

THE TWO DUALITIES: SOUL & IDENTITY AND MASCULINE & FEMININE

The question arises, 'alignment with *what?*' The rationale for SMA's strong focus on the Soul-level of being comes from the idea that *one's own source* should be one's compass in life. And knowing that source should be one's work in life. SMA terms this source 'Self-Essence,' or the deepest layer of one's individual nature which does not source from one's humanity but rather is the source of it. Self-Essence is the essential level of our being animating and guiding all other levels. It is the origin of our identifiable uniqueness. It is our natural intelligence. It has memory. It can learn. But it's housed in a cloak. This cloak, or wrapping, or vehicle, SMA terms Self-Identity. This provides our understanding of humanity's first inner conflict: that between Self-Essence and Self-Identity. If we examine this, we find the Soul's urge – its desire for greater realization of its nature – leads us into unknown places, while the Self-Identity's needs of safety and familiarity strives to keep us in the known.

There is a second conflict or energetic argument not only within us, but in all of life as well, which might be seen as that which is both the first and last obstacle to liberation. It is the encounter between the masculine and feminine urges. The masculine and feminine natures are inextricable from each other. One cannot be separated from the other. Together they are called the Primal Pair. All individual manifestation – subtle or gross – is the result of the Pair's unending 'Conversation' striving for new resolution. The Pair's Dialogue is an endlessly morphing, ecstatic, intensely creative, uber-archetypal engine which produces the necessary raw energy and directional intent for specific components of consciousness to be made known and 'resolved' in awareness (personally and collectively). However, this type of 'resolution' is not concerned with producing an 'answer' to a 'question' or resolving a conflict *per se*. The Dialogue instead seeks to stabilize the components of consciousness being 'discussed' and thereby expand the range of possibility for attaining greater coherence, syntropy, understanding, and harmony. When applied to the Soul, an individual's *Soul's Desire* describes a conspicuous aspect of the Conversation striving for and working towards greater coherence. We humans are thus fated to experience the dual nature of ourselves through the experienced dual nature of our Soul until such time that we have attained an alignment not only between our masculine and feminine urges but also between our Essence and Identity. A tree needs to root as deeply as will support its growth upwards, *and also* to interact with its environment in a mutually supportive balance of give and take. We humans have much the same dual task.

MASCULINITY AND FEMININITY

Let's look closely at the masculine-feminine conflict. Herein, 'Masculine' and 'Feminine' do not refer to gender roles, patriarchies and matriarchies, men and women or ideas of maleness and femaleness. They refer to the two underlying principles within all creation.

Masculinity and Femininity fundamentally exist *beyond our ability to conceive of them*. The following descriptions do not try to define them, but to trigger our inner experience of their qualities.

> *The Masculine principle in creation is the urge to move away from its own source, to penetrate into indefinable spaces, and forever seek. It is chaotic in its absence of pattern. It will disrupt and shatter structure, organization and stagnancy. The Masculine evolves in humanity from additive subjective consciousness into reductive objective consciousness. Masculinity houses the archetype of the individuation impulse, the urge to develop a singular, defining identity. Its experience exists within a context of singularness, and has a natural antipathy toward being consumed, overwhelmed, or homogenized. It is the Masculine that seeds creation to occur through its instigating, fertilizing, energetic nature. The Masculine part of humanity can be individualistic, inconsistent, eruptive, solipsistic, competitive, hierarchical, and alienating, but also progressively idealistic, non-violent, entrepreneurial, visionary, emotionally powerful, detached, and deeply committed through a service-oriented vision.*

Without the masculine, there is no activating principle to ignite life to begin. When we lose touch with our masculine, we lose our Desire; we forget what Desire is.

The feminine principle can be described as the urge to return:

The Feminine principle is the source of the impulse to retract, to return, and to move inward; to dissolve uniqueness into a totality of sameness; to draw all with which it is in relationship into itself. The Feminine is the origin of the cyclic nature of physical existence. The Feminine part of things is so ubiquitous as to be both invisible and unknowable. It is both the source of and the final resting place for the essential vitality of creation. It evolves in humanity from reductive subjective consciousness into additive objective consciousness. The Feminine qualities arise from the archetypal predisposition to relate, to contain and to live/die. Feminine humanity can be jealous, rageful, intensely myopic, parasitic, and threatenable yet fiercely protective. It can also gives rise to the qualities and archetypes of: conceding, harmonizing, accommodating, compassion, receptivity, inclusiveness producing depth insight, essential and unending nurturance, dark balance, and non-differentiation.

Without the Feminine, there is no creation to be ignited and no form to manifest. When we lose touch with the Feminine, we lose our Source; we forget where we come from.

The natural conflict between the Masculine and Feminine impulses reveals itself in the human psyche at the level of our Self-Essence or Soul, within the incarnational realm. Here, we simultaneously desire to move away from our *innerness* to experience ourselves in our *outerness* (or *otherness*) while also desiring to return to our deep innerness to re-source ourselves. What's a Soul to do?

A resolution does exist and it takes as many forms as there are individuals to house the conflict. We can see the harmony of the masculine and feminine urge in the growth of a tree. The tree *requires* its inner conflict to grow: it needs both its deepening roots and its expanding trunk, branch and leaf structure. Only because of the action of both does the tree grow. The same applies to us. We *require* our conflicts in order to evolve. Such is the context of this reality we call Earth-living.

Applied to astrological practice, these notions give space for the necessity of duality within and without all things. Duality – and ego – become something not to be avoided or disdained, but to be deeply examined. The more that duality – and our ego and fear and habitual patterns – can be explored, the less we assume duality to be the only feasible reality paradigm. Likewise, the more the Sacred Marriage Astrologer legitimately honors the necessity of the dualistic paradigm, the more s/he is able to guide others in transcending it for themselves. The astrologer becomes an initiator for the client's Soul-level of being. After all, the Soul only knows itself as this oneness.

NOTES:

[1] The *ecliptic* is the circular band of space created from the mean orbit of our solar system. For a complete explanation of the ecliptic, see chapter 11.

Chapter 2

The Astrological 'Agents'

A good foundation of astrological wisdom must incorporate an understanding of basic celestial dynamics. It is the observable sky dynamics that greatly enhance insight into the psyche. Familiarity with the unique qualities of astral bodies forms a basis for accuracy and effectiveness in prioritization and interpretation.

In SMA, there are two general types of astrological bodies known as *agents*. Each group of agents are general categories and are fundamentally different. Where one is observable, the other is invisible. Where one describes the movements and relationships of physical orbs in space, the other encompasses terrestrial-based confluences of hypothetical points and planes. Therefore, each group of agents describes unique functions within the human psyche. Understanding the differences between them effectively *brings down the sky* for us to illuminate the unique, psychological imprint for our lives. In so doing, we also earn a look at what we are destined to become.

Physical Bodies

In ancient times, the observation that some stars or 'sky lights' actually *moved* while others remained still, birthed the idea-seeds of what we now call astronomy, astrology, religion and later society.

Any planet, asteroid, star or other physical body in space comprise the first category of agent. Astrologically, these are most directly involved with the major and minor *psychological* influences, imprinted at birth and strongly influential at various stages of life (the LifeCycles[1]). Their physicality reveals their influence: they each exist in physical reality which we in ours can identify and point to. This captures astrology in its most basic formulation: the observation and corroboration of *As Without, So Within*. Each body moves in the physical universe in at least two ways – rotation (on its axis) and revolution (around the Sun). These motions create an electromagnetic influence on other bodies, while they are in turn influenced by forces from other bodies nearby (or not so nearby!) Science is now revealing and observing more subtle (and therefore more powerful) energetic influences on physical bodies in space. The photon belt, the galactic super-wave, and 'M' Theory are a few of the contributors to the conception of physical reality as even more complex than ever imagined.

Each planet in astrology (or 'astrological planet') symbolizes one of the twelve astrological signs which operate in us at the level of our psyche. These physical bodies accurately lay out our psychological makeup. They, along with the *aspects*[2], reveal the full dynamic blueprint of our psychological workings[3]. This community of planets, asteroids, and stars reflect for us that we are a social species who relies on social interactions with an Other not only to survive but to thrive. Humans are born, live and die through their interactions at numerous levels and spheres with Other, be they another human, an animal, a different reality, a new environment, an angelic mes-senger, or an altered psychological state. In fact, humanity *requires* Other to actualize its deepest self (Self-Essence)[4]. Humanity needs mirrors.

POINTS OF INTERSECTION

The second category of astrological agents are comprised of mathematically-derived non-physical points which are computed to exist at certain points at certain times. Almost always, this group results from the intersection of orbital paths and the spatial planes they create. They are points of intersection between spatial planes. Yet we should not make the error that these agents cannot affect us simply because they are not physical. It is quite the contrary.

Relative to a human's experience of himself and his life on Earth, the four *Angles* and the *Lunar Nodes* are the most popular in this group.

Angles are the intersections of two of the three main 'hoops' around any point on Earth: the horizon, the local meridian, and the ecliptic. The four Angles are the Ascendant, Descendant, Midheaven and Lowheaven. Angles are determined by the observer's location on the globe of the Earth at a unique point in time. As an example, just as a child is born, look to the Eastern horizon for the child's Rising Sign or Ascendant.

The Lunar Nodes are created from the two points of intersection between the Moon's orbit around Earth and the ecliptical plane, while the other planetary nodes result in much the same way: the orbital path of the planet intersecting with the ecliptical plane.[5]

These agents do not deal directly with psychological influences *per se*, as the first group does. Instead, they address *spheres of potential*. For example, the Ascendant (rising sign) is not addressing the same domain of the psyche as the Mars sign. The sign of natal Mars indicates *how* one is psychologically predisposed to accomplish what one wants, while the sign on the Ascendant describes a much fuller, more mysterious picture: whom you are to realize yourself *as*, distinct from anyone or anything you've known yourself as in the past. All the Angles utilize the individual planetary bodies (agents of the personal psychology) as their fuel to self-realize in the direction of the signs on the Angles[6].

The *Lunar Nodes* signify the full spectrum of karmic and future Identity. In this way, they are defining our Soul-level sphere of Identity potential. While the SouthNode is our past karmic Self-Identity, the NorthNode is our current-life goal of Identity.

The Points of Intersection describe 'that which we are meant to embody and embrace ourselves *as*'. They are intimate and widely relevant pathways into the mysteries of our center. It is useful to look at the philosophic rationale behind these ideas. Because these points are not physical bodies, we can say they represent 'what's not yet manifest' or even 'what may never manifest without our working at the manifest level'. But this does not mean they are unobservable or unattainable. We can observe them *inside of ourselves first*, and then use this intuitively gained information to enrich our observation of our sky and future experiences. In this way, we have the Hermetic principle leading us in the opposite direction: *As Within, So Without*. This is also consistent with the notion that the Angles and the Nodes and *not* the planets in signs are the most unique, individuating and deepest descriptions of who we are as individuals.

The Points of Intersection enlarge the notion of a personal center into a mythic and mystical space. Here the Soul-level conflicts mentioned earlier – the sources of much if not all of an individual's personal unconscious motivations – are resolved. It is important to remind ourselves this resolution is not a technique, a religion, a mantra, a partner or a creative outlet. The deep 'resolution' of our inner conflicts are held in our Center. Working with any one set (all four Angles together, or both Nodes) fortifies our Center as *a dynamic, flexible state of being and awareness* rather than a static condition or a familiar feeling.

There are additionally many other points one can use in interpretive work. While not all of them are technically Points of Intersection, they are not physically existing yet have been demonstrated to varying degrees to point to specific qualities of human nature and motivation. Examples are midpoints, hypothetical planets, and Arabic parts.

THE DANCE TOGETHER

Naturally, every individual has the full potential of both groups of astrological points because each planet, Angle and Node is working *in* them. Actualizing this potential requires moving through levels. We first become aware of ourselves at the most basic level in childhood and adolescence[7]. Eventually, we are challenged with difficult life circumstances. 'A path' of spiritual awareness or authentic self-inquiry then may begin. Fed enough attention, energy and time, we begin to recognize patterns of behavior and thinking that have been with us throughout our lives. Here we are working with the first group of agents – the planetary bodies – because we are addressing ourselves at the level of our psychology.

If we continue in compassion and honesty, we may become aware of what I term *essential conflicts*, those imbedded unconscious beliefs we are wired into which we inherited with our DNA. Examples of these essential conflicts are: *powerful-powerless* and *loved-forsaken*. If for example we are running (and therefore run by) the *powerful-powerless* pattern, we must realize first that this dichotomy is part of who we are in the current life to the degree that our challenges create our strengths and reveal our gifts. We will utilize our psychological understandings – the functioning energies of the planets – to do this. With this understanding and considerably more compassion and honesty – these apparently insurmountable dichotomies eventually reveal their hidden gems through profound discoveries of new opportunities of self-definition, relationships and life purpose! We then utilize the second group of agents – the Points of Intersection such as Angles and Nodes which symbolize the wide open space of our potential – to activate this type of shift. In the *powerful-powerless* example above, we may *unconsciously* believe that we are completely ineffectual in our lives, that we have no true power to create what we want no matter how much money, charisma, or influence we wield (powerless). And, *at the same time(!)*, we also carry the knowing that we *are* the very power without limit which we seek (powerful). This simultaneity is a core understanding of the nature of the human psyche and thus the human dilemma. It is also at the root of any inner sacred marriage.

Only when we have developed the self-understanding represented by the planets, stars and asteroids, can we effectively convert the huge potential stored in the symbols of our personal Points of Intersections into a full evocation of our Soul's Desire.

NOTES:

[1] LifeCycles are the consistent phases of life each human goes through at roughly the same period in life. For example, the first Saturn Return occurs for everyone at 29 years of age, the Venus Return occurs every eight years, the Mars Return at the same, yet irregularly spaced ages of 15, 32, 47, 64, etc.

[2] Aspects are the relationship *between* the physical bodies. Aspects represent the strongest case for humanity's inherently social nature. (See Chapter 8).

[3] Psychology is the name we in western cultures give to the layer of our Being that is the intermediary between the gross realm – the below place, the self that dies, the unconscious, the hidden joys and fears, the survival instincts and the primal brain – and the etheric plane – our vision, our purpose/destiny, angelic messengers, the heavenly mysteries, our ideals, the self that does not die, unity consciousness, cultivated spiritual awareness. It is in the realm of this in-between space that psychology exists and addresses, to be a bridge to something deeper/higher. It is within this realm that the planets, asteroids and stars mirror for us the numerous influences being exerted on us in the depths of our psyche.

[4] This requirement obliquely points to humanity's inherently *expandable* nature as well. Our social nature is first and foremost a primal impulse. It is rooted deep within our primary brain (brain stem) as a means to procreate ourselves. There may be a second, no less important goal of the impulse – to survive through social methods, so apparent in the actions of the leaders of our families, friends, groups, gangs, communities, nations, and alliances. I suggest it is the simultaneous desire to return to the source of our being with a greater consciousness/aware-ness/presence/attention /power/Love than that with which it departed. It is *through* socializing with the myriad world of social *difference* that we realize ourselves and thus re-attain the source of that self. We return to the same octave but not the same

note on the spiral of our evolution. We are expanded through the social interaction with Other. Even those on a path of solitude are labeled hermit, from the Greek, which originally implied a religious motivation for one's reclusiveness. And religion as it is exists in full power, in contrast to what it has been reduced to, is a path of re-union with the mythically real in an engaged, enlivened and God-like manner. There is, in my estimation, nothing *more* social than true religion.

[5] See Chapter 11.

[6] See Chapter 5.

[7] These stages do not necessarily imply an age range. How many 'little boys' are residing in adult male bodies (and the same for 'little girls' in adult women bodies)?

CHAPTER 3

SIGNS, PLANETS & HOUSES IN SMA

SMA sees the sign energy, the planetary function and the house area of life *emanating from the same source* and thus expressing that source. Specifically, a sign expresses Mystery as a 'domain of consciousness energy,' a planet as 'a function of the psyche', and a house as 'an area of life.' So for example, the Gemini/Mercury/3rd House trinity would play out like this: Gemini is that facet of total consciousness which we might describe as Logos, Mercury is the human being's left-brain, cognitive functioning, and the 3rd House is one's education, learning and communication styles and activities. Each of the other 11 trinities follow the same idea.

This orientation to the signs, planets and houses greatly reduces the apparent complexity of learning how signs work with planets, or signs with houses or planets with houses. It doesn't reduce the importance of learning what each sign, planet and house signify; rather it assists our learning of *how they each pragmatically inter-weave with each other.*

SMA teaches that Sign energies infuse into Planets and their innate function. This inner alchemy of a distinct Sign energy infusing or 'characterizing' a Planet's function then manifests or becomes expressed through the specific domain of life signified by the House. For example, if Jupiter is in Virgo in the 11th House, we would interpret this signature by observing how the Virgo consciousness will infuse into the inner, psychological function of Jupiter and then become most prominently expressed in the 11th House area of life.

SIGN ENERGIES

One way of understanding the astrological Signs is to look at 'where' they are in the sky. Contrary to much popular belief, an astrological Sign is not determined by stars in the sky. The stars we see twinkling at us in our night sky are responsible for our *constellations* or star-patterns. It is said that the mythological Greek centaur Chiron was the first to introduce the pre-Sumerians (which we loosely know as the Ur cultures) to the practice of 'connecting the shining dots' to form recognizable patterns in the sky. What we know as Signs today didn't come into full use until the ancient Greek civilization several millennia later. It is a widespread error to equate Signs with constellations: as an example, the constellation of the 'Twins' formed mainly from the stars Castor and Pollux is simply not the same thing as the Sign of Gemini. The same goes for the Ram and Aries, the Bull and Taurus, the Crab and Cancer, and so forth. And perhaps more importantly, the *interpretations* derived from Signs compared to those from constellations emanate from a significantly different level of consciousness, and thus will address different manifestations for human life on Earth. Where the Signs speak directly to actual consciousness – quite separate from our ideas *about* them – the constellational interpretations deal more with *how life manifests in a social or 'knowable' sense.* Thus, constellational interpretation will address political, social, cultural happenings. Sign interpretation will address the actual energies inhabiting those individuals or organizations which choose to act in certain ways. For those interested in exploring star-pattern astrology, known as 'fixed star astrology', I recommend the work of Bernadette Brady.

Each of the twelve Signs is identified from a starting point on the *ecliptic*, and from the constellations in our skies. But first, what is the ecliptic? The ecliptic is the mean path the planets follow around the Sun. A good way to imagine this is to remember that every time we see a planet in our skies – the Sun, the Moon, Mars, Venus, etc. – it is traveling along the ecliptic, which can be said to be an imaginary circle in space around our Sun. The Earth travels the ecliptic just like every other planet in our solar system. There is always one, distinct path that the planets will appear to us to be tracking along in the sky. We will never see a planet anywhere that is not along the ecliptic. Figures 1.1–1.3 offer three views of the ecliptic.

So, where is the starting point and how are Signs divided along the ecliptic? Well, the starting point on the ecliptic is said to be the beginning of the sign of Aries. This is known as the Vernal Equinox, or the moment that the Sun enters Aries in our calendar year. In the northern hemisphere, this is also called Spring Equinox and lands on March 21 usually. With this Equinox, springtime is said to arrive, bringing the growth of new life

Figure 1 - Top view:
Actual planetary orbits

Figure 2 - Side view:
Actual planetary orbits

*Figure 1.1 - 1.3 – Three views of
the our solar system's ecliptic*

Figure 3 - Side view:
Mean orbit = Ecliptic

and the sloughing off of winter's hibernating hidden-ness. In this, the choice of the Vernal Equinox to 'begin' the year is understandable: new growth, new births, new year. Throughout history, many cultures chose the December Solstice and some even the September (or Autumnal or 'anti-Vernal') Equinox to begin the year. And some used both points to begin different calendars which tracked time for different applications.

As to the second question – how are the Signs divided on the ecliptic – the ecliptic is divided equally into twelve sections of 30° of arc or spatial distance for each Sign. This never changes. We can understand this by imagining that we are standing in the middle of a circular room. The circumference of the room – its walls – are divided into 12 equal sections. Each one of these sections is one Sign and the entire circumference of the room is the ecliptic.

Let's apply this image in two different ways, to give you an understanding of the ecliptic from two perspectives. If we imagine that our position in the middle of our circular room is at the center of the solar system, on the surface of the Sun, then the ecliptic can accurately be thought of as the walls of our room, as stated above. But now if we imagine that our position in the middle of the room is the surface of the Earth, then we will need to adjust our view of the ecliptic to be not parallel to the floor, but higher at one point and lower in another, creating a sort of canted circle. This distinction is important because it reminds us that our position of observation determines our spatial reality (if we're on the Sun, the ecliptic will appear to us differently than if we're on Earth), and more specifically because it sets the stage for the next important understanding, the difference between signs and houses. From Earth, the ecliptic is perceived to be tilted because the Earth herself is tilted by 23.5° from 'true' north.

Once again, astrological Signs are nothing more than equal divisions of the ecliptical plane. Our Earthview of the inside of the 'wheel' of the ecliptic is what the ancients termed the *zodiac*. The word 'zodi-ac' traces its roots back to 'a way, a path' (*sodi*), and *not* to 'a circus or grouping of animals' as is *so* popularly thought in much astrological literature. Thus originally the idea that later became our word 'zodiac' was used to demarcate the path that the Sun follows amongst the backdrop of stars of the sky in the course of a year. This precisely points to our notion of the ecliptic's function, but adds the important idea of passing through the star-patterns (constellations). Today when we say 'zodiac' what we are invoking is *both* the idea that the Sun follows its path along the ecliptic and that in the course of its journey it will pass in front of the various star patterns called constellations.

One final explanation that may serve to clarify not only the difference between signs and constellations, but also how each began to be used. What follows is by no means a comprehensive description, but hopefully serves to give you the basic idea of the genesis of today's popular, yet unrecognized error in equating Signs with constellations. The earliest meanings derived from the night sky were based on *stars* and the *patterns* they formed in the minds and imaginations of those early sky-watchers. For them, it was the *star patterns themselves* which might have been called 'the Gods'; it was the star patterns which exuded different energies. Planets were seen to 'move into' and 'move out of' the area of space owned by one of these patterns (constellations). The net result on Earth would be potentially predictable events in the lives of the most important figures in society: kings, queens and state affairs. The main idea for us in this method is that they were utilizing the star patterns to determine which energy the planet was being infused by. And they knew which pattern controlled which part of the sky because the path (eliptic) which planets would move along through their skies would naturally align with certain patterns. In other words, because all the planets in our solar system move along roughly on the same plane, there will be predictable star patterns behind them from our Earthview. This is similar to the image of peeling an apple around in a consistent direction so as to return to the point where we began the peeling process. If we then look at the partially peeled apple, we have a 'track' marked for us all the way around. This track is the ecliptic. And this ecliptic will naturally align with some constellations and not with others.

About 1800 years later, the earliest Greek astrologers introduced a new way to identify which energies were infusing into planets. They detached the planets from the stars in the sky and instead divided the ecliptic into precisely equal sections of 30° each, and assigned each of these new divisions – which we call Signs – the qualities of the star patterns used previously. In other words, the planets were understood to be entering different *Signs* rather than different constellations. Anecdotally, because of this, it is technically incorrect to look up in the sky, see the stars Castor and Pollux and exclaim 'That's Gemini!' In fact, these two stars mark the constellation of *the Twins*. Gemini is a Sign, the Twins is a constellation. The same goes for the rest: the Ram and Aries, the Bull and Taurus, the Crab and Cancer, the Lion and Leo, the Virgin (Priestess) and Virgo, the Scales and Libra, the Scorpion and Scorpio, the Archer and Sagittarius, the Fishgoat or Goatfish and Capricorn, the Water Bearer and Aquarius, and the Fish and Pisces.

In a forthcoming booklet, I will be presenting SMA's view of galactic *precession* ('pre-cessing' or moving backward) and how it applies to the practice of Soul-focused SMA. In short, the phenomena of precession is the result of the *difference between signs and constellations where Signs are seen to 'move' over long periods of time, while constellations remain fixed* resulting in an increasing offset distance between the two. Such is the case currently. In fact, in the near future, we will be seeing the Sign of, say, Cancer overlayed onto the constellation of the Twins, or the Sign of Aquarius overlaying onto the constellation of the Fishgoat. It is precession that is responsible for what we know as 'ages', as in the Age of Aquarius. It is precession that is explained in the Indian *yugas* and Mesoamerican Great Cycle. And it is precession that is at the heart of the Mayan end-date of Fall/Winter 2011 or 2012.

Let's return to more astrological considerations. What is the nature of Signs? Signs are too big to be known directly by man. They are too high in their frequency, too broad in their scope, and thus too transcendent to be known directly. Thus the SMA term, 'domains of consciousness,' attempts to imply a vastness, an entire region of consciousness, or the enigmatic energy of existence. It is the Signs which determine the raw materials of our solar system's evolution. Each Sign obviously contains different sets of qualities within the totality of consciousness, as is evident from a symbolic understanding into the idea that each Sign is located in a *unique position* along the ecliptic. Once these qualities infuse Planets and then express through the Houses, we can identify the Sign energies; they then become knowable to us. When a planet moves from one degree of a sign to the next, there is an energetic, evolutionary progression happening. A Sign's essence will be expressed in unimaginably huge amounts of variation across all dimensions and realities, depending on which planet one is orienting from, one's evolutionary status, and one's evolutionary goals. Once again, Signs are too vast to be known directly; human consciousness (at this stage of its evolution) requires intermediate structures, or vehicles, to know them. And these structures are first astrological Planets and then astrological Houses. Through both Planets and Houses, the Sign energies find a form to express through and be put into use by human effort.

PLANETS

Planets are visible, unlike Signs. They exert and are exerted upon by electromagnetic, gravitational and other types of forces. They exist in physical space and thus are more recognizable and definable. They each have specific physical and energetic properties. From these types of ideas comes a powerful way to understand Planets in an astrological context. In SMA, the term astrological 'Planet' (capitalized) does not refer to the physical body in space, with its physical and orbital characteristics, but to a specific function within the human psyche. We can always remember that a (lowercase 'p') planet's physical body corresponds to a (capitalized 'P') Planet's identifiable function within the human body-mind. Once this is established, we then can examine the physical characteristics of a planet to augment our understanding of a Planet's function within us. For example, Uranus rotates on its side (its north pole is roughly horizontal), which is a highly unique physical characteristic. This points directly to Uranus' function within the human being: that of uniqueness, originality, and unexpectedness. Similar correlations can be discovered for each planet, asteroid and other body used in your astrological practice.

In SMA, a Planet can answer the question 'which aspect of myself am I working with?' The Mercury function is quite different from the Venus function for example. *Planets* are the mini-engines of our capacity to live and operate on many levels, which combine to form the macro-engine of our functional and integral lives. If my Jupiter (that function of my psyche) is in a *catalyzing aspect* from Saturn, then it may very well be that I do not know how to rely on my intuition (for more on catalyzing aspects, please refer to the Chapter 8). This may cause throat problems for me which may then connect to my self-image deficiencies. Planets indicate the inter-related functioning of all levels of the human being.

HOUSES

As previously mentioned, Houses are areas of life in an explicit expression. In most applications, there are twelve Houses. Each represents twelve different domains in which a human will express her/himself. Examples would be: one's family, parents, children, vocation, career, finances, relationships, sexuality, etc. While Houses never correspond to only a few expressions, they each constellate around a few core ideas, which not surprisingly, correlate to the qualities of the 12 Signs and Planets. For example, the 1st House is thought of as how one is carried into and through life in an instinctual way, so one's physical appearance is a 1st House symbol. This in turn is very close in concept to one of the core ideas of astrological Mars (Planet) – a symbol of one's willfulness and self-assertion into life – as well as to that of Aries (Sign), the instinctual drive within consciousness to come into life and engage oneself actively in it. Each of the Sign/Planet/House combinations work in the same way in terms of referencing the same domain of total consciousness through three different expressions. It should be pointed out, though, that some combinations are more closely aligned than others.

House		Element	Mode	Subjective † Development	Objective † Development	Relational † Development	Individual † Developement
1st	M	Fire	Cardinal/ Angular	self-existing	----	----	self-existing
2nd	F	Earth	Fixed/ Succeedent	self-stabilizing	----	----	self-stabilizing
3rd	M	Air	Mutable/ Cadent	self-informing	----	----	self-informing
4th	F	Water	Cardinal/ Angular	self-defining	----	self-defining	----
5th	M	Fire	Fixed/Succeedent	self-expressing/ creating	----	self-expressing/ creating	----
6th	F	Earth	Mutable/ Cadent	self-accuracy	----	self-accuracy	----
7th	M	Air	Cardinal/ Angular	----	self relating with other	self relating with other	----
8th	F	Water	Fixed/ Succeedent	----	self-transforming with other	self-transforming with other	----
9th	M	Fire	Mutable/ Cadent	----	self expanding through other	self expanding through other	----
10th	F	Earth	Cardinal/ Angular	----	self leading other	----	self leading other
11th	M	Air	Fixed/ Succeedent	----	self improving other	----	self improving other
12th	F	Water	Mutable/ Cadent	----	self returning into Other	----	self returning into Other

† Indicates the Hemispheric locations of each house. Hemispheres are discussed in chapter 6.

Table 1 – House qualities comparison

Houses can also be thought of as the *triggers* for certain psychological dynamics, physical expressions, or circumstances to occur. For example, with Neptune conjunct the Moon in the 3rd House, it may be that time spent with one's siblings (3rd House) may trigger greater receptivity to past-life memories (Neptune conjunct Moon).

But actually, what *are* Houses? They are simply twelve areas of space created from a set of geometric and trigonometric rules centered around a specific point on Earth at a specific time. Houses are the result of, among other factors, the rotation of the Earth around its axis. Earth's rotation is of course the cause of our day and night. It is the spinning Earth that also 'creates' astrological Houses. The birth location strongly co-determines (along with the birth time) an individual's natal house divisions. Most basically, houses are created from the 'cardinal directions' of a person's birth location: the extreme east, west, north or up, and south or down positions along the ecliptic. These four cardinal points – east, west, north and south – on an individual's natal chart are known as an individual's personal Angles. The east point is the Ascendant or rising sign, the west point is the Descendant, the north or up position is the Midheaven and the south or down position (through the Earth and out the other side) is the Lowheaven. For more about these, please see chapter 5.

If two people are born at the exact same time on the same day in different parts of the world, then their natal charts will show planets in matching Sign positions (indicating their location on the ecliptic), *but very different house positions*. In Figure 2, both charts show nearly identical *sign*

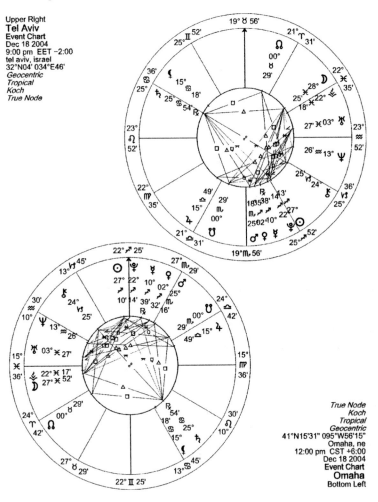

Figure 2 – Same time and day, but different locations (12p Omaha is 9pm Tel Aviv)

positions for most planets, yet the Tel Aviv chart places 10 planets in *different houses* than the Omaha chart. In addition, the House divisions (normally called 'cusps' though this may not be the best term for them) are quite different as well.

HOUSE SYSTEM

There are over 20 different house 'systems' used by astrologers today. Each one is unique in its philosophical and computational bases. How the Angles are computed, the importance of the Angles in calculating house cusps, and which meridian to use (local or prime) are just a few of the many factors involved. It should be clear from this that there is no one 'correct' house system agreed upon by astrologers. This reminds us to follow our intuition about which House system produces the most effective results.

SIGNS & HOUSES

For beginning astrology students or enthusiasts, it can be confusing to wrap the mind around the difference between how planets move through Signs and how they 'move' through Houses. In the simplest way, planets actually move through Signs as they orbit the Sun. But planets technically do not move through Houses; rather, they appear to us on Earth *in* different houses as our view of the sky changes.

The Sign wheel (of twelve 30° sections) and the House wheel (of twelve irregular sections) are independent of each other. While the Sign wheel is determined by the ecliptic, the House wheel is determined by the birth location on Earth. In almost every house system, a point on one wheel can find itself anywhere around the other: a planet in a Sign can be in *any* House and a planet in a House can be in *any* sign.

To review, Signs have as their center the Earth, while Houses have as their center a particular location on the Earth. We can say that Houses describe how the sky appears from any position on Earth as a result of her rotational motion at any moment in time, while Signs are the result of the planets' orbits around the Sun (including Earth).

Let's now look at how planetary movement through Signs is different than through Houses. When a planet moves from, say, 3° Virgo to 4° Virgo, that movement describes *a Sign or zodiacal movement*: the planet has traveled along its orbital path around the Sun by 1° and we as a total planet (Earth) are affected by that movement. But when a planet is positioned *in a House*, that determination does not describe where the planet is in its own orbit, but where and when the planet will be passing through the visible sky above or the invisible sky below our horizon. Thus houses can be seen as Earth-centric views or frames of space. This points back to the idea that Houses are the result of the rotation of the Earth, which creates for us day and night.

⚓ Planets moving through Signs (ie., 3° Virgo to 4° Virgo) signify the process of evolution of consciousness; while

⚓ Planets appearing in Houses signify specific circumstances or areas of life for those evolutionary intentions to be expressed and worked out.

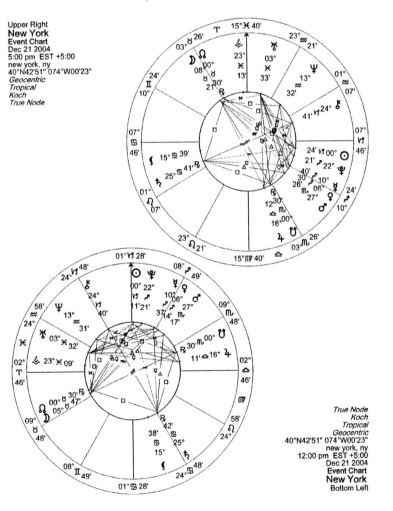

Figure 3 – Same location, day and year, but different times

With some practice, you will come to understand *that normal, forward movement on the astrological chart will produce planets simultaneously moving forward zodiacally through signs (ie., from 3° to 4° of Virgo) and also backwards in terms of houses (ie., from the invisible 1st House to the visible 12th House).*

Let's look at two examples to illustrate the difference in practical terms. If two people are born at the same location on the same day five hours from one another (Figure 3 on the previous page), we know their planets' positions in Signs will be relatively identical, because in merely five hours they will not have traveled far along their orbital path. But their house positions will be quite different because in five hours, the Earth will have rotated through (usually) two houses and be into the third.

If we now change our example to two individuals born at the same

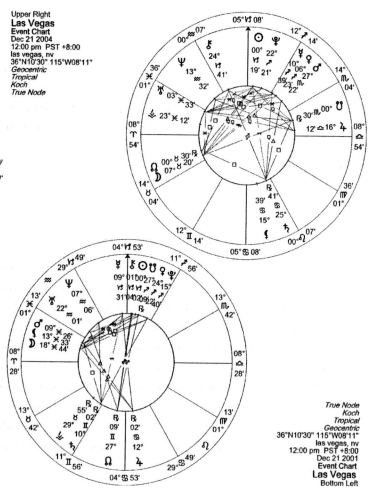

Figure 4 – Same location, day and time, but different year

location on the same day of the year but three years apart from each other (Figure 4), then we know their Houses will be nearly identical, because on the same day in consecutive years, the Sun rises and sets at the same time. Once again, Houses are determined by the rotation of the Earth creating our view of above and our lack of view of below the horizon. This shouldn't confuse you, if you always remember that houses are the result of the rotation of the Earth and not planet's movements in space.

If we comprehend the difference between planetary movement through Signs and 'through' Houses, we can understand that although a planet will always be seen to be moving forward (retrogradation not-withstanding) through a Sign, that planet will also be seen to be moving *backward through the Houses*. For example, if a planet shows up in the 6th House just after sunset, that planet will show up in the 5th house about 2 hours later, and then in the 4th House after that. Again, the *appearance is that the planets are moving backward through the Houses: 6th, then 5th, then 4th*. But the Planet itself is clearly *not* moving backward through a House, it is only appearing to do so because of the rotation of the Earth. The twelve Houses are location- and time-specific lenses or filters of per-ception through which we view up, down, east and west. Change the location on Earth and the House divisions too must change. Change the time of our viewing and they will also change, albeit in different ways and in different proportions.

Let's now apply these ideas to a deeper level of understanding. There are two useful examples I like to use here. One is a kaleidoscope. When we peer through the kaleidoscope aimed at a tree, the particles inside the tube or the tree in the distance remain what we are looking at. The tree itself or the pieces of glass inside the tube do not change shape. But when we rotate the tube in our hands, a new fractalization of the perceived image occurs, creating new, as it were, divisions. This is just like Houses. In the second example, we can think of a House as an ever-changing twelve-faceted clear quartz crystal which we look through to observe the space all around us. Some of the facets will be bigger than others and will refract light differently. If we then rotate the crystal in our hands while continuing to gaze into it, the larger facets will land in different positions, causing different areas of the space around us to be accentuated. This idea of larger facets is analogous to the idea of larger Houses.

THREE HOUSE SYSTEMS IN SMA

In SMA, we utilize three different house systems for various applications: Koch, Whole Sign and Planets on 1st House. Koch is used in a majority of applications, from natal work to transits to progressions. I have come to informally call the Koch system 'terrestrial houses' for it frames our Earth experience. The Whole Sign system is used to unlock certain archetypal patterns within the collective (however we define that for ourselves) which the individual is expressing in their incarnational embodiment. It therefore lends itself well to archetype and mythic considerations. The Whole Sign system literally does not have its feet on the ground (it summarily avoids any accurate pinpointing of house cusps and thus avoids the matter of cusps altogether by equating the first degree of each house with the first degree of the Sign occupying it). In SMA, it is almost never used on its own in natal work and even less so in transit work. It proves itself very useful for refining interpretations of one's higher octave (archetypal) contributions to the collective unfolding. I have come to informally call the Whole Sign system 'galactic houses.' The Planets on 1st House system – placing any planet at the Ascendant position – is used to re-cast an entire chart from within the context of a specific planet's position. This illuminates one planet's function within the psyche and how every other planet or point supports or challenges that function. It works well for contextualizing the entire chart around one planet as the center-pole. All others are thus seen in relation to it.

SIGNS INTO PLANETS, INTO HOUSES

To integrate each basic component – Signs, Planets and Houses – into an understandable flow is to birth within us the magic of astrology.

First let's discuss one method for understanding how a Sign, which as we've seen is 1/12 of the ecliptic wheel, actually enters a House, or is rendered knowable within phenomena. The traditional way astrologers refer to the beginning or ending of a House is as its *cusp*. A House's cusps are normally the divisions between the Houses, where one ends and the next begins. This shift from one House to the next indicates an energetic opening or portal in the psyche. House cusps specifically open a new domain of expressed life to begin. House cusps are the channels or entry/exit points through which the Sign energies 'enter' a house. Signs require this because they are un-manifest on their own. They are only 'made effective' in the spatial, environmental, and knowable domain signified by the House. Without the Houses, Signs remain unmanifest.

A Sign, at the House's cusp, will initiate or infuse that House. When one Sign ends and the next begin within a House, that transition also characterizes the energy of a House. For example, if Sagittarius becomes Capricorn at some point within the 5th House, then that House will incorporate both energies and also their transition energy. There are two ways to determine which Sign is dominant or most-influential of a House's character. We can look to the Sign that begins the House – the Sign 'on' the House – or we can determine which Sign owns more of a House's real estate. Identifying the Sign energies associated with (infusing into) a House is very useful, *even if there are no planets in that House.* This is because the Sign on each House indicates an individual's *projection* onto others of how s/he feels others should express their House's domain. For example, Libra on the 3rd House will reflect an individual who naturally assumes that others *should* listen well, communicate clearly, not offend, and take interest in others. Yet when this individual meets Sagittarius on the 3rd House, they will not have their expectations met. (Each House description in chapter 4 includes its area for projecting onto or assuming about others in this way.)

I teach two different ways to structure one's interpretation of an astrological signature (such as a Planet in a Sign and House). The one which seems to be the more popular with students begins with the planet. In this method, first identify the function of the planet by recalling both the left- and right-brain information about it... in other words, the data about and the feeling of it. Let's take as an example Venus. Venus is our feminine nature, how we root in the world, how we manage our money, the quality of our ability to receive from others (or Other) and our sensuality (among many other things too!) Once we've recalled for ourselves the meanings symbolized in the Planet Venus, then turn to the Sign it is in. Perhaps our Venus is in Capricorn. Recall your knowing of Capricorn, which might produce the associations with leadership, social position, responsibility, wisdom, career, and organizing groups. Next, consider how 'Capricorn would infuse into Venus (Venus as a function within the human psyche).' How might this look or feel? If Venus has much to do with our interior (feminine nature) and Capricorn has much to do with one's position within a social context of some kind, then Venus in Capricorn may express as someone with a strong proclivity to take responsibility for the group. This is but one interpretation. There are many, many more valid possibilities.

The last step is to then place that Capricorn-infused-Venus *into* its House. Let's say ours is in the 7th House, which is the area of life (House) containing one's relationships of all kinds and how one learns about oneself

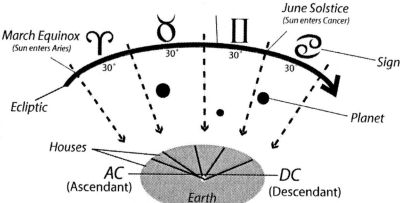

Figure 5 – Signs (Aries, Taurus, Gemini, Cancer) infusing into Planets (three black circles) being seen from within the Houses on Earth.

through those interactions. First, feel this. The 7th House is realistically about our exposure and learning about Other. When we place our Venus in Capricorn into the 7th House, we see that we might find ourselves being drawn to positions of leadership or responsibility through which we come to form friendships and contacts with all kinds of people. In other words, our self-stabilizing ability (Venus) will grow stronger from any positions of authority (Capricorn) which we accept, and this will directly occur through and be supported by our experiences of engaging with people of very different political, religious, or social backgrounds (7th House).

Let's now re-interpret the above example (Venus in Capricorn in the 7th House) from the Houses-as-*trigger* (of experience), rather than House-as-environment (for experience to occur in). As mentioned above, we may have discovered that we have a natural leadership ability, that we take on responsibility well, effectively administer it, and are known as 'pragmatic' or grounded by others (Capricorn). But in other times we may also have intentionally avoided interacting with certain people or certain businesses because we were rubbed the wrong way by them (7th House). We may thus come to discover that our ill feelings about some people will *trigger* or *cata-lyze* our doubts about our ability to manage our affairs, which is so crucial to our self-stability (Venus). Our past pattern of avoidance is then revealed at a deeper level: we've avoided people and situations which we could *not* manage in order to perpetuate a self-image that we can effectively manage our life. Thus, the 7th House exposure to others will trigger us to strengthen our abilities by illuminating a weakness. This exposure can be triggered by natal strategies and/or by transit cycles of various kinds.

CHAPTER 4

SIGN-PLANET-HOUSE MEANINGS

In SMA, it is seen that signs, planets and houses emanate from the same core Mystery and thus can be understood to be similar.[1] Where signs are domains of consciousness, planets are innate functions of the human organism, and houses are areas of expressed life. This understanding gives the astrological student a way to understand the complete cycle of consciousness development on three different planes: Aries to Pisces describes consciousness itself prior to expression, the Sun to Pluto (or beyond!) describes a complete picture of the cosmically-attuned human being, and 1st House to 12th House provides for every possible area of one's life (creativity, career, relationship, etc.)

The notion that a sign, planet and house share the same origin should not be taken to mean *that the manner in which* each sign, planet and house will relate with another will be the same. The distinctions will naturally arise from the nature of that facet of consciousness. Thus how femininity will express through Venus in relation to Taurus is not homologous to how *logos* will emanate through Mercury in relation to Gemini. Those signs of a watery nature will naturally tie more to operations within the subconscious while air energies will reflect those of the mind. Those of a fiery nature will tend to be instinctual, intuitive and excitable, while more earthy tones will revolve around degrees of stability and definition.

Clearly, astrology as we know it is in need of a re-invigoration of the original mystery teachings which seeded it thousands of years ago.[2] We can see this in the popularity of superficial, personality-driven Sun-sign astrology. But to make a shift like this requires going beyond the comfort of the ego-based mind with its need to define and label in order to remain in the *known*, and into the deeper *unknown* with courage and intelligence. And it asks for a quantum leap of trust in ourselves and in life.

This chapter is devoted to illuminating how consciousness itself evolves through the *signs*, how we humans are electro-biologically wired with each *planetary* energy in our perfect and right proportion (for our growth goals), and how each *house* or area of our life (work, family, relationships, etc.) might see consistent expressions of these energies manifest before our eyes. And from the level of Soul, it presents a way to understand each stage of consciousness the Soul will encounter (Signs), each cloak or Identity the Soul will use as its vehicle while in incarnation (Planets), and each sphere of expression the Soul will experience itself through (Houses).

If this is your first astrology study, I encourage you to read and understand as much of what follows as you can. It is written in order to activate understanding, rather than to relate data. If however this is not your first investigation into astrological Signs, Planets and Houses, then I invite and encourage you to approach this information with an energetically open mind and heart. See what might want to be resolved, what might want to be changed, or what might simply want to be glossed over!

NOTES:

[1] However, mainstream astrology is grossly oriented in the *other* direction in its practical applications across the globe; that is, it seeks to dissect, classify, categorize and intellectually box up the innumerable expressions of unity it finds within and without itself. This is because it has simply lost the underlying intelligence or love or knowing of the essential nature of being, which in SMA is named Soul or Self-Essence. It is one chocolate chip within a larger cookie looking around and seeing everything it shares the space with as different than itself; it has forgotten that in the deepest way, it is first and foremost one component of the unifying cookie.

[2] We no longer need to break apart inherent wholeness just to be able to wrap our minds around another of life's mysteries. We are inevitably forced into reducing the mystery to fit our boxes, as we've now proven to ourselves for thousands of years. The distinctions between signs, planets, houses, aspects, and all other components of astrology need to be re-framed in order to cellularly support each Soul to awaken to its own uniqueness within a

heart of oneness. Astrology should be returned to its proper function: a mysterious telling of mysterious things evoking our own mysteries and celebrated in full mystery-drenched regalia!

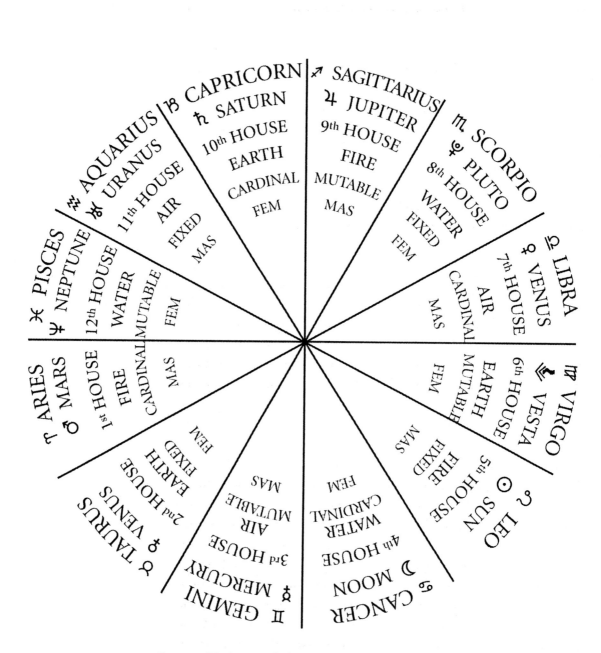

Figure 1 - The 'master wheel' correlating signs, planet, houses, elements, modalities, magnetic polarities and glyphs.

"Be the future you now." – Bashar

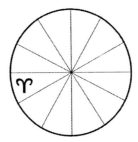

♈ ARIES

MASCULINE – CARDINAL – FIRE

Engaging in life experience to discover authentic Desire.

Why is Aries seen to begin the Journey through the Wheel of Consciousness? Aries is the initial, automatic, instinctual move outward, away from the past and the known, in order to individuate its Self within existence. Aries correlates to the Masculine urge within consciousness.

Just as the child emanates out from the womb of the mother, Aries emanates out of Pisces, the state of unified, undifferentiated consciousness. It is the first move *into* life, or the first subjective consciousness of one's existence. But Aries isn't necessarily conscious of what it does. Its quality of self-awareness is closer to the idea of *pre-consciousness*. We might think of Aries as *the urge to subjectify*. Aries correlates to all aspects of us that determine our basic uniquenesses, but not those we have developed in a deliberate way. Aries domains would be the uniqueness of one's physical shape, one's face, and one's body in a general way. These are all beyond our control, as if they occur *'to us'* to give us our shape. Our born physical characteristics are one of the most instinctually-derived domains of our subjective nature. They define us, even beyond the bounds of our choice of them. This does not mean however that Aries is deeply *aware* of its physicality. It is more that Aries is *discovering* its physicality, as a child would. Aries people often have a difficult time being fully in their bodies in a conscious way though they may be quite athletic and enjoy sports very much. Through Aries is the possibility of one's body being a focus of conditioning, strength-training or refinement, but also a target of one's unconscious or imbalanced behaviors of denial or excess such as pushing one's physical limits without consciousness. In this light, Aries can be associated with the amount of pain the body can withstand in the pursuit of competition.

Aries encompasses the *primal urge* within all creation to live, to come into life, and to engage, invest and embrace life and one's ability to experience basic aliveness. It is the Soul's first subjective consciousness that 'I exist.' And what does this impulsive nature require? Lots of energy invested toward *maintaining* that existence. This perhaps explains many of Aries' expressed qualities: aggressive, go-getter, brash, impatient, and uninterested in a closer look, deeper meanings, or another's experience.

Aries is pre-cursory to a deeper self-consciousness or sentience. On its own, Aries is incapable of and quite uninterested in accessing its deeper experience initially, as its duties are to experience its aliveness in its own way. Aries will gravitate toward (or demand) plenty of room to explore and to experience this thing called existence, or its own life.

Human-embodied Aries consciousness is streaming, impulsive action and thought in an automatic, natural and instinctual manner. There is an inner resourcefulness, a courageousness, a tremendous willfulness or commitment, and an instinctual self-reliance in Aries that will be seen by others as either charismatic and attractive or immature and childish. However others may perceive Aries, it needs to be this way because it alone is responsible for kicking off the entire Journey around the Wheel of Conciousness.

As the first move within consciousness away from the womb-like Pisces, Aries consciousness will necessarily include a separation anxiety. This will be expressed as a strong urge to remain constantly active, in motion, always thinking, always progressing toward some goal, in order to allay the fear of abandonment. As an archetype, this is an attempt to continually 'do something with' its strong and demanding cellular imperative to forever come into life, to activate itself, engage itself, and *to viscerally experience being alive in each moment.*

Because of its inherently unpredictable and unbalanced expression, Aries has a reputation of being immature, 'like a child', and often competitive or combative. But we mustn't make the mistake of relegating Aries exclusively to the archetype of the misbehaving child. As an intended goal of realization, Aries can serve to teach strength, courage, persistence and focus, which may represent a high attainment of consciousness for a particular Soul.

In adults, Aries can produce a natural type of animal magnetism quite attractive to others (Scorpio is another) in light of its total focus on viscerally engaged experience.

ARIES POLARITY: LIBRA

To balance and thus to evolve, Aries is required to draw on the Libran 'focus on Other.' An authentic interest in another person's reality, opinions and needs can often be the most difficult attainment for the Aries individual because it psychologically symbolizes the loss of self, or the negating of the subjective context so crucial to Aries consciousness. Yet those Aries who do find themselves following their innocent interest in others – even through the fear that they will be slowed down and thus be rendered weak or vulnerable – will uncover new domains of themselves attainable only through this expression of the sacred marriage, or union of opposites.

ARIES SHADOW

Quick to anger and violence; frenetic; impatient; uncaring or uninterested in others; myopic; energetically un-balanceable; immature; dominating; demanding; brash; reactionary; shallow; bossy; fickle; violent; unpredictable; stubborn; overly competitive.

ARIES SELF-REALIZATION

Aries self-realization occurs through a complete and total immersion in its task, action, movement, goal, effort, competitive battle, game, strategizing. In its complete engagement, all aspects of the Aries self-ness align, working together, focused on the goal, like a perfectly tuned athlete. Aries self-realization occurs when there are no doubts, no 'individual' or 'separated' components of the personality within the activity, when there is the complete focused integration of all one's 'bodies' toward a specific goal or effort. Within Aries, this unification brings about a non-dual state of being, transcending the small self and its needs.

♂ MARS

NOTE: Mars and Venus are the symbols of the Masculine and Feminine impulses within consciousness. That they are the 'first' two planets in the archetypal development of consciousness points to their primacy in that process.

On the level of the Soul, Mars symbolizes how we are wired to act on, express and realize our Soul's Desire (the Soul's intent for its own evolution) in life. Within our psyche, Mars is our Masculine impulse – the primal impulse within us to come out, to actively engage in life, to individuate ourselves, to assert ourselves – our inner, divine masculine nature. Mars signifies how we assert ourselves willfully in the world, how we move toward what we want. As with the sign Aries within consciousness, the planet Mars within the psyche reveals how spiritual energy manifests into matter through us. Mars contributes to understanding our pattern of anger, impatience, aggressiveness, competitiveness, as well as our desires.

1ST HOUSE

The 1st House symbolizes our intentional and automatic efforts at individualizing ourselves: our subjective discovery of being; our self-hood; our automatic or 'given' individualities: our face, head, and how we energetically assert ourselves in the world (less of our physical appearance *per se*); our independent, sovereign freedom; our raw existence; the instinctual domain of our behaviors and psychology; our anger pattern; our self-assertion style and domain; and our upbringing and how we energetically carry ourselves in a physical body throughout life.

"What the...1st House actually represents is the area of life which sees the expression of] *the original impulse of the original being*, or we might say, the self as a particular vibration and rhythm, and the unique destiny of the individual ever so little different from all other individuals. This impulse has to acquire substantial material around it in order to exist as a truly functioning human being."[1]

The signs of the 1st House signify our orientation to our most basic individuality and how we assert ourselves in the world. They will thus reflect how we project or assume others should assert themselves. For more information, see 'Ascendant' in Chapter 5.

NOTES:

[1] Dane Rudhyar, *The Astrological Houses*, 1972.

"You can have anything you want if you give up the belief
that you don't have it." – Robert Anthony

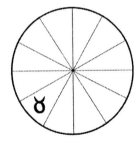

♉ TAURUS

FEMININE – FIXED – EARTH

Embracing physicality as inwardly and outwardly supportable and self-sustaining.
Stabilizing within oneself.

After Aries, consciousness will next seek to balance itself within its environment in order to ensure that its existence continues, just like the body of a developing child grows bigger and more substantial to ensure its survival. In Taurus, consciousness needs to *feel itself as a physical being in a physical world*. Incarnation happens within physicality, so a sustained physical existence is necessary for the Soul to meet it evolutionary purpose. Coming from Aries, consciousness here learns how to survive within physicality *instinctually*[1]. In order to do this, it must learn to *identify* what it needs (transform instinct into awareness), and then learn *how to obtain* those things (effective management of all resources, both inner and outer). Whatever Taurus consciousness identifies as a need will create its survival reality.[2] And these core needs in turn define its values and value system which then produces its core beliefs. The psychological domain Taurus occupies thus is deeply rooted in one's survival *instincts*.

These will include everything that plays a part in how one physically orients to life, including one's procreative instincts: sexual values, desires and needs. Our sexual instincts emanate from our survival needs as well as the species-level imperative to continue its existence. This creates the need to have a very immediate bond, again instinctually, with one's body, because one's body is the most immediately accessible resource for survival and thus the personal vehicle for our necessary participation in physicality. Taurus is the sign most associated with the sensuality of one's body. In this participation – for example the need to find food and water – we become aware of our physical environment and those others who play a part in our interaction with it.

As we embody our own physicality, we successfully interact with the larger physical world. We ground in the physical experience, a clear Taurus reference. This produces various characteristics and tendencies. We tend not to bond with those others of different value systems or beliefs because we are striving to stabilize our own. It is natural for Taurus to want to be with others of similar value. As our embodiment deepens, we come to see anything of beauty or of value as particularly attractive because, in the externalized beauty or value, we are (desiring to be) seeing ourselves as something beautiful and of value. We also become very good at managing our resources – both gross and subtle. In so doing we progress toward *exteriorizing our individuality* – which was begun in Aries. In other words, through the Taurean need to survive and thus to support our evolution, we are supported; through our impulse to build and form ourselves in the physical world, we ourselves are built and formed. Here in Taurus, we 'realize what we are by using what we have'[3] through the right use of and relationship with matter.

Taurus/2nd House is also the place where we enjoy physicality the most through all the senses. We are enriched by our deep exploration of the sensate experience. Beautiful images, fragrant aromas, wonderful music, sumptuous foods, and physical pleasures draw us. We explore (or we might say descend into) enjoying and balancing matter and our physical experience. We learn to manage our money and care for our home and body, for example. We learn to *enjoy* our environment because enjoyment signals an acceptance, a presence and a resilient stability within.

> *"...for that called Body is a portion of the Soul discerned by the five senses."*
> – William Blake

Once we are cognizant of what our physical and emotional needs are, we then begin to develop the ability to *acquire* those things for ourselves and *receive* those things from others. To receive means to acknowledge the 'other' though the acknowledgment is still quite pre-conscious, just as in Aries it is the self which is acknowledged in more of an instinctual, pre-conscious manner.

In Taurus, the 'other' appears on our radar screen only in the context of *what we need*. Experiences of or with 'other' remain instinctually subjective.

We choose our close relations to reflect and support our own developing ability to stabilize ourselves.

If Aries uses Earth to instinctually engage in its own Fire, then Taurus uses Earth to instinctually stabilize in its own Earth.

POLARITY: SCORPIO

Scorpio symbolizes others' possessions, and interactions with others to reveal/get to the truth of what motivates them, in order to reveal one's own limiting ideas or realities around survival and interaction with the outer environment. If Scorpio produces the need to go deep into others' motivations and thereby understand oneself, then Taurus is the instinct to identify one's needs in order to understand self-within-the-environment. So, Taurus needs to pull on or draw from its polarity in order to recognize how it is myopically limiting its ability to in fact stabilize itself.

SHADOW

Stubbornness; intractability; gluttony; lethargic; lustful; passive; possessing; 'bull'-headed; greedy; uncommunicative; selfish; insensitive; over-reliance on someone or something to fulfill one's own needs; denial of the reality that we cannot do everything for ourselves; addiction to a survival-based reality.

SELF-REALIZATION

When Taurus transforms its instinctuality into consciousness, a magical alignment between self and perceived environment happens. The self finds itself *everywhere* – in every cell, in every space, in each of its interactions with 'other'. The outer environment transforms into the inner environment. Indeed, the self numinously inhabits all of itself, producing a blissful groundedness which is rooted in an unshakeable self-reliance.

♀ VENUS

Venus[4] is the primary symbol of the Feminine principle in creation. *In context of its connection with Taurus,* Venus represents the instinctual, lustful, sensual, tantric, resourceful, wild, rageful, brash, impetuous, surviving, and Earth-goddess Feminine. This can express as the Tantrika and the Daka/Dakini, the epicurean, the esthete. The sign/house/aspects of Venus symbolize our inner goddess; for a woman, this is her femininity, for a man, this is his feminine nature and the inner sacred partner to his masculine. In ancient Sumeria as well as in Mithraism, the goddess Inanna (or Queen) was portrayed with scorpion-men attendants (Scorpio is the polarity energy to Taurus). The Taurus Feminine surrounded by her Scorpio polarity servants symbolize that she is in the appropriate balance with her polarity – not denying or being consumed by it – and thus they are her 'servants' rather than wrathful deities overpowering her. Venus can correlate to the Empress in the Tarot. Venus signifies how we receive, our relationship to relationships[5], to money, to intimacy, and our comfort in 'being' (rather than Mars' 'doing').

The actual name Venus has an interesting history: "The name 'Venus' comes from the Latin 'venustus,' which means graceful. This ancient Italian goddess was seen as the growth and beauty inherent in nature's bounty and spring's rejuvenation. She was worshipped in Rome where Julius Caesar claimed to be her direct descendant.... [Venus] is related to the goddess Charis (charity) who was the Greek goddess of grace and embodied the concept of human love."[6] In her Taurus aspects, she is closely aligned to the goddess Aphrodite as well, who is a master of self-stability in her beautiful physicality and desire to gaze at her reflection in mirrors and in water.

2ND HOUSE

The 2nd House expresses (one-half of) our Feminine-impulse activities (the other half coming from the 7th House): our income, our stability in the world; our resources for living; our values; our sensuality/sexuality; our ability to receive; our relationship with our finances; our familiarity and comfort with our physical environments.

The 2nd House symbolizes where the self uses what it finds available within and without itself in order to exteriorize and thus stabilize itself. Its inner resources are its survival instincts, level of receptivity, intelligence, and its values, while its body, physical possessions, money, and attractiveness are its outer resources.

The signs of the 2nd House signify our orientation to physical life: how we interact with it, how we stabilize within it, etc. They will thus reflect how we project or assume others should interact with and stabilize in their environment.

NOTES:

[1] The first quadrant of signs – from Aries to Gemini – symbolizes three different *instinctual* modes of discovery of the self. See Chapter 6 for more about these hemispheres and quadrants.

[2] In fact, the 'root chakra' of one's entire reality is symbolized ultimately by Aries, Taurus *and* Gemini. From this view, the remaining signs seek to alternately strengthen, develop, transform and evolve one's reality eventually to fully align with one's Self-Essence.

[3] From Rudhyar's *The Astrological Houses.*

[4] Mars and Venus as the symbols of the Masculine and Feminine impulses are the 'first two planets' in the evolution of consciousness. This points to their primacy in that process.

[5] There is a very interesting aspectual relationship between Taurus and Libra, the two signs 'ruled' by Venus. For information on this relationship, please see note 2 in the section describing Libra.

[6] Reprinted with permission from the author, astrologer Julie Gillentine. The full description originally appeared in *Atlantis Rising,* Vol. 48, October 2004.

"My joy is to convey the urgency of beauty." – David Hayward

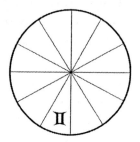

♊ GEMINI

MASCULINE – MUTABLE – AIR

Developing left-brain function to successfully participate in physical existence. Exploring duality.

The instinctual relationship of one's physicality with one's physical environment (Taurus) here is explored *cognitively* by a strong impulse to *learn about that environment.* Like the child beginning to identify objects and people in its environment, Gemini introduces a drive to identify and learn as much as one can about the world one operates in – systems, rules, people, nature, etc. In the ability to *know* its outer environment, the Soul here takes the next step toward securing itself emotionally and mentally. Its increasing familiarity with its environment later crystallizes as a highly-developed awareness of the *inter-relatedness of all things.*

Gemini moves quickly because the mind moves quickly. The normal notion of 'mind' – jumping from thought to thought, constantly categorizing and deducing, and difficult to tame – is very close to a basic understanding of Gemini. Quickened speech, speed-reading, and a fast learning ability are Gemini qualities. Gemini instinctually prefers to move at or near the speed of thought, once again because it is through the mind function that Gemini evolves. The mind is its 'home turf.' In a sense, an individual's initial learning of Gemini will require s/he learn how to balance the consistent need to 'keep up with the mind.'

It may not be surprising to learn that the ability to 'remain in cognitive movement' is perhaps the core goal of the Gemini ego identity. Ways of learning, understanding and communicating differ with each Gemini/Mercury/3rd House combination. If these archetypes are emphasized on the birth chart, then the Identity will depend on its cognitive processes for emotional (ego) safety. In other words, the Gemini Identity is predicated on its ability to understand its world: to the Gemini Identity, the world as it appears to the mind *is* its Identity in a deep way. Gemini is thus the domain of feeling trapped by non-understanding or ignorance.

Because this stage of consciousness development requires the mind to be developed, it will focus on that which the mind can identify; namely, *phenomena* (see Glossary). That which the mind cannot perceive directly and thus not identify or classify will not be of interest.

Gemini learning happens quickly, and it just as quickly moves on to the next piece of data. It does not necessarily connect personally with *what* it is learning. In another way of saying, though incessantly focused on the outer world of matter, Gemini does not necessarily focus on *its place within that world*. As Aries and Taurus before it, Gemini orients to the world instinctually; together, these three signs form the quadrant of "Discovering Self" (see chapter 6). It is very difficult for Gemini to discover its deep emotional or feeling experience if not forced to by challenges to or breaks in its ego identity. The Gemini depth will surface into awareness instead through its great capacity to understand or cognitively absorb the infinite complexity of the *inter-relatedness* of life as it appears (phenomena)... when *logos* reveals itself.

The Mutable Air of Gemini is not only quick-minded, it is also quick-tongued. Verbal, visual, and sonic communication is under the domain of Gemini because the Soul is here required – along with its desire for data, details and whatever is new on the scene – to learn how to *interact with* the environment, the source of those data and details. Gemini serves its purpose as an intermediary for meaning through its strength of communication and fluency with language. Communication is an archetype of bridging or connecting. When something – an idea, an emotion, or an image – is communicated between two, it is as if it crosses a threshold between the invisible and visible realms. It is brought out from within and presented to another, at which point the dynamic inverses. The receiver then takes into itself what is offered, thereby re-locating the communicated into an entirely different world. When framed like this, communication is truly a 'bridging of worlds.'

As modes of communication[1], the first three sign energies develop the Identity's capacity *to communicate with life in the most basic ways*: Aries communicates what one experiences; Taurus what one needs; and Gemini what one understands. To understand is to have successfully integrated thought energy into one's reality frame. The frame is either strengthened or challenged to change because of the introduction of the new energy. It is a question of relatedness at the level of thought-energy. In the physical body, Gemini corresponds specifically to the left-brain function – where new data is received, processed and communicated – and obliquely to the general function of the nervous system – which includes the brain, spinal cord and peripheral nerves – to be the body's intra-communication network.

As an archetype, duality itself is a Gemini sphere. Inevitable to any Gemini-influenced life will be the exploring of all manners of opposites, complements, dyads, trios, partners, friends, enemies, comrades and friends. In essence, the entire range of expressed difference.[2] It will seek out greater levels of *distinctions* between things in order to understand them further. It will revel in details, minutiae, order, and relatedness. Any industry, career, or area of life which needs constant updating – such as the computer software industry, the stock market, and 'modern' medicine – is a flame for the Gemini moth.

It is Gemini's fascination with duality itself that produces our understanding that alchemy itself is a Gemini expression. True alchemy requires knowledge of dissimilars in order to create the *third*. Alchemy intends to merge opposites to create a higher form than either of its two components express.

Gemini is the last step in the completion of the DISCOVERY OF SELF quadrant, and it is a mutable sign. Thus, we see cognition- and communication-developing Gemini paves the way for the arising of self-consciousness to come (in Cancer). In Gemini, how much one knows and how one demonstrates that is assumed to be who/what one is. And rightfully, richly so!

GEMINI POLARITY: SAGITTARIUS

Where Gemini is the search for *knowledge*, Sagittarius is the search for *wisdom*. Where Gemini focuses on the intellectual identification of its immediate environment, Sagittarius is the learning and identification of one's larger reality. Where Gemini is one's opinions, Sagittarius is one's deeper knowing. All Geminis can draw from Sagittarius' intuitive ability to balance its rational dependence. As Gemini grows, it will find itself increasingly interested in broadening its cognitive terrain. It will come to magically find itself exhibiting the Sagittarian qualities of integration (not just education in differences), *deeper* understanding, and higher cognitive flights.

GEMINI SHADOW

Incapacity to commit, solidify, or constellate around any one idea or path (symbolizing an archetypal fear of fully entering life); evanescent; irresponsible; indecisive; fickle; insensitive; prone to gossiping; inconsistent.

GEMINI SELF-REALIZATION

"The enlightened person is he who is freed from opposites."[3]

When one fully aligns with the Gemini Mysteries, one experiences the magical departure from ordinary reality which has been described as 'threading the eye of the needle with a sword', and is associated with the Coyote or Heyoke, the Magus of the Tarot, and Hermes Trismegistus. It is the direct cellular experience of being separate or outside of any duality. The Zen tradition calls it the non-dual, non-abiding mind. And this experience is profound as it releases the self *from* its obsession with mental labeling and *into* a place of serenity, peace and profound *presence*. This is the liberation from our addicted dependence on the left-brain function to understand reality. It is one path to the Creative Will of God, or Logos.

"Through outer circumstances which constantly appear and disappear before us, we learn what within us is real and what is illusion. We eventually come to know they are both and neither."[4]

☿ MERCURY

The symbol in our psyche for our cognitive process; our left-brain function; our intellectual processing speed, style, accuracy and thoroughness, as well as our mode of learning; our speech pattern; our communication style and learning style; our inner mental reality; how we process new information; and how we integrate and communicate that new data. Also, reading, contracts, basic education, and the archetype of studying or learning are Mercury significations. Mercury is crucial for determining how one's ego 'thinks' or rationalizes safety-seeking thought- and behavior-patterns.

3RD HOUSE

The 3rd House expresses through our siblings; trips or vacations; our basic education; our mental or inner reality; our cognitive abilities and functions; our opinions and mental habits; our style of communications (speaking, writing, etc.); and our area and level of interest in phenomena.

Experiences which bring us to understand the relationship between being and using, between subjective self and objective reality of the actions we take. The assumed beliefs from childhood, which operate (initially) subconsciously. Also, the collective thought patterns the individual is cognitively oriented to express personally.

The signs of the 3rd House signify our cognitive orientation, our learning and communication styles, and how we view the phenomenal world. They will thus reflect what we project or assume others should think, learn or what defines a useful or interesting education.

NOTES:

[1] Please do not limit the notion of communication to only verbal speech. Implied here are also all other types, such as emotional, mental, empathic, psychic, and in other ways.

[2] Deeper than the level of the physically manifest, there are other distinctions which give rise to outright psychic conflicts. The first one is of course that between the Soul and the Identity. Another is that between Masculine and Feminine or *yang* and *yin*. It is this pair that reflects the nature of Creation itself: as an ever-changing dance between *stasis* (balance, unchanging, syntropy) and *ex stasis* (imbalance, changing, entropy).

[3] The ancient Indian Upanishads.

[4] Adam Gainsburg, 'The Final Laugh' (essay).

"The seen is the changing. The unseen is the unchanging." – Plato

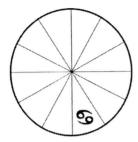

♋ CANCER

FEMININE – CARDINAL – WATER

Forming an independent self. Nurturing life. Developing emotional awareness/ maturity.

NOTES

Cancer begins the second quadrant, the "Exploration of Self" (see Chapter 6), and symbolizes a major shift in how consciousness orients to its lessons. Where the first quadrant represents instinctual learning, the second quadrant sees more self-consciousness developing.

In Cancer the Soul is required to consciously form a relationship to itself as an independent self, so it must formalize this self-image into something tangible, into a structure that can maintain itself. This is the *ego*. The ego is the most basic component of the Self-Identity, which itself is the vehicle for the Soul to inhabit and discover itself through. It may change in density or definition, but its inherent imprinted presence remains.[1] As cardinal water, Cancer flows out into life through its caring, empathic, emotional nature. We might understand this Cancer impulse as the child who transfers her imaginary friend into a physical doll or toy: she is *forming* the Identity of her friend into something identifiable.

The ego's main role is to maintain self-security, however it defines that for itself.[2] Essentially, the ego projects the self-image in a process of creation. It takes what it knows (the past), uses that information through which to filter the current experience (present), and then manifests within itself a projection of what that current experience *means*, and what the self should do or feel about it. But the meaning itself is a projection created through the lens or filter of the pre-existing identity needs. Depending on what the ego defines as safe and allows in or as unsafe and rejects, the actual present moment – the is-ness of what is occurring – may not be experienced at all. The ego may only allow in a small amount of information. In other words, the vehicle or *container* of self – the ego-based Identity – has replaced the *contained* – the Soul – in its role as captain of the ship. This separation and incorrect hierarchy between ego and Soul is the basis of all human fear. It is also the source of the painful fact that one's self-image is not the same as others' images of us.

To clarify a point often raised by students in SMA classes, the function of ego itself is a Cancer domain. However, the specific ego definitions a Soul is meant to develop can result from *any* sign or combination. For example, Moon in Taurus indicates an egoic identity (Moon) built from within the Taurus mysteries.

Cancer is also the archetypal source of *emotion*. Emotions usually result from the collision between our instinctual desires (Aries), our values and belief systems (Taurus), and our inner cognitive reality (Gemini) *on the one hand* and *on the other* our moment-by-moment raw experience of ourselves, others, and our environment. Emotions usually seem to arise mysteriously from our depths. But we can understand this strange trait of humanity if we examine it as a Cancer domain. We begin to see that the unexpected arising of intense emotions is a pressure release for built-up energetic tension to be purged. This applies to *both* enjoyable and difficult ones. An emotion can also be addressed as a signal that an unfamiliar idea or circumstance is in contact with or has reached the threshold of one's Identity. If the meaning or personal symbol of an emotion poses a (ego-perceived) threat, then the arising emotion will communicate that. If the newcomer is seen as a friend, the emotional experience will be pleasurable. Emotions thus are strong signals that something is trying to make itself known. They are the immediate result of ego-sourced and mind-categorized beliefs.

While Cancer is the home of our emotional life, it often is not the home of our *feelings*. The distinction between emotions and feelings is an important one. In SMA, the difference is simply this: feelings are the direct result of our direct experience, whereas emotions are the result of how our ego orients toward or away from those feelings. Emotions always are the product of beliefs held within the structure of the Identity. Feelings can arise not only from experiences we are aware that we are having, but also from those we are not. As humanity progresses along its path of growth I see our capacity for a deeper, richer, 'cleaner' feeling experience to dramatically increase.[3]

A powerful way to frame Cancer's domain is to think of it as a *bridge*. It has one foot in the subconscious waters of our beginnings – the womb – and the other foot looking for *terra firma* in the developing Identity. And as a bridge, our Cancerian focus will gravitate to one or the other at various times in life. When we lean more toward our origin, the subconscious areas of life – emotions, dreams, journeying – will draw us. And when we meet challenges to our Identity with courage, self-love, and trust, we will be more 'visible' or conscious in our lives.

This bi-focused development ultimately is designed for us learn *how to structure ourselves as both an individual and as a member of a collective.* The Cancer symbol of the *ego* clearly illuminates the individuality of this intention. But how Cancer reflects us as a member of a collective asks that we take a closer look at the sign. Though Cancer is clearly the stage around the Wheel of Consciousness which requires self-definition, it also reflects the idea that all humans come into life in the same way: from fertilization through gestation and into birth. In this archetypal and deeply meaningful light, Cancer is our collective womb (as well as our personal one). The Native American Moon Lodge ceremonies and practices reflect this idea.[4]

As we gain familiarity with a fuller range of Cancerian meanings, we begin to *feel* how they connect. As SMA students have expressed, we come to understand how the individual is the natural extension of the source of All Life and further that the individual *reflects* that source, just as the source *promises* the (birth of) the individual. "Individuality is the centeredness in a self that is a rhythmic power that resides at the very center of concrete existence."[5]

Anything that supports an individual to root in self as an autonomous being may be thought of as a function of Cancer, the Moon, or the 4th House. The autonomy which Cancer learning demands exists on the level of ego and is revealed emotionally. To tell ourselves, 'I know who I am without others making me who I am' may often not be as true as we would like to feel it is. Cancer initiations bring us deep into our selves, to face the bedrock of our Identity which we can see in 4th House archetypally beginning from the Lowheaven or IC ('lowest heaven' – see Chapter 5). We become individuals with generally unshakeable self-images – those that both allow for deep and wide emotional richness but do not topple us.[6] To evolve out of the pattern of requiring emotional validation from others in overt or subtle ways as needed indicators that we are cared for, nurtured and loved by others, is ample reason to move one's home onto a houseboat! This new position would in fact symbolize being *on top of one's water*, rather than drowned in its perceived absence (while in truth being surrounded by it).

As a cardinal water sign, Cancer correlates to healers, nurturers, massage therapists, etc. Cancer will then also refer to one's origins, childhood, mother and/or parents, family, and in general the contexts for them.

The distinctions between Cancer and Aries can often confuse those new to astrology. The difference might be easily expressed as this: where Aries is the intent to pre-consciously discover one's aliveness as a self, Cancer is the intent to consciously *form* a self-image.

CANCER POLARITY: CAPRICORN

To balance itself, Cancer needs to draw on the self-regulation and self-responsibility of its polarity Capricorn. Capricorn's focus on being known within society or a group (as its path toward growth), its self-autonomy, its dedication to a social purpose will all lift Cancer out of the waters of self-instability. When Cancer is too dependent on others for its self-image, it can draw on Capricorn's ability to be not only self-defining but also self-regulating.

CANCER SHADOW

When the self is summarily projecting a self-image based in others' needs of it rather than on its own authentic images, or when the self refuses to cease the addiction to outside approval or validation.

Uncontrollable emotionality; pessimistic; fearful; moody; co-dependent; overly sensitive; controlling.

Resistance to needed changes in self-image; unconsciously pouring one's life energy into others without regard for itself.

CANCER SELF-REALIZATION

The Cancerian experience of self-realization is the profound experience of being one with one's source. But this does not occur through mind-based practices, like meditation or astral projection. It is produced from the maximum alignment with one's natural ability to love and to nurture the growth of all life. When this occurs, there is the simultaneous experience of one's love and deep support for others as limitless — which creates a profound self-empowerment feeling as well as the experience of cellularly residing in the great mystery that gives rise to life itself. In other words, the self simultaneously knows it is the vessel, the recipient and the source of divine nurturance.

☽ MOON

"The nature of our natal Moon energy, just like the nature of ego in general, is to be a bridge between the known and the hidden, the safe and the unsafe, and between my experience of 'me' from 'you'. It is the self which has the experiences and that moves through life with relative self-acknowledgement. It does not correlate with our genetic or karmic past as its primary function."[7]

The Moon symbolizes the psychological nature of the current-life ego identity; the nature of the emotional body (and the issues within it); the subconscious environment and its demands; 'how' we dream and 'what' we dream about; our connection to ancestors, to family and to places of origin (our source); how we feel within our mysterious interior (consciously and subconsciously); and our psychic and intuitive abilities, along with Sagittarius, Aquarius and Pisces symbolizing other constituent parts of these functions. The Moon is an important indicator for determining an individual's or couple's resistance to change (see chapter 15).

⚷ CHIRON

First discovered in 1977, Chiron has been associated by astrologers alternately with Virgo and the 6th house, the Virgo-Libra/6th-7th transition, and with others. I do not use Chiron as a ruler of a sign or a house. Chiron essentially symbolizes the original wounding at 9-10 months, the first *experience* of being split from or different than mother, but also the first opening for consciousness to arise within the new being. Therefore, Chiron reveals a 'tender spot' within the self-definition, a place that cannot be strengthened through outer achievements or outside validation. It is *both* a place of a very deep pain — one that the self has already built up strong protection around well before it begins to speak — *and* it is also the precise location within the psyche for a truly profound experience of the quality of one's love for all of life. We see this in the Sufi depiction of the spiritual seeker coming into a love relationship with God.

"Ecstasy is a Feeling that comes
Only when the Heart is tuned to that pitch of Love
Which melts it...
Which makes it Tender...
Which gives it Gentleness
Which makes it Humble" – Hazat Inayat Kaan, *The Sufi Message*

Chiron's natal house, sign and aspects reveal an individual's Sacred Wound, the intended mode of learning to be developed through its efforts to come into wholeness, and also the individual's Sacred Medicine. The Chiron 'sacred wound' is one of the deepest wounds the individual carries, *relative to the current life intent* as it symbolizes the primal experience of being split from its source and the pain that that brings. Thus, the natal signature of Chiron will also reveal precisely how the self has been crystallized to protect future encroachments toward this place or issues.

SMA does not see Chiron as a 'ruler' of any sign or house but as its own archetype with its own symbols and interpretive applications. There is agreement in SMA with suggestions that Chiron can effectively be used as an alternative 'ruler' of the 6th-7th Houses and the 7th-8th Houses, which have been proposed by many excellent astrologers.

Chiron is included here within the Cancer family of archetypes to acknowledge its unique relationship to the Moon within the psyche: as the Moon's higher energetic function. As Dane Rudhyar has pointed out, Chiron can be seen as the higher octave of the Moon.

An extended essay on Chiron is included in Chapter 15. For a comprehensive treatment of Chiron, the Sacred Wound and the Sacred Medicine archetypes, see the companion book *Medicine Making Through Chiron: The Evolution of the Sacred Wound* (SMA Communications).

4TH HOUSE

The 4th House symbolizes our first awareness of the mythic realm of self; what we are as a concrete, identifiable, and sustaining self. It expresses through our origins, ancestors, traditions, roots, and foundations; our mother or parents; the beginning and ending of physical life (or of the life of the known self); our parents' attitudes; our emotional basis; our private life or inner home; and our domestic affairs.

The signs of the 4th House signify our emotional orientation (safety needs) and how we root in ourselves (deep self-acceptance). They will thus signify what we project or assume others need for emotional security. For more information, see 'Lowheaven' in chapter 5.

NOTES:

[1] The ego may have a physiologic location within the human. As my work with Chiron suggests, this location may be the brain stem, the location of our genetic prehistory. It controls basic functions of the body, such as respiration, heart rate and blood pressure. *Medicine-Making: The Evolution of the Sacred Wound* is a new book project due out late 2005 in which is an exploration of how Chiron correlates to the physical body.

[2] See essay titled 'The Nature of Ego, the Function of the Moon' in chapter 15 for an examination of the ego within the Self-Identity.

[3] The human organism is a massively complex hologram or multidimensional template for the cosmos. As such, it is wired into all of creation. This idea of a greatly increased capacity for a wide array of feeling-experience (unmitigated by fear issues) is based on these understandings.

[4] In these rituals, women experiencing their monthly Moon-time will be with each other. I see this reflecting for us that all life begins in the same 'place' or space.

[5] Dane Rudhyar, *The Astrological Houses*.

[6] What are too often categorized as 'dark nights of the Soul' are actually deaths to certain aspects of those egos too afraid to believe that they will in fact live through the experience. The forthcoming book *Bridges of Union: The Archetypes of Masculine & Feminine Transformation* (2006) includes a thorough essay on the topic of the dark night of the Soul misnomer. It suggests instead 'the dark night of the ego.'

[7] Excerpted from the essay, 'The Nature of Ego, the Function of the Moon' in chapter 15.

63

"Be a lamp unto yourself." – Gautama Buddha

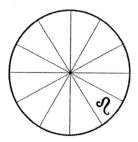

♌ LEO

MASCULINE – FIXED – FIRE

Learning and radiating self-love. Developing the capacity to create.

When an old light bulb is replaced by a new one, we discover new light with which to see. When Leo follows Cancer, we discover our Self-Identity in an entirely new light – complete and radical focus on the development of subjectivity. We discover a new light, a new depth, and a new excitement in creating and giving life (and light) to things.

During its course of evolution through the Wheel of Consciousness, a Soul will need to develop an Identity in balance: balance within itself, with others and with the larger world. A Soul must know itself before it can successfully participate with others. While in Cancer the Self-Identity initially rooted itself in its own water, here in Leo that Identity becomes owned, personified, substantiated, actualized, concretized, embodied, and inhabited in the fire of its own spirit. Leo is the fullest exploration of the nature of being a unique self. Its mysteries are the mysteries of subjective consciousness themselves: 'What is it to fully experience oneself as a self?', 'How do I – as a self – fit into a world with lots of different others in it?', 'What do I desire to create and to create myself to be?', 'How much does Other pay attention to what I create?'

The consciousness here intends to realize itself in a subjective way[1] – *to discover itself at and as the center of itself, its domain and its world.* From this arises the Leo tendency toward narcissism. The core of narcissism is 'consuming self-love' (Freud) and the narcissistic *tendency* is absolutely appropriate within a Leo context. Of course, this *tendency* needs to be balanced by a quota of humility and respect for others, the balance of which will look differently for each individual.

If in Cancer the Soul 'becomes a self' through the *internal* functions of emotion, security, and rootedness, in Leo it 'becomes a special self' through the *external* activities of being visible (to others), being an original, and interacting with others as such. Yet they both operate within the context of a self learning of itself as a main evolutionary drive.

Leo is a highly creative sphere of consciousness. In the process of a human being authentically creating anything – bringing something into form – the Self-Identity within that human being will necessarily feel empowered, will experience itself as able to influence the outer environment and others in that environment. This becomes the initial discovery – which is fully developed later in Virgo – of one's capacity to have a direct effect on its outer environment – here in Leo it happens through the creation process. The creation process also feeds the Leo development through its results: the actual manifestation of the creation – the artwork, the project, the deal, the retreat center. In other words, to produce something that is desired, valued, or praised by others. Thus, a prized creation becomes an egoic extension of the self which allows more of the self to be made visible, known, adored, praised and validated.

With Leo at the center of a family unit, it can feel itself in power because the family itself is in fact its creation. Again, through Leo, a Soul comes to know itself through its creations, whereas in Cancer self-knowing occurs through its security and self-rootedness. Hence the association of Leo and 5th house with family, and with being the 'center of the household'. The Sun as the center of our solar system speaks to this as well.

Recognizing that one can place oneself at the center of whatever one chooses – consciously or otherwise – the Soul through its Identity will experience its first taste of power. In this context, power is three things: 1. the experience of being imbued with a fullness of purpose and of being aligned with a flow of natural energy which is bigger than it; 2. knowing and feeling its right to exist and its right place within existence; 3. and being imbued with energy by the recognition, validation and adoration from others. In its ongoing attempts to be the center of everything it is involved in, Leo can very easily lose perspective. It will eventually realize that this driving need is a subconscious one, that it has not yet *actually* contacted the reason for its presence. The individual will move through experiences designed to challenge its subconscious 'assumption' or addiction to self-prioritizing oneself into the center of attention. It will come to understand by observation how its needs affect others.

It is quite important to remember Leo operates *subjectively*, from a complete *I-centered* context. It is inaccurate to think that Leo is normally aware of how self-centered it is. Rather, it needs to be grasped that through the extreme subjectivity, it is *developing* its awareness of itself and how others can be there for it. Leo intends to learn about its needs as a self, inhabiting the role of *center* within a larger environment. This must be remembered in counseling Leo clients as it will allow your understanding of the sign energy to translate to others as honor and acknowledgment of its importance, rather than summarily labeling clients as narcissistic and ego-based.

The Leo consciousness can be visualized as a vortex of energy, with the individual at the center. Leo draws into its self-vortex all that is around it in order to realize itself. It *requires* others and their attention in order to develop itself. But this is one-half of the Leo dynamic. The other half is what happens when these narcissistic-type needs come into balance. If Leo can appropriately alchemize its need to be seen by others into a deep centered-in-selfness, the energy previously moving inward (as a vortex) will begin to *radiate* outward. This radiation occurs only when the energy coming in (from Other or others) has first been cellularly integrated and hasn't fallen through the cracks of an insecure self-definition. Assuming that, the radiating energy becomes for others like sugar to a hummingbird. This is then felt by others as charisma, magnetism, popularity, attractiveness and even glamour, the qualities Leos are (in)famous for. When Leo can balance its drawing in of energy from others with substantiating itself on its own terms, energetic balance is struck. When this occurs, the egoic structure becomes the container for the balanced state. The Identity experiences itself as if for the first time simultaneously *in*-powered and also self-generating. It discovers an inner 'light' or radiant quality of awareness. Archetypally, Leo is the first position through the Wheel of Consciousness which approximates the ability of the Identity to know itself as a Soul vibration, an entirely other level of being. For more along this idea, see the 'Leo Self-Realization' section below.

An ancient Egyptian constellation appears to have been named for this alchemical result. The constellation of the Lion which we now associate with the sign of Leo is translated as 'pouring out.' This image may refer to the Sun's heat and light pouring out of itself into the space around it.

LEO POLARITY: AQUARIUS

To balance, Leo can draw from Aquarius' detached, objective manner which often expresses as a strong focus on social or political concerns. Where Leo will naturally want to relate life to self, Aquarius will want to dedicate self to improving life. While Leo is subjective consciousness, Aquarius is objective. Aquarius can assist Leo to temporarily depart from its subjectivity for a more spacious view of itself. This will often create an initial conflict and an arising of Leo's fear of 'losing itself.' The degree to which the Leo Self-Identity is fearful of not being seen will be inversely proportional to the level of its ability to take a break from its incessant subjectivity, laugh at itself and perhaps gain needed space.

LEO SHADOW

The endless need to be approved by, fulfilled by, surrounded by, adored by others (the 'black hole' of self-esteem); an insensitivity to or manipulation of others; an inability to center oneself without others being present: the circle's center that can't find its circumference and thus loses itself; self-obsession; vain; narcissistic; solipsistic; manipulative; selfish; needy; arrogant; myopic; haughty.

LEO SELF-REALIZATION

Leo self-realization is the experience of oneself as a Divine and Beloved being, one that is an agent of God's will. It is so full of its unique essence and this experience is so healthfully integrated with the egoic level of being, that there is nothing the individual experiences that is not a source for the reflection of its own self-mastery and divinity. The person 'becomes a translucent and perfectly shaped lens through which light is condensed and brought into form.'[2]

☉ SUN

The symbol for the quality of life-force animating and infusing every aspect of the being. Sun sign energy is one's energetic methodology for living, for participating in physical life, for being alive, being seen, and being who one is. One's Sun energy tells us *the way* a person is to be *pranically* alive. Therefore, it will also reveal how one is seen by others. The Sun sign is *not* the main identifier of Self-Essence nor is it the main identifier of Self-Identity. It is the type of electricity one is wired for to be alive. It also reflects the type of energy one attracts (because it is the energy or personal quality one puts out).

Along with the Moon, the astrological Sun paints the full picture of a Soul's incarnational Identity (yet they do *not* include that Soul's prior, karmic Identity nor its future Identity to be). With the Moon as the inner stability of self and the Sun as the outer radiance of self, the Self-Identity can be identified and illuminated for others.[3]

5TH HOUSE

The 5th House expresses in our father; our children; the 'method' or path of self-love; our creativity and creative expressions (art); the family we have created for ourselves; our experience of our raw originality; our sexual experimentation and eroticism; our appearance to others; arts, games and entertainment which we are attracted to; personal love, dating, and courtship; our productivity; and our beneficial acts. Planets here indicate which domains of our psyche will be sources for creative expressions. The condition of the 5th House may challenge (square) our ownership of our possessions (2nd house): ie., our financial support (2nd House) of our children (5th House) reduces our financial support for our other creations.

The signs of the 5th House signify our orientation to the creative process (or to ourselves as creators). They will thus reflect what we project or assume others should create and be in their life.

NOTES:

[1] Use of the word 'realize' here suggests enlightenment, or 'en-lightening' one's awareness to something. This connotation includes not only cognitive understanding, but also cellular (genetic) alignment and an alteration to consciousness.

[2] Dane Rudhyar, *The Astrological Houses.*

[3] There is a powerful method for working with one's Sun and Moon signs throughout one's life. This method was introduced to me by astrologer Carolyn Brent of Shamanic Astrology. It is explained and tailored to fit into a Sacred Marriage Astrology context, in chapter 15.

"The highest reward for a person's toil is not what they get from it, but what they become by it." – John Ruskin

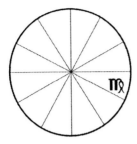

♍ VIRGO

FEMININE – MUTABLE – EARTH

Developing self-accuracy. Devoting the self to selflessness. Performing a greater function.

Virgo is a transitional sign (as is the 6th House): it marks the transition between the direct development of subjective consciousness (Aries to Leo) and the entry into one's social environment or beginning of objective consciousness development. If Aries to Leo symbolizes the Soul's entry and exploration of the pool of subjective consciousness, then Virgo represents the Soul's emergence out of that pool in order to examine itself and understand who it is more accurately. Virgo is the sphere in which the subjective identity – which has been developed up to this point – must now be balanced, reduced, and integrated into a more accurate, realistic sense of self. Without this, the Soul is not ready to enter the social environment. When the identity begins to release its overly-subjective self-image, it will necessarily begin to see things in others – people, ideologies, etc. – that it does not have itself. It experiences, perhaps for the first time, the feeling of self-insufficiency or wrongness which emanates from within itself.

At the Virgo stage of evolution, the self has not yet developed an objective foundation strong enough to balance the inner self-critic, which seems to be ever-present with self-doubting comments. Initially, Virgo will not know how to work with the voices of criticism because the self has not been weathered by a balance of subjective experience and objective distance. This is in fact one way of framing the Virgo goal.

Examining its placement within hemispheres, Virgo is located in the Subjective and Relational hemispheres (see chapter 6). This suggests that Virgo can only relate *personally* (Subjective-Relational) to its physical form (earth sign) as a controlling parent relates to an impudent child (mutable). Virgo will thus subconsciously perceive that it itself and its immediate physical environment (body, home, work, etc.) requires constant disciplining or *improvement*. In its attempt to control, it will also subconsciously assume responsibility for what it perceives to be an absence of perfection.

A Virgo Self-Identity will naturally perceive its emotions arising from these feelings as something to correct. One way to alleviate this is to improve or better oneself, to grow out of the pattern responsible for producing them. The Identity will seek to educate itself about why it feels, acts and thinks the way it does. Though it will gain valuable insights about itself – such as its strengths and weaknesses, how it feels to be in service, how it balances its intensely self-critical nature with its heartfullness – it will not find the final, rational answer to its question of 'why it is the way it is' within itself alone. Virgo is incapable of attaining an answer because such an answer does not reside in a realm Virgo can access (Virgo is still *below* the horizon). In other words, the answer to 'why is it the way it is' is *rationally* unknowable. Virgo will continue self-analyzing, self-victimizing, or self-criticizing until it realizes this, until it recognizes that it has reverted back into the swimming pool of subjectivity (see above). Once realized, it will then be able to re-exit the pool and dry off once again. With practice, Virgo can develop into one of the most effective, balanced Identities of the zodiac because its impulse is to thoroughly inhabit the Earth element as its means of devotion and service (mutable) to something greater than itself.

Only with the acceptance of its nature can Virgo begin to sense something larger – the idea of a divine presence, love or intelligence – which it can open to. Experience of this connection will eventually catalyze the feeling of self-understanding, acceptance and compassion for itself. Symbolically, this 'greater than self' domain which Virgo seeks a connection to, points to the world of social Other, which begins in Libra and is developed through the entire upper hemisphere (Libra/7th House through Pices/12th House archetypally). Virgo will see the need to simply accept its nature, as it is. Once it begins to accept itself for who it is and who it is not, it will naturally want to expand or *do something with* (mutability) what it has learned. This impulse is still the same impulse from its beginning – to move towards becoming that which it perceives it is not currently. This is actually the source of the Virgo qualities of tireless service, deep devotion, attention to detail, and being a team player. It may also feel drawn to help others find the same solace within themselves. From this, we see Virgo is also the place of conscious service to something greater than just itself but *through the vessel of an accurate self-image*, which requires the inner ability to see itself clearly – strengths *and* weaknesses – as well as the ability to know how to serve and to give of oneself selflessly.

In Virgo's strong nature to analyze all aspects of itself and its experience, we can see it as a type of reporting engine – 'how am I doing', 'how did they like me', 'what could have been better', 'what should I have done', 'what should they have done', 'what needs to be improved on', etc. From this we see the Virgoan:

- addiction to lists, schedules, the prescribed, proper order of
  things, and attention to detail;
- extreme focus on one's body and maintaining the 'right waist-size',
  the right clothes, the right workout regimen; and
- tireless commitment to one's work and self-analyzing
  one's performance.

All outer expressions of Virgoan inner drives can be seen as attempts to 'control matter' (Earth). Its body, its work, and its ability to shape or control its physical world are examples of this, which we can see in the trine from Taurus.[1]

There is a powerful association between Virgo and the archetype of masochism, which says 'the suffering of others, the breakdown in efficiency, is inherently my fault because of something I've done or not done in the past. I therefore need to atone for my sins perpetually.'[2]

But let us understand where this really comes from. Virgo represents a crucial threshold between subjective consciousness trying to evolve into the seeds of objective consciousness seen in zodiacal placement which ends the lower (subjective) hemisphere and prepares for the upper (objective) hemisphere to be started. The 'heavy burden syndrome' found in all Virgo pathologies is the archetypal result of the individualistic self (Aries through Leo) evolutionarily coming up against the limitations of maintaining that self-image and orientation to life. Virgo is a transition consciousness, just as all mutable signs and houses are. It strives to reduce its intense focus on its own perfection through greater self-acceptance. It must be noted that Virgo's striving for perfection actually emanates out of the subconscious belief that one is never good enough. If one believes in one's lack of quality, then one remains safe in one's own subjectively-defined world and increasingly cements in this Identity. But if one transitions out of this belief, then one is left with far greater self-acceptance, but not necessarily one which is accompanied by the knowledge of which direction to move in with it.

"...there is no coming to consciousness without pain." – Carl Jung

In order to make the transition, all assumptions about itself as inherently responsible for others or insufficient in crucial ways (which otherwise produce an incessant striving for perfection) *must be met by the light of one's awareness and trust in oneself.* If not, then an individual heavily endowed with Virgo energy will naturally develop a guilt program which produces passive-aggressive behavior, masochistic desires, or other aberrant behavior.

As Virgo is the transition between the lower and the upper hemispheres, we can see it as the transition between the known and unknown, the attained and the aspired to, the self and the other.

The Virgo mentality is intense and is a storehouse of motivation to work on oneself, to become what one wants to become (who one fears one is not), to associate oneself with something greater than oneself (Pisces polarity), and to transform one's heavy commitment into loving devotion. This requires the individual learn discernment about which self-analyzing voices it needs to heed and which it can ignore, as well as trusting which activities are appropriate objects of its devotion. Any errors in these processes will necessarily produce a humbling effect as one is stopped by one's own issues of negativity or guilt. With compassion and consciousness, the lessons that arise from these experiences can be cultivated into humility and a greater self-acceptance.

When a Virgo-influenced individual comes to a place within their growth where the subconscious needs to take unnecessary responsibility, to guilt oneself, and to incessantly control their physicality are no longer driving factors of the psyche and its life choices, Virgo's profound capacity for heartfullness, wisdom and insight activate. They become beacons for *what the moment is asking*, and this knowing does not source from them. Rather, it emanates from a greater source (Pisces polarity). The individual is uniquely, cellularly prepared for enacting this higher inspiration in the world and through itself. The archetypes of the Priest/Priestess, the Sky

Watcher, the Sacred Homemaker all apply to Virgo.

Virgo Polarity: Pisces

Pisces is the archetype of the final merging back into Source, Christ consciousness, or God. To balance itself, Virgo can learn from Pisces' acceptance of all things and people as expressions of the Divine, from its mastery of timelessness, in that time and the accompanying constriction or limitation of possibility is the cosmological reason for the Virgoan intensely controlling nature. Through Pisces, Virgo can aspire to something greater than itself, something it recognizes it itself is not (yet).

Virgo Shadow

Narrow-minded; hyper-critical; perfectionist; dogmatic; superior; judgmental; masochistic; self-abnegating; overly responsible; guilty; harshly ascetic; tight; fixated on outcomes.

A perpetual addiction to a masochistic self-image based on any number of factors; assuming the burden of guilt for others or defaulting to guilt when there is no guilty party; refusing to release control (mental, emotional or physical); intense workaholicism accompanied by equally intense feelings of not having done enough; an intense controlling nature based in the existential fear of being too flawed for return to God.

Virgo Self-Realization

The Virgo self-realization experience emanates from a complete self-honoring and selfless devotion to something greater than oneself. In this experience, the natural mutability of the Virgo consciousness – which previously found expression mostly through the mental function – expands into the trans-mental or a larger, spiritual directive. This produces the living experience of being an instrument for something much greater than one's egoic desires and needs, which frees the boundaries set by the Identity to allow the Soul to inhabit a fuller residence.

⚶ Vesta

This is a non-traditional assignment. The traditional ruler of Virgo is Mercury which we can see in its overt symbolism with our intellectual activity. But for me and for other astrologers, that's where the usefulness ends. There has been good work to correlate the asteroid goddess Vesta with

Virgo's mysteries. The mythology says Vesta was one of Saturn's daughters, which we can see from the natural Capricorn-Virgo square. The location of natal Vesta can indicate the individual's Virgoan orientation to life, its qualities, and psycho-dynamics of devotion and commitment, cultivation of the sacred (both inwardly and outwardly), and the search for self-improvement. Ceres, another asteroid, is also used as an alternate Virgo 'ruler.'

Vesta's synodic return: 3yrs. 3mos. 1wk. (39 months).

Sign periodicity: 3¼ mos.

Degree periodicity: 2¼ days.

6TH HOUSE

"If you had known how to suffer, you would have had the power not to suffer."
– attributed to Jesus or Yeshua from a Gnostic hymn.

The 6th House expresses in our physical health; vocational work; employers and employees; daily tasks; our peers; our diet; our personal crises and defeats, and how we internally meet and externally express them; our healing experiences (how we meet the limitations of our body); our inner-then-outer response to a social situation.

The sixth house test is that of patience, endurance and suffering.

The signs of the 6th House signify our work ethic, physiological predisposition, and orientation to self-control. They will thus reflect what we project or assume others' work ethic, physicality and picture of self-control should be.

NOTES:

[1] A trine is a 120° aspect. For explanations of the aspects used in SMA, see chapter 8.

[2] I was originally introduced to this idea through the work of astrologer Jeffrey Wolf Green, founder of Evolutionary Astrology.

"May we devote our thoughts to understanding, our words to truthfulness, and our actions to peace." – Interdependence Day Prayer (July 4 in US)

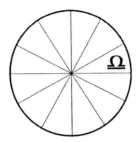

♎ LIBRA

MASCULINE – CARDINAL – AIR

Exploring 'other' as mirror/window into the self. Learning harmony/balance through exploration of extremes.

In Libra, consciousness is exposed to an entirely different psychic context – the world of Other. It is like we discover a new room within us which we hadn't known was there. Upon entering, we come to find we are inexorably drawn to other people: their opinions, their activities and their understandings. Up to this point, we've been in a self-centered world where everything learned was in a context of the self (subjectivity). Now though, Libra signifies something quite different: *the self's first exposure to others.* As the 7th sign, Libra is halfway around the Wheel of Consciousness; as such, it is the seed or initiator of our eventual and inevitable return back to our source.

Aries to Virgo shows us the various 'skills' or awarenesses we need for a clear, balanced self image and context. Here in Libra, we enter the reality of others. This new domain is vital for the Soul's growth because it cannot remain within in its own context forever. Its nature as an evolving Soul prohibits it. In addition, the nature of creation or manifest life is to interact with itself in *all* its myriad expressions. For one expression of creation to remain isolated from the rest of creation is contrary to life.

Consciousness which is only familiar with its own subjective reality will naturally experience strong conflict within the egoic identity when it begins to incorporate other people and their ideas into its reality. *How to be with others* is an ongoing Libra learning. This will force not only conflict, but periodic breakdown of the entrenched self-image. It can't continue from its ego-centric position. So the Libra mysteries arise from all manners and

75

expressions of relationship. Libra requires a wide array of interactions with others – all kinds, flavors, variations and iterations of interactions, engagements, conflicts and experiences in a social context. In other words, Libra will necessarily gravitate to relationships – either many at once or one after another. This is its developmental modality. And this makes sense as it would be quite impossible to learn about oneself through the interactions with others if we had no sense of ourselves first.

In Libra we learn about other people's realities, ways of communicating, assumptions, beliefs, expressions, strengths, weaknesses, prejudices, attempts to manipulate, and hidden fears. We then discover how we naturally respond or react to them. This provides a whole new methodology or resource for self-learning. For example: 'what do we do, internally and externally, when we realize our friends and supporters aren't there for us anymore?, ...when we experience strangers trying to coerce us into something not so integrous? or... when our Soul mate simply isn't?', 'Who does that make us, and why did we believe what we believed about them in the first place?', 'What's wrong with the way we're thinking of ourselves?' This can be very intense and very disturbing for the Identity. Through Libra the Identity's safe zones are strongly encroached upon, and it is forced to deal with its many assumptions it has been carrying about others. Disillusionment is always right around the corner for Librans, yet one's ideals, or perfect pictures can be so strong that their absolute adherence to those ideals will prolong the evolutionary point from being realized. The point is twofold: what Libra is thinking or assuming to be true is not necessarily true for others, and how Libra is basing its social and Identity reality on those assumptions is not sustainable because it is not necessarily true.

From this, we can see that Libra partially contains the archetype of idealism, in its most dry, intentional, and intellect-driven sense. (The other sign in this regard is Pisces, which contains the archetype of idealism in its wet, subconscious, unintentional and naively-innocent sense.) Like everyone, Libra wants self-security, which it attains by providing others what they need or by making itself into what (they believe) others want. As the Libra logic goes, 'if other people have what they need from my efforts, they will naturally approve and accept of me.' The problem is, Libra cannot accurately sense what others need; but they assume that they do.

Librans share the gift of communicating in ways to make others feel authentically heard. Librans are the consummate conversationalists for this reason. The real Libra lesson though is to learn that they are not responsible for the other person, or that the harmony of the relationship or community is not a reflection of their self-worth or their security.

Ultimately, the learning is how to *be with others* in an authentic manner, without agendas and false ideas. It requires the development of an ability to listen to others not from our context, but from theirs: 'What is it for you to experience what you are experiencing?' This in turn requires the capacity to cease projecting, assuming, or stubbornly adhering to one's own ideas of what is best for others. These obstruct the realization of the whole intent: to authentically relate with another. Libra is always on the search for, always interested in and always self-realizing through this type of motivation. And, again, all of this perhaps is based on how the egocentric context is being tempered, whittled down and made more realistic (begun in Virgo).

Libra qualities include compromise, mediation, harmony, and balance. All of these naturally arise when an individual learns to be with others in a simultaneous self-honoring and other-honoring manner – when neither is abnegated.

This in turn creates the lesson of flexibility and being willing to change oneself to meet the needs of the social moment. The archetype of adaptation[1] is inherent in the human species, on the biologically primal level. But to bring our adaptive capacity into our *conscious* dealings with others is not always an easy transition. It requires flexibility – both around the intended outcome *and* around our self-definition – as well as the ability to stay on course relative to the original intent. It can require humility and acceptance that often we don't know (what to do next, who we're becoming, etc.) Practically, some Libras need to be forced into adapting, while others are quite ready to change the plan.

Libra is an air sign – thinking, analyzing, judging, and comparing – and it is cardinal – initiating, active, moving. Put these two together and we have a consciousness – Libra – that must evolve through an active, initiating, and seeking mental function. A huge potential for projection, don't you think? When Libra has not *incorporated and taken into itself* what it is learning from all its cognitive activity and social interactions, it is like a jar full of holes – always needing more to fill itself. As mentioned earlier, this can manifest into an ignorance or a blindness to what is actually happening around it. In other words, it remains focused on the goal of the ideal outcome (but again it is only *its own ideal*) to the exclusion of the reality of the group (or relationship). The element of air, is naturally un-contained, LOVES to be activated in a direction. It provides it purpose.

Projection is a classic Libra trap. For Librans though, it is an honest mistake in the right direction, in terms of what projection ultimately provides: self-discovery *through* the other. When an individual projects onto someone or something, at core what is happening is they are in some way trying to discover those qualities they perceive in others – consciously or subconsciously – within themselves. They are striving to discover new aspects of themselves from the reflection of those qualities within another person. Once Libra can recognize it is projecting, it can then begin to identify which of its latent qualities are trying to make themselves known through the pattern. Again, this whole domain of self and other, projection and inherent qualities is how Libra actualizes itself – *through the other*. Eventually, Libra will learn it can stop project-ing and will realize that its immediate, reactionary need to either adjust to others, or adjust others to itself is unnecessary. It can instead learn to honor others for their own uniqueness and from within their reality.

Libra consciousness is thus directly associated with the maturation of the archetype and experience of duality (begun in Aries). On the gross level, it asks, how can an individual *connect* itself to others who are fundamentally different than it? On the subtle level, it requires the individual root itself more deeply (rather than defining oneself through others or the quality of one's relationships with others). This produces the awareness that our view of things, even *our* view of ourself, is actually relative; it is only our view. From this can then arise a deeper honoring of life and other people *as it/they actually are*. It can engender the wonderment of the diversity of life minus the sub-conscious need to be taken in and cared for by others. The Libran tendency of creating high ideals can eventually produce great results through resolution, mediation, and settlement of issues between people, countries, etc. as well as a truly egalitarian, self-responsible society. Ultimately, Libra growth leads to the feeling or sense that everything has value, all manifestations of creation emanate from the same source, and all are sacred. Libra can lead us to deep experiences of witnessing the divine in others and Other.

LIBRA RELATIONSHIPS

Libran relationships are relationships of purpose. They will need to know what it's for, and maintain an active monitoring and working at it. If anything should come up that's not 'good', they'll naturally want to work it out (talking/processing - air) in order to keep the relationship moving (cardinal). It is through the 'doing' of their relationships that Librans find their dharma.

LIBRA POLARITY: ARIES

If Aries is our raw experience of our individuality and how we instinctually experience ourselves to be alive, Libra is how we instinctually relate with others. To balance its tendency to require Other in order to complete itself, Libra can draw on Aries' fire of independence and comfort in aloneness. If Libra's striving for partnership or some type of related-ness is accompanied by an absence of autonomous self-definition, then Aries independence will act as a challenge to strengthen the Libran Identity in its own soil.

LIBRA SHADOW

An identity built around fulfilling others' perceived needs, producing for example: 'I am good if my partner is devoted to me, if my relationship is going well, if I am loved and cared for.' This identity definition is destined to be broken down because it is summarily created from within the other's reality, which is *not indigenous to the self*. Libra asks that we root our self in our own soil, but learn how to do so *through* the Other. While the Libra lesson is indeed relativity, the application of that lesson is a consistent identity formed *from* one's many experiences with others, and not *defined by them*.

Attaching onto the ideal or desired outcome or 'pretty picture'; co-dependent; over-accommodating; unrealistic; indecisive; fickle; opinion-less; over-processing; utopia-manic; disconnected to feelings; prone to act from ulterior, selfish motives.

Mental illness (schizophrenia, neurosis or worse) from the lack of a structured Identity.

LIBRA SELF-REALIZATION

Libra's self-realization will occur through the direct experience of being profoundly *received* – being accepted, welcomed, and honored by Other. This produces a cessation of the familiar Identity structure and results in the visceral, cellular awakening to its profound belonging within all of creation. Stabilizing its relatedness with Other (through a committed relationship, peace-making activities, or social successes) can unify the Libra consciousness within the cells of the body to create a consciousness expressing a deep caring *and* a far vision.

♀ VENUS

The 'other' side of Venus and Femininity (begun in Taurus) is relatedness. As the Feminine principle requires Other to exist in its unique way, its association with Libra, the sign of relatedness, is appropriate. This other side of Venus points to a deep understanding of Femininity – 'the impulse to draw all with which it is in relationship into itself.'[2] It rounds out the picture, along with the Taurus side of Venus[3], for a person's intimacy needs. (For a full description of Femininity, see chapter 1).

Libran Venus qualities are good listening skills; a strong importance placed on communicating (everything); desire for harmony and balance; a natural orientation to partnering in all ways; an innate skill at finding middle ground and understanding many sides; wanting social acceptance; and a consistent focus on the (perceived) needs of others.

7TH HOUSE

The 7th House expresses through our partnerships; agreements; marriages, competition; allies; foreign places we moves to; our listening abilities; how we as individuals interact with others; our first place of relationships: meeting, courting, dating, etc (because all our interactions with others for a larger objective); our legal bonds, agreements, and cooperative ventures (like relationships); our legal results in court; consulting, advising, and relationship counseling; and mediating, harmonizing, and conflict resolving skills.

Planets in the 7th can reveal the qualities we want in our relationship partner.

The signs of the 7th House signify our energetic orientation to personal relationships, or our 'sacred relationship' self. They will thus reflect what we project or assume others' should be as well. For more information, see 'Descendant' in chapter 5.

NOTES:

[1] I was originally introduced to the association of adaptability with Libra by the work of astrologer Jeffrey Wolf Green.

[2] For more on femininity, see chapter 1.

[3] As mentioned above, Venus also is closely associated with the sign energy of Taurus. These two signs, Taurus and Libra, naturally create an aspect of 150° known as a *quincunx*. (For more on the quincunx, refer to chapter 8.) In one of the strongest ironies of the astrological mandala, these two signs, said to be the two main symbols of the Feminine, share a 'no-relationship' relationship, one in which there is no clear communication happening between the two. The 150° quincunx between the two directly suggests that *the role or job of the Feminine is in fact to create relationship*. And further, the Feminine is the domain within which true relationship with others (Libra) is possible only when we have successfully stabilized ourselves enough to be able to 'cleanly' receive from others (Taurus).

Association of Venus to Taurus is a *yin*(-) planet to a *yin*(-) sign, while Venus to Libra is a *yin*(-) planet to a *yang*(+) sign. This accurately reflects the intra-dualism within Femininity. That, as the source or container for life, the Feminine 'contains all within itself'.

"My death will be my wedding with eternity." – Jalal al-Din Rumi

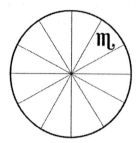

♏ SCORPIO

FEMININE – FIXED – WATER

Effectively aligning one's will with the force of creation. Developing the power to transform oneself.

Just as the discovery of a new element in the universe (Libra) will then transform (Scorpio) our periodic table of the elements to reflect the new knowledge, Scorpio consciousness seeks to deeply apply what it has learned in Libra through a process of inner transformation. It strives to transform those aspects of itself which prevent a deeper experience of itself. This will include those limitations, restrictions, repressions, obstructions, patterns, or habitual behaviors standing in its way. The limitations experienced of course emanate from within the self, and so the Scorpio mysteries revolve around learning this for oneself and how to transform them. In other words, Scorpio symbolizes the archetype of evolution itself[1] : the genetically-aligned change of consciousness, which spiritual teacher Andrew Cohen describes as the 'focused intensity' of the unmanifested's ecstatic urging for/into manifestation.

Generally speaking, these self-created limitations are an attempt to hold onto what is known in order to maintain security – a secure self-image, relationship, wealth, etc. Yet security is a passing cloud, so the limitations created by the self are only useful to perpetuate the past. Scorpio becomes the stage of consciousness where we must experience and practice transforming these vain attempts to maintain what is known. At core we are Soul: pure, consistent sparks of divine consciousness. To resist our nature will eventually show itself to be futile. This idea refers to the tag line above: 'Effectively aligning one's will with the force of creation.'

How is Scorpio a response to Libra? Scorpio takes the Libran knowing and sensitivity to other realities and perspectives, how to function within that world, how to relate effectively with others, and how to build an authentic self-image from our relationship experience, and seeks to *apply that information to ourselves* (feminine fixed water). Scorpio seeks to go deeper into its own motivations, limitations, and sources of power, passion and life force. As Scorpio is located in the Relational and Objective hemispheres, this internal exploration will necessarily occur *through* its interactions with others (Relational) and will eventually produce a greater ability to identify the parts of itself preventing further growth (Objective). (For more about the Hemispheres, see chapter 6).

From the Scorpio perspective, all of creation is the environment for battling and conquering limitations. Something is a limitation when it obstructs the otherwise natural flow of growth into new spaces. Yet Scorpio within human psychology will invariably reframe the battle as that between security and insecurity. Security arises from what is known, insecurity from what is unknown. For most, the Identity is the known part of self, the Soul is the unknown.

Scorpio has a strong connection to the Soul. Let's re-examine (from Chapter 1) what we mean by Soul. The Soul is divine and timeless. The Soul *knows*, in the sense of being in full presence, which we understand in its unboundedness (by time). The Identity (ego) is not capable of the same *knowing* because it operates within linear time and thus its reach is more limited.

When a Soul enters or vibrationally associates itself with/into an Identity (an individual) before its birth, it is entering a completely foreign world (to it) – an unknown world. The Identity will instinctually resort to absolute diligence in fending off any threat to itself. Yet again, the Soul itself in its own domain still *knows*. It is still whole and will remain that way forever. The Soul does not die, as energy does not die, though it will undergo changes in its energy structure. These changes result from changes in how the Identity utilizes (fixed signs) its life force, those beliefs or perceived needs it constellates around, and how it views itself in relation to an Other (hostile) environment. In other words, an Identity's approach to its growth needs, ways of thinking, behaviors and self-image will necessarily reflect how much of its essential nature – its Soul – it remembers. The 'thicker' the forgetting, the more the Identity's needs for security will dominate.

Further, because the Soul knows itself outside of any belief context, it also knows what it wants. In SMA, the general term for what the Soul wants is the *Soul's Desire*. The Desire can be seen in several ways:

1. It is that which at the deepest level *motivates us to grow*. Again, the

Soul doesn't die, so its Desire also does not die.

2. It creates both the Identity's *insecurities* (when our Desire makes us aware of our internal limitations) and its *transformations* – our striving to overcome them. What in humanity I name the Soul's Desire may also be described more generally as the primal force 'moving' creation to perpetually occur.

3. It is our *deepest longing*, as it is what we are and thus what we desire as well.

For a thorough discussion of the Soul's Desire in an SMA context, see chapters 9-11.

Scorpio is a feminine penetrating energy. It needs to enter experiences deeply in order to uncover the information waiting there, in order to understand itself at that level. Therefore, Scorpios will be attracted to anyone or anything that symbolizes or reflects what it more deeply desires for itself. Examples would be: mandalas, sacred geometry, words of power, lovers, disciplines, certain careers, evocative images, sexual expressions, or spiritual, military, tantric, shamanic, and other practices. But the lesson here is appropriately hidden. The very things Scorpio is attracted to – people or external symbols of power, depth, mystery, and the "hidden" of any kind – are actually representations of what it *unconsciously* recognizes itself as. So it will consciously pursue these qualities in the outer world because it subconsciously believes it does *not* possess those qualities itself. It strives to feel/know itself more intensely. But the balance between pursuing external symbols of its as-yet-unrealized self or power, and the realization that the qualities it seeks through outer forms already exist within itself, must be struck.

Because in Scorpio the self is intending to become aware of and then transform its limitations to its further growth, it is also the archetype of suppression or repression[2], processes through which we 'keep back' or 'press down' awareness or information about ourselves either from ourselves or others. This then reveals where the Scorpio traits of suspiciousness, mysteriousness and brooding silence come from.

"What has no shadow has no strength to live." – Czeslaw Milosz

Scorpio is the domain of the archetype of power as it is the first place the Soul comes into the experience of itself as powerful – again, this can only happen in the world of Other (the upper and right hemispheres – see chapter 6). It will desire these experiences of itself more and more. If the authentic, progressive self-image is buried in heaps of guilt, past trauma, masochism or self-denial, then it will subconsciously create situations that re-create experiences of itself as those qualities. If it is instead overly ego-centric, then it will create experiences in which it feels supremely powerful, sexy, deep, or intense, and may lead to becoming overwhelmed and thrown into a 'personal hell.' A 'personal hell' is the acute experience of being unavoidably faced with one's limitations.

Ultimately, to transform one's own limitations, one needs an awareness of what those limitations are, as well as a sense or a way to transform them. The Scorpio method of realizing one's blocks is through the experience of overwhelm, or the 'dark night of the ego' experience.[3] And its way to transform them is through a courageous immersion in levels of power greater than one's own. So the process of Scorpio mastery requires that one learns how to be energetically overwhelmed (revealing where the limitations are) and then maintain an active presence within the experience (method of transforming those limitations). Bona fide tantric practices – not just sexual – are great examples of this. This eventually produces the evolved Scorpio traits of trust, dependability, great *in*-sight, and managed responsibility.

In no specific order, Scorpio domains are: psychology; sexual intercourse; evolutionary processes; cultural mores and taboos; consummations of relationships; our genetic material; the colon and the elimination of waste; the Kundalini energy intending to enter every cell; sexual union in that the lovers access what they cannot on their own; the act of sexual intercourse in the penetration or enmeshment into another's energy/body/psychic field.

Its positive qualities are regeneration, rebirth, positive will power, positive self-motivation, non-defensiveness, deep strength and resiliency, and the ability to change as necessary.

Scorpio Polarity: Taurus

To balance its intense or willful penetration into others' hidden interiors, Scorpio can draw on Taurus' ability to self-stabilize in its own identity, power, and value. From Taurus, Scorpio can gain self-acceptance, a delight in physicality and its pleasures, a greater capacity *to receive* from others and a quality of foundation-ness (fixed earth). These qualities can balance

Scorpio's rather constant need to push one's limits, to feel intensely, to pursue external sources of feeling deeply while ignoring one's own, and to carry ulterior motives in engaging with others.

SCORPIO SHADOW

Compulsive; manipulative; jealous; defensive; hidden; intractable; possessive; obsessive; suspicious; sadistic; vindictive; controlling; selfish; hurtful; mean; narcissistic.

SCORPIO SELF-REALIZATION

Scorpio's self-realization includes the experience of a far greater energy flowing through its circuits. It will also feel that it somehow knows *how* to manage in its own 'red zone' of amped-up energy. What is actually occurring is the release of Kundalini energy. It produces the experience of being far more greatly infused with life force (prana) itself or its own higher power (foreshadowing the key meaning of the next sign, Sagittarius). The maximal infusion of greater aliveness causes a transformation of the normal experience of the self. The individual becomes an agent of the 'force of creation'.

♇ PLUTO

In general, Pluto is the symbol for *both* our deeply unconscious fear *and* our deepest knowing of ourself (the Soul).

As the symbol for death/rebirth, metamorphosis, transmutation and regeneration, Pluto describes where in the psyche we are afraid of our inherent lack[4], or that which we *subconsciously believe* we are permanently lacking in some fundamental way to our existence. Therefore, Pluto symbolizes a place of potential abuse, manipulation, or death of *any* kind, as we will either try to avoid discovery of this information (by remaining in self-abusive situations overtly or implicitly), or convince ourselves it doesn't exist (through the over-powering or manipulation of others). Further it signifies how we are meant to transform ourselves out of patterns, beliefs or other limitations which hold us back.

Pluto is also the symbol for the position of the Soul in its current evolutionary journey (see chapters 9-10), and the karmic Soul's Desire. Pluto's sign/house/aspects are the deepest and widest context for understanding ourselves and our purpose.

8TH HOUSE

The 8th House expresses through experiences of 'little' or 'ego' transformations – the act itself of dying; powerful attractions/repulsions; psychic experiences; taboos; occult; our legacies; our eroticism; our relationships' possessions – how we substantiate our bond with the other; our symbols of power; what we die to; how we are transformed and then resurrected/rebirthed; where we are meant to break down in order to reveal our limitations; orgasm in the sense of the transformation of normal consciousness; and the focus and reason for our manipulating or overpowering others.

The signs of the 8th House signify our orientation toward personal transformation and 'what' we tend to deem as taboo subjects. They will thus reflect what we project or assume others' focus for and method of transformation should be and what others should not speak about (taboo).

NOTES:

[1] There is a growing popularity in studying the evolution of consciousness, or how consciousness itself develops. This study differs from traditional human developmental models in that developmental models tend to work from the outside-in, meaning that they are formulated predominantly from studies of human behavior at different stages of its development. Individuals are then placed *into* one or more positions within the model. Studies of consciousness evolution by definition cannot be exclusively based on human behavioral trends because they are studying consciousness, which expresses in everything, everyone and everywhere (for more about this, see 'Pisces'). The perceived will truly arise from the perceiver's orientation to it. Thus consciousness evolution must be discerned from the inside-out and then refined through statistically defendable models.

When examining the evolution of consciousness itself, one finds that one's position of observation will largely determine what one sees. Ken Wilbur states, 'From the inside, evolution is like riding a psychotic horse toward a burning barn. The evolutionary urge is deeply erotic in an intense form. Half of the [evolutionary] experience is a blissful pushing into newness, while the other half is a carpet burn from a death of the old.'

[2] I was first introduced to this correlation by the work of astrologer Jeffrey Wolf Green.

[3] What are too often categorized as 'dark nights of the soul' are actually deaths to certain aspects of those egos too afraid to believe that they will in fact live through the experience. The forthcoming book *Bridges of Union: The Archetypes of*

Masculine & Feminine Transformation (2006) will include a thorough essay on the topic of the dark night of the soul misnomer. It suggests instead 'the dark night of the ego.'

[4] For a description of the archetype of lack as it emanates from the Pluto archetype, and as it fuels the Soul's Desire, see chapters 9–10.

"To fear anything is to believe you are separate from God." – Emmet Fox

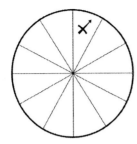

⚹ SAGITTARIUS

MASCULINE – MUTABLE – FIRE

Seeking and expanding into higher intelligence (spirituality). Learning to connect to a greater reality.

As a mutable energy, Sagittarius represents an upward and outward-type movement in consciousness where one's evolution requires that one discover how one is meant to be drawn higher. Sagittarius is the first place where the archetype of spiritual expansion appears. After Scorpio transforms any resistance to a fuller, more empowered self thus engendering a more deeply-aligned Identity, the embodied Soul next seeks to discover the broader sphere of consciousness it operates within, just as the mountain climber has his eyes set on the top. And we see this illustrated in Sagittarius' archetypal culmination at the highest point of the birth chart, the *medium coeli* or 'middle heaven' known as the Midheaven. Sagittarius asks us to face the challenge of a new type of unknown: the mystery of a greater reality. This is an awareness which requires a new opening to occur.

Through Sagittarius, we learn that there is indeed a reality or dimension which is more broad in scope than our normal perception would allow access to. We discover that this broader field is in fact greater than we are. The Sagittarian Identity therefore desires to experience for itself this expansive-ness. The Soul here is stretching upward to remember itself, and of course brings the Identity with it. It ultimately seeks to experience its relationship to this greater-ness. The Fire of Sagittarius burns on the action of seeking... seeking for understanding of this greater-ness as well as itself within it. The wisdom gained from Sagittarian learnings is of a more subtle realm than the phenomenal world. It represents a body of information which can only produce a reformulated Identity, one that can include a higher reality in which its ego is not the director of the show.

That which Sagittarius seeks is ultimately *to find meaning in this greater reality*. Discovering meaning, or understanding, is the ultimate Sagittarian Holy Grail. This fact explains several domains of human life associated with Sagittarius: philosophy (meaning of life), religion (connection to God), spirituality (our essence or nature), and illumination (experience of more light within). In order to have new experiences (whatever 'new' might mean), we need to be open to them. Once we experience something new, Sagittarius urges us onward *to understand what we've experienced*. In other words, to find meaning in them: 'What does this mean for me?' 'What should I do about it?' 'How does this change my current beliefs or opinions?' In order to find meaning in these initially foreign experiences, we again need to be rather flexible in our beliefs... if we are too fixed on believing that we already know, then our Sagittarian function within will never get off the ground or we won't ever board the plane in the first place: 'Why fly if I already know where I'm going *and* how I'll get there *and* what it will mean for me?'

Sagittarius is the stage of development where we identify our truth – what we believe to be true and why. The full picture of one's 'truth' must include not only Sagittarius but aspects of *every* sign. Where some deal directly with how we create reality and our truth, others provide a foundation of Identity and relatedness which support our creation of them. For our purposes, the idea of Sagittarian 'personal truth' derives from the combination of both cognitive and intuitive formulating, ordering, and prioritizing the invisible aspects of life into a workable schematic. Our personal truth also includes our opinions and ethics, but encompasses much more as well. Inhabiting our truth will only begin to mature in Sagittarius because prior to it there has been no exposure to a greater reality; before Sagittarius, personal truth can only be created from subjective and early objective understandings. It is in fact the Scorpionic ego-death experiences which are responsible for the Sagittarian personal truth to be sought after. In other words, if we have gained the capacity to know that we are limited and are responsible for those limitations (Scorpio), then we will be ready and indeed desirous of discovering ourselves anew in more *un*-limited ways. When we connect to the higher order of creation – Nature – we find ourselves to be limited only by our own imaginations.

This connection *is* our personal truth. It is what we *believe* about that bigger order, or Nature, or God, and how and why we are a part of it. It is important to remember that Sagittarius is the place of our truth, rather than final Truth. For example, my truth might be that astrology is the path to happiness. But I will need to learn that that's not true for everyone, that it is a facet of my personal truth. But a final or universal Truth might be *all things change*. One way to understand this distinction is to ask, 'Is my belief actually applicable to all of life?' If not, then you know you're in the realm of Sagittarius. If so, then think about Pisces.

The archetype of belief itself is quite central to Sagittarius. The etymology of *belief* is *'that which we hold dear to or trust in.'* And the verb *to Believe* is quite close in origin to the verb *to Love*. When we believe in something, we are 'giving permission' or *taking lieve* for that idea to enter us. In other words, a belief is an idea or a concept which we invest in, attach to, or identify with. If we have not consciously chosen our beliefs, then our inner body-mind relationship will be built with at best temporary and at worst false beliefs. True Sagittarius demands we never stop searching for our truth, that we never stop seeking out those beliefs which might bring us higher in our understanding of ourselves and the universe. As we reach higher in our understanding – as our understanding grows to include more of a universal understanding – our reality will change eventually bringing us to the point where the beliefs themselves no longer serve our enlightenment. Sagittarius is the component of personal reality in which the self comes to *know* itself as part of something larger.

When we stop the true search for understanding our connection to the universe, our Identity crystallizes around the specific beliefs invested in at the time because those beliefs represent the known, the familiar and the safe and reveal where we've stopped. We become close-minded to other beliefs, religions, and philosophies if they are different than or challenge our own. This is the familiar pattern of the ego's function to maintain self-stability (see Cancer). Through Sagittarius, ego stability is sustained by our closely-held philosophical, religious or spiritual definitions.

The Sagittarius square (90°) to the Virgo-Pisces axis reflects one way this works. The square from Virgo to Sagittarius is the argument between the self striving to improve itself by its own (human) efforts and its seeking of a higher connection, which is certainly another kind of improvement, through forces greater than itself. The square from Sagittarius to Pisces is the conflict between one's personal truth and the greater truth applicable to all, or that between the upward expansion to higher realms (Sagittarius) and the *omnidirectional* expansion of consciousness encompassing everything and everywhere (Pisces). Thirdly, it is the argument between the need to discover, establish, and follow one's own truth, and the unavoidable, final release of that truth back into the One Truth of all Life, or God, at death.

With its focus on the search for truth, Sagittarius is the sign which symbolizes the religious or spiritual head (and maybe the political proselytizer), the guru, the philosopher, and the traveler or adventure-seeker. Through teaching or spreading our wisdom, we attempt to make our outer environment more like our inner (belief) environment. When this occurs with consciousness and integrity, real learning and expansion can occur for both. But if our desire to seek, travel, teach or to religiously lead others emanates from the belief that our way is either 'the only way' or 'God's only way', then there is a selfish (or self-righteous) and egoic motivation present.

SAGITTARIUS POLARITY: GEMINI

This axis (Sagittarius-Gemini) is the axis of the human mind or development of mental balance – left-right, inner-outer, and lower-higher thinking. In order to grow, Sagittarius must draw on the Gemini appreciation for a wide array of paths and information. This will keep Sagittarius from solidifying in its own beliefs and needing for others to believe the same. As Sagittarius symbolizes one's personal truth, it will need Gemini to make sure that its relative version of truth is seen as such and to balance its perpetual seeking for a personally-experienced higher connection/deeper meaning with a large acceptance of others' paths.

SAGITTARIUS SHADOW

"A great many people think they are thinking when they are merely rearranging their prejudices." – William James

Self-righteous; blind faith; dogmatic; blatantly insensitive; spiritual or religious naiveté; impatient; superior; spiritually superficial; deceptive; emotionally disconnected; false idolizing.

The mutability of Sagittarius can lead to a life lived as an 'endless search' in which there is never any 'finding' due to the addiction to searching; reliance on a non-specific understanding of what truth is; dogmatic assumption that 'we already know'; assuming that 'others should believe as we believe' which can be traced to an egoic need to have others believe as we do in order to feel safe, not threatened, and to protect the deeper suspicion that one's truth or beliefs are small-visioned, foolish or simply wrong.

SAGITTARIUS SELF-REALIZATION

Sagittarius' self-realization archetype is perhaps the closest to what is commonly known as the *samadhi* experience. It is the experience of an inner a-ha!, a full awakening to one's innate nature as spiritual essence, and the embodied realization (beyond the mental) of one's direct connection to spiritual Light.

♃ JUPITER

The largest planet in our solar system. Within our psyche, Jupiter is the function to expand, grow, explore, leap, and to understand the broad design of life. Its effect is to expand us in some way. This expanding within consciousness can also have a frequency-raising effect, which can force any flaw in that system to show up (a blown gasket, a deceitful business partner, a dormant disease). Jupiter's expansiveness is the cause of its association with spiritual pursuits, religion, teachers, certain expressions of the father archetype, and most kinds of beneficent results from our efforts (windfalls, new career success, inheritances, etc.) Also, Jupiter points to how the human psyche comes to absorb its experiences of greater realities, more intense experiences (Scorpio and 8th House), and broader consciousness. To do this, the Jupiterian individual will be less focused on the minutiae and more on the 'big picture.' In this way, Jupiter's effect is to assimilate us into something; or something *into* us.

9TH HOUSE

The 9th House is symbolized by our long travels; our higher education; our intuitive abilities; our right-brain functioning; our personal truth; what for us are foreign cultures and ideas; our spiritual practices, teachers and pursuits; our religious beliefs and practices; our style of integrating new understandings; how we move toward either group harmony or dogma through our own beliefs; our 'big' dreams; and our symbols of spiritual connection and understanding.

The signs of the 9th House signify our orientation to attaining higher awareness and its integration into our lives. They will thus reflect what we project or assume others' path of spiritual development and integration should be.

"To be a human is to feel that one's own stone contributes to the edifice of the world." – St. Exupéry

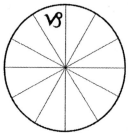

♑ CAPRICORN

FEMININE – CARDINAL – EARTH

Appropriate application of wisdom/authority/responsibility. Effectively managing within the constraints of time and space.

Here in Capricorn, the Earth element goes cardinal. Cardinal Earth is a good way to understand the general intent within consciousness of Capricorn. It says: apply and implement, out in the world, with others, in society. Capricorn intends to make use of the wisdom gained in Sagittarius. The image of a mountain is a good one to describe the relationship between Sagittarius and Capricorn. The journey up its slopes to connect with greater reality is Sagittarius. The return trip down the other side to disseminate the information for others symbolizes Capricorn. Moses returning to the Israelites from his Mt. Sinai meeting with the Lord carrying the Ten Commandments in his arms is a good example of this image.

Capricorn people do have a natural knowing of how best to manage, organize, administer, lead, or teach. It includes an awareness of the past and what has and hasn't worked, so that it can bring those experiences to bear on the present. In this we see Capricorn corresponding to the archetype of elders, teachers or ancestors, those who have come before us and from whom we can learn. Interestingly, Cancer, Capricorn's polarity, is also directly related to ancestors.

Some Capricorn expressions will include a quality of far-seeingness, or vision. And as a feminine sign, Capricorn desires to give form to the wisdom it carries. How that comes about is to a large degree known as community. The activities which make up communal functioning include leadership, group rules and laws, individual responsibility and loyalty, trust in fellow members, willingness to voice personal concerns, consensus mentality, taboos and forbidden behaviors, the limitations of any organization, and entrusting personal concerns to the group wisdom. It is primary in the Capricorn awareness that individual effort serve the collective goal: "Individual success is a myth. What succeeds is the society – and ultimately mankind – through an individual who has developed power of mind or skills which are actually the result of the endeavors and struggles of countless preceding generations."[1]

An individual's involvement in a group or society reflects their individuality within a larger universe. So Capricorn also symbolizes how we function within linear time and definable space. It is within this domain that we can understand the crux of the Capricorn psychological conflict: how can it apply its innate wisdom within a constrained, physical world (earth sign) which is filled with human dynamics (square from Libra) and which together produce a limited, inconsistent, myopic, and error-prone field (human society) in which to do so? Capricorn carries a very deep desire to implement organization among people, yet it will be constantly faced with these facts.

In other words, Capricorn is the stage within consciousness where we come to face the truth that we have a limited amount of time, resources, or personal capacity to structure life in a positive way for the whole. Much of the Capricorn psychology can be understood with this as a starting point. For example, Capricorn's trait of *duration* or lastingness allows it to 'go the distance' in light of the ever-present feeling of being limited or restricted by prior or current forms and structures. *Nobility* is another Capricorn quality which emanates from its innate, pragmatic, managerial-like counsel which often expresses an uncanny awareness of past ideas, successes and failures.

The intrinsic relationship between Capricorn and the past is an interesting one to explore. I suggest that its placement *after* the Sagittarian stage of consciousness (the seeking of greater understanding) and *opposite* the Cancer stage (the subconscious relation with ancestors/the past as one's origins) seem to combine to create the Capricorn desire to consciously apply the wisdom of the past on present circumstances. Further, its feminine and earth qualities would naturally create a solid storehouse for memory of past deeds, both personally and collectively.

Capricorn will naturally take responsibility or positions of leadership because it subconsciously knows that its evolution depends on its experiences of responsibility and leadership, and ultimately on its ability to operate effectively in a social setting. For example, if I decide to build a new house, and four months into the project, I've fired every contractor or worker I've hired because I perceive they've failed to perform their jobs in the way I deem correct. Despite the actual progress being made, I may in fact be sabotaging the plan's completion due to my inability to release attachment to the ideas of how things should be done. In Capricorn fashion, I may then legitimize my actions with rational explanations of the faults of the project and the need for my increased control of the situation to manage things properly. In this example, the project itself is a metaphor for life; the constant replacement of personnel is the result of a misplaced Capricorn initiative to apply one's expertise in the world with others.

To evolve the pattern of struggling against the nature of life as it really is requires we bring ourselves to deeply understand that our lives are limited. We have limited time on Earth, plans don't go as planned, and accidents and changes happen. Acknowledging these truths is important for building a more accurate relationship with the natural limitations of our lives: once again, time and space. Then re-discovering our authority within these unavoidable constrictions becomes the seed for a self-sustaining Capricorn contentment and marks a high attainment within consciousness.

More often, Capricorn initially will become depressed, as a way to eventually reach this same awareness. The archetype of depression[2] is a bona fide strategy for deep self-inquiry. In relative moderation, it is healthy and useful. Too much of it is a Capricorn shadow expression. As we go within, we become clearer about our limitedness and more realistic about ourselves. Perhaps we cleanse ourselves of some of the deep resistance to the natural limitations of the world and our lives. As we become more realistic about ourselves, we become more realistic about others and our expectations of them. We eventually re-calibrate our psychological orientations and interactions with others in social or hierarchical relationships.

The Capricorn Self-Identity is thoroughly wrapped up in the social identity – its successes, failures, reputation and level of social acceptance. Capricorn is highly sensitized to what the culture says it should be – sexually, politically, gender-wise, religiously, professionally, etc. This naturally creates a huge pressure within the self to conform to those outside definitions. If an individual is pressured to conform and s/he is not in full alignment with the end result, the psyche must suppress some aspect of itself to allow the conforming to occur.

Why do conformity, suppression, and distortion arise from Capricorn? It seems to be because all three are the result of the general dynamic of an individual self trying to manage or administer a larger-than-self system. Capricorn strives to structure reality in a pragmatic way for all. In outwardly structuring our reality (cardinal earth), we can effectively and relevantly participate in what is otherwise a chaotic, anarchistic and time-limited universe. We counteract the internal pressure for acknowledgement, acceptance, and approval from the consensus as a mark of security. Once again, these drives emanate from the impulse to formalize or systemize successful methods and structures of living in harmony with one another, with the Earth, and within a larger universe.

Looking deeper at the personal cauldron of inner experience, we see that we are constellated around discovering ourselves as part of or at the head of a larger system: to feel ourself as the center, the leader, the organizer, or simply the one holding it all together and to feel legitimately credited for our role in the success of the group. Through this, Capricorn feels a measure of autonomy and influence within the limitations. Here we see the Capricorn domains of social position, professional or personal reputation, and one's leadership or management skills.

And this self-experience is a window into understanding Capricorn intimacy and sexuality.[3] For Capricorn to be validated is to be, in a sense, seen or exposed around a tender issue: one's effectiveness. Due to its heightened sensitivity to the group mind, the Capricorn experience of 'being seen' will trigger a deep safety or security feeling, which will naturally give rise to a desire to open up from a deep place, which in turn can trigger sexual arousal and desire. In light of the heightened repression on our emotional, psychological, and sexual self-expressions from our culture (mass consciousness) and the Capricornian sensitivity to this societal pressure to 'obey', we can understand how deep the Capricorn feeling function runs and how much opening has to occur within a psyche in this culture to produce a feeling of freedom of self-expression.

Dark Eros is an archetype most closely placed in the domain of Capricorn[4]. The dark side of Eros arises when the light side is either unavailable, feared or we are ignorant of its existence. If sufficient healing, integration, or transformation of the inner need to conform and to have others conform to one's authority has not occurred, more than likely this repression will lead to sexual or creative repression.

The goal of Capricorn within consciousness is to realize one's innate self-authority and inner wisdom accurately and effectively by reconciling oneself to one's powerful inner energies, needs, and conflicts. This will require the reformulation of one's Self-Identity, which can harmoniously occur with the healthy acceptance that the self exists within limitation, is thus limited in its abilities, but is unlimited in its capacity for long-seeing wisdom.

CAPRICORN POLARITY: CANCER

From Cancer, Capricorn is reminded that one's deep roots of identity ultimately are the source of self-authority and effective expression of wisdom, rather than the outer success of its managements. Cancer assists Capricorn to maintain awareness and make important its own emotional life (rather than repressing it) while trusting that emotional caring must be present for all true leadership to exist.

CAPRICORN SHADOW

Dictatorial; aloof; depressive; energetically heavy; apparently unfeeling; tight; 'by the book.' Staying trapped or hidden behind powerful forces of repression or unresolved inner frustrations and anger; intense needs to control situations, one's emotions, or those of others; demanding respect without having earned it; needing to lead; being unable to learn from others.

CAPRICORN SELF-REALIZATION

The Capricorn self-realization experience is one of a profound realization of personal purpose in the context of collective effort. When one has realized oneself to be an effective, caring, generous and wise leader or administrator of wisdom, self-realization becomes an ongoing experience. Specifically, the trigger for the experience is the cellular recognition that one has been effective in one's duties and has served others well. Though it may sound rather dry, the individual who is, in a bona fide way, destined for Capricorn self-realization will be highly sensitized to the powerful trans- or supra-personal experience of utilizing man-made rules and regulations to transcend them. The results can bring the individual to a highly realized status of something along the lines of a saint.

♄ SATURN

"Saturn is a planet of strength. Wherever it moves, it seeks to strengthen what it touches." – James Kelleher

The ordering/structuring/forming function in our psyche, Saturn represents the process of densification (ie., as higher energy states transduce into lower vibration states) and how we are meant to *strengthen*[5] ourselves. Without Saturn, nothing can happen because nothing will ever form within time and space. Saturn can represent the Father, the Authority – government, church, etc., society in general, and mass consciousness or any figure in a superior position than the individual. Saturn also indicates one's personal wiring into the mass consciousness: how one is more vulnerable to societal pressure, and thus perpetuates mass consciousness (progressively and regressively); how one is meant to transform personally and collectively a particular expression or embodiment of consciousness; how and what one learns to organize, structure, and/or disseminate one's innate wisdom and earned authority around; how one acts in positions of authority, and in positions of hierarchical inferiority (ie., as an employee or child); and what one feels pressured to conform to.

Saturn represents the father or other authority figures in one's life; the way one is destined to strengthen one's resolve within society; how one is meant to form and psychologically function within a career or long-term commitment.

10TH HOUSE

The 10th House is symbolized by our father or authority figures (but not God); our career, reputation and in other ways our earned public notoriety; our social position within a group; our best achievements or accomplishments; our areas of responsibility in life; our teachers and leaders; our social morality and ethics; our larger contribution to society (6th House is more of our personal work); our bosses or employers; our religious structure and how we uphold/contribute to it; our government/nation/state/community and its laws. The 10th House also contains what we repress in order to 'fit into' our society; and thus correlates to our dark eros; our depression-tendency; and what we assume to be true for us from our cultural values.

The signs of the 10th House signify our picture of social order and how individuals are best meant to contribute to that structure. They will thus reflect our projections and assumptions about how others should function within social structures. For more information, see 'Midheaven' in chapter 5.

NOTES:

[1] Dane Rudhyar, *The Astrological Houses*.

[2] I was first introduced to this idea by the work of astrologer Jeffrey Wolf Green.

[3] It seems astrologers in general fail to explore this side of the Capricorn consciousness.

[4] Some wonderful work has been done by various Evolutionary Astrologers to examine deeply the dark eros of Capricorn.

[5] I was first introduced to this idea by Vedic astrologer James Kelleher.

"A truth once seen, even by a single mind, always ends by imposing itself on the totality of human consciousness." – Pierre Teilhard de Chardin

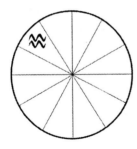

♒ AQUARIUS

MASCULINE – FIXED – AIR

Commitment to innovating impassioned change with detachment. Learning to bridge between consciousnesses.

If Capricorn represents the crown of consciousness development on the level of matter and the highest realization attainable in form – symbolized by the archetype of the Elder, then Aquarius is the intent to transcend one's own crown in exchange for newer heights unknown. Where Capricorn's impulse is to order and structure, Aquarius seeks to go beyond those structures and envision new forms.

Through Aquarius, this will occur outwardly (masculine). Aquarius will naturally avoid or try to break any structure (Capricorn) which binds, defines or limits it, such as an organization's rules, social pressures, a political party's agenda, a family's requirements, a religion or spiritual group's dogma, or an intimate relationship's vulnerability. Rather, it will seek to identify with those social forms that offer freedom of expression without ties as well as individuals that think like it (fixed sign).

On the worldly level, the ultimate intention of Aquarius is to create new, improved systems of social organization from one's own unique orientation to life. Aquarians are the social rebellers and activists pining for improvement. Essentially, all these 'external' organizations from which Aquarius tries to extract itself or improve upon are actual reflections of its own needs to realize more freedom. In fact, the Aquarian Self-Identity is predicated on being free from (what it perceives to be) any limitation. Where Scorpio is transformation from within, Aquarius might be described as freedom through (or into) without.

Aquarius desires to know itself as boundless. Yet it finds itself within a frustratingly-limited human context. It will initially think of its body, emotions, fears, and habitual patterns as insignificant to its goals because it operates mentally. As the fixed air sign of the zodiac, Aquarius assumes it can *think* anything into or out of existence and will exhibit a strongly determined and persistent mind whose core drive is to create life to be as its own nature: objective, unbounded, creative. Aquarius will rationalize its detached orientation to life and those 'messy' human domains of emotionality, intimacy and commitment, with questions like 'Why go into the emotions?', and 'Why become personally involved?' It may even respond with 'They're too messy, too unclear, too unnecessary.' This excuse-making exists on the level of the mind and derives from its egoic fear of being held back or losing itself. Though the Aquarian Self-Identity is highly intelligent, visionary, objective and creative, it will lack a direct knowing of its more human qualities of emotional vulnerability and physical inconsistency.

This creates a schism within the Identity. It is as if its vision lives on one side and its human experience on the other. It will require a tremendously convincing argument to attempt to bridge the gap between the two. This is usually provided only by repeated failures of its revolutionary projects, futuristic plans, or attempted friendships. What is missing – and therefore what must be cultivated – is meaningful, *personal* connections with others. With enough failures at *what could be*, Aquarius will eventually look to or be forced back into itself to examine 'what's not right.' It will inevitably experience deep frustration because it will be unable to identify itself as the source of the disconnect. Rather, it will believe itself to be interminably blocked by the stupidity of others, by unseen forces, or because the world is simply not ready for its 'advanced' ideas. But these beliefs are only beliefs; the reality is that the only way it will be able to bring about positive change is for it to locate and inhabit its human context more meaningfully. This will require actual emotional or psychological transformation. It is insufficient for Aquarius to simply analyze its situation or itself, as analysis usually remains on the level of mind. It will need to enter the deeper feelings and allow that mysterious intelligence to guide the healing process.

Aquarian psychology is one of constant innovation and creativity, a tendency toward dissociation, an avoidance of deep emotionality or commitment, and an ongoing need to differentiate oneself from the norm. Aquarius will often mask its denial of its humanity as a way to avoid dealing with psychological and emotional issues. Aquarians will carry an angry frustration about not being understood or seen for their brilliance or uniqueness, and may easily hide this fact from themselves and others. Indeed, repressed anger and/or frustration is a very common trait of Aquarian individuals today.[1] Further, Aquarians will desire to separate those aspects of self which they perceive keep them bound to rules: fear, physicality, insecurities, uncertain or overpowering emotions, doubts, and karma (on the personal level), and any participation in rules-based, consensus-minded groups or organizations (on the social level). Aquarians will bounce between periods of self-isolating behavior and impassioned commitment to a cause or alternative group. The Aquarian isolation pattern is evolutionary designed as an opportunity for self-inquiry; by retreating to its familiar space of feeling alone, it can view itself objectively and take stock of the current situation. But as a fixed sign, its tendency to hold to the known initially may not allow its self-inquiries to bear any deeper fruit. Gradually, Aquarians will discover a far greater capacity to realize their purpose – to meaningfully contribute to a better society in unique ways – once they accept more of themselves. From this angle, an Aquarian lesson is to realize that no matter who we are or what we do, we each exist within a physical, emotional, social, familial, communal, vocational, national, and planetary context, and that each not only does not have to restrict us, but also can create opportunities for more fully *inhabiting* our Identity so that we can more effectively and efficiently contribute our vision to the future.

"The finger of God never leaves identical fingerprints." – Stanislaw Lec

As mentioned, Aquarius will gravitate to a detached self- and world-view. Separating or distancing from one's emotional reality, immediate experience, or pre-set ways of thinking is what is known as *objective consciousness*. Objective consciousness also allows us to gain perspective about intense or confusing situations. The 'observer' is the voice within us which observes what we are experiencing; it is known as the seat of the witness. For Aquarius, this comes quite naturally. Aquarius will seek to change, innovate, improve, create, radicalize, or re-invent its social or personal structures because the unshackling of itself from the bonds of restrictions symbolizes what it strives to know itself as: unbounded and unique.

If Aquarius succeeds in transforming the ingrained psychological patterns of perpetuated self-isolation, it will no longer need to remain isolated in the name of being misunderstood or different. It will no longer have need of overemphasizing the importance of uniqueness for egoic reasons. It can then inhabit a more mature Self-Identity – one that does not subconsciously depend on outer success or social uniqueness but on the quality of one's contribution to changing the world through creativity, far-seeingness and community. When the Self-Identity shifts in this way, *the former fear issues transform themselves into new tools of insight and understanding.* In Aquarius, these tools create a *deeper* human experience within, which supports its capacity to envision more clearly.

Either way Aquarius goes – either evolving out of self-isolating and frustration-causing belief patterns or remaining entrenched in them – it will naturally gravitate towards creating its own social circles and connections. This happens for two reasons: to give to itself what it feels the world cannot – recognition as a leader or visionary or simply unique – and to form a new association of like-minded individuals constellated around a common dream or mission. In this way, its pattern of feeling like a permanent foreigner in the world is temporarily alleviated. With enough of these experiences over time, the pattern itself is transcended, and the individual then begins *to live as that which s/he is moving towards.* In other words, one becomes a channel or vessel not only for what socially needs to change but also how that change can happen.

When Aquarius is able to balance its objective nature with its more human qualities, it strikes a resonant chord within the heavens: *heaven gains another messenger.* This does not necessarily refer to a religious or blatantly spiritual expression of heaven, but to a more universal one. It suggests that individuals are the representatives of a larger intelligence which require nothing outside of themselves to receive instructions. Indeed, Aquarius' nature is as a receiver of communication (fixed air). If we think of a central computer communicating with many individual workstations to perform individual tasks in synchrony, this gives a picture of how the heralded Aquarian Age may look.[2] The success of this organizational scheme is dependent on the absence of the automaton (consensus) mentality; it requires true individuality from each member. With each individual following their individual purpose which only they 'know' at any moment, a greater pattern of development is revealed over time. Each individual is thus responsible for listening and following their own inspiration/intuition/guidance. Each individual becomes a 'channel' of sorts.

It may be surprising that the archetypes of channeling information or modeling a different reality in present time are rooted in the human body's electrical nature. Through the electrical acceleration of the human body-mind, Aquarius reveals why it is known as the zodiacal 'bringer of the future.' As seen in its glyph (≈), Aquarius is the domain of electrical energy – within and without. And if electricity is the flow of energy through a conductor, then Aquarius is truly the electrical conductor of the zodiac and Aquarians are the human conductors of the human species. Aquarians 'conduct' all types of new ideas, new visions of the future, and new improvements on prior conventions. They receive this information due to their heightened electrical functioning. In this we can understand why Aquarius is considered the Sign *least* defined by the cycles of Gaia, such as day/night, the solar year and the lunar cycle. It operates exclusively from how consciousness itself is structured and infuses everything.[3] Consciousness does not require wires to run through. It is ubiquitous. Consciousness as a self-evolving flow seeking new directions is an Aquarian archetype.

The Aquarian orientation to *collective change* and its close relationship to the 'structure' of consciousness can help illuminate why the sign has been associated with the personal unconscious.[4] The level of personal or *individual unconsciousness*[5] holds all an individual's self-denials and unrealized patterns of manipulation, invisibility, and psychic violence; all of its unacknowledged and un-enacted dreams for itself and its world; and all its memories of past incarnations and contracts for the current one. An individual's 'personal' unconscious is that which chords him/her into the collective unconscious (Pisces).

The Age of Aquarius refers to the time when societies will operate with higher efficiency, more vision, and through new forms of social structures. In essence, Aquarius teaches that while individuals are the building blocks for a collective vision to come to pass, it is equally true that a collective vision can inspire and motivate individual purpose. Aquarius reflects the interdependence of the personal and the collective spheres of activity and inspiration. It thus requires access to an unrestricted flow of inspiration and opportunities to communicate and implement its futuristic vision.

AQUARIUS POLARITY: LEO

The *self-focused* perspective of Leo can balance the one-sided *collective-focused* perspective of Aquarius. Through Leo, Aquarius can discover that it is not only safe but it can feel good to embrace the full range of one's humanity, and to be seen by others. It can learn commitment does not mean death but a richer opportunity for realization of its dreams. And it can embrace itself as an inherent part of a universe that requires each individual to make up a successful whole.

AQUARIUS SHADOW

Dissociated; austere; superior; unrealistic; idealistically manipulative; self-righteous; blindly hopeful; inconsistent; consumed by ideas; emotionally absent; critical; ungrounded; imbalanced; intimacy-averse; irresponsible; and self-isolating through idealisms.

AQUARIUS SELF-REALIZATION

The Aquarian self-realization experience can take many forms, but the essence of the inner transformation which gives rise to it is the cellular release from an I-based context. This shift can be momentary or long-lasting. It is the direct experience of pure objectivity overtaking the normally subjective-dominated Identity. When this occurs, it frees the individual from individual-ness and releases him/her into an unbounded state of awareness. In any typically Uranus transit or effect, the most unexpected, unprepared-for thing happens. In this is the subtle hint that seems to say 'if you flow with rather than against this influence, you may discover yourself quite freer than you might have imagined.'

♅ URANUS

From ancient myths, we learn Ouranus was birthed by Gaia. Natal Uranus signifies what the individual is meant to free him/herself from and how. It also signifies the individual unconsciousness, the nature of an individual's electrical communication of brain to nervous system throughout the body. Uranus' effect is to accelerate consciousness through electrical magnification. Uranus symbolizes higher communication and the drive to rebel, innovate or improve on social or technological status quo. Transiting Uranus will trigger experiences which ultimately arise from one's unconscious wiring (these will be seen as shocks, or at least be very unexpected). The distance of Uranus to the Sun is twice the distance of Saturn to the Sun, meaning that the unknown (Uranus) requires at least two times the effort to access than the known (Saturn). "Uranus is the power of the Universal Mind."[6]

11TH HOUSE

The 11th House will express through our social and political circles, and circle of friends; our socially-acquired resources such as money, contacts, and a personal network; our social skills, shared visions, dreams, and aspirations, global ideals; the group identity we choose to incorporate into our personal identity; our level of social/political involvement (indicated by number of planets in 11th). Also, the electrical circuitry in our body; our unexpected visions; our ability to channel; the quality of our connection and communication with other realities; and the objective (social) 'results' of the subjective (personal) seeds sown in the 5th House.

The signs of the 11th House signify our definitions for friendship, what and how we uniquely envision for the future, and our ideas of a more-perfect, improved society. They will thus reflect our projections and assumptions about how others should orient to friendship, what others' dreams and aspirations for the future should be, and what their ideas for a better world should be.

NOTES:

[1] Let us remember that, as an archetype, repression is more of a Capricorn dilemma. In this light, the Aquarian dispensation to repress any of its experience indicates in fact its impending disillusionment when it perceives it cannot change outer structures fast enough for its own speed of vision. And underneath this, is the egoic imperative to maintain its secure stability, Aquarian style. For more on the Aquarian ego definitions and resistances to change, see chapter 15.

[2] My personal view of societies in the Aquarian Age is that of many individual workstations or human-stations operating independently in their external lives, while internally being 'guided' or intuitively instructed by the same 'central computer' as all others in that society or group. Of course, this prediction relies exclusively on how well the individuals within these future societies are embodying their innate Aquarian traits.

[3] However, consciousness itself as a component of existence is a Pisces archetype.

[4] I was first introduced to this association by the work of astrologer Jeffrey Wolf Green.

[5] The term 'individual unconscious' was first introduced by Carl Jung.

[6] Dane Rudhyar, *The Astrology of Personality*.

"...the field of infinite co-relation." – Deepak Chopra

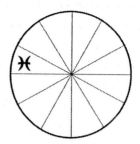

♓ PISCES

FEMININE – MUTABLE – WATER

Evolution of the personal space to empathically merge with all. Developing awareness of actual reality/Truth.

Pisces is the cosmic Water within which the Aquarian Air cognizes the future and all activity within existence occurs. Piscean Water is not flowing on Earth, but rather is the Water of Life: it is consciousness itself or the most fundamental and knowable nature of existence, which we call God.

In Pisces, the Soul approaches the highest understanding: that it has never been separate from its source and that its journey through individuality (ego) and duality (time-space) was designed to prepare it to return to that source with greater awareness of All That Is. Pisces symbolizes our unknown source, the unity of all life, and consciousness itself in its omnipresence. Pisces dissolves any egoic strivings for security based in self-separation, in order for the Identity to return to its essential nature – as Soul and in balanced relationship between self/God, known/unknown, and safety/insecurity.

If Aquarius represents the impulse to liberate from conformity, Pisces returns the impulse back into the self...more specifically, the transcendent self. In order to return to this state of transcendence, the self will need to release those beliefs and patterns which prevent it from experiencing a unity within and among all things. It will become exposed to the falsity of its own assumptions and beliefs. If these assumptions have been held very deeply within the psyche and the egoic structure has been largely dependent on them, then this realization will be traumatic within the Identity. It will release an onslaught of doubt about the existence of God, the quality of one's belief in God, or the quantity of worthiness one has earned to be graced by God. The Piscean Identity will necessarily be formed around one's beliefs (usually subconsciously) or automatic assumptions about the nature of true reality, beyond phenomena. This can take shape as notions of one's origins, how to care for others, how to remain unattached to worldly affairs, what happens after death, what constitutes selflessness or ego-less-ness, or even how to worship God. When the Piscean Identity is revealed to its erroneous safety needs, it will become profoundly disillusioned.[1] We can think of this experience as the beginning of either accepting more worldly reality or opening to a greater one which includes a divine source.

"Pisces represents the whole mechanism of life which operates regardless of the individual's understanding."[2]

Any aspect of the human psyche which emanates from the under-standing that everything has consciousness, that consciousness of a person is the same as that of a star as that of an ant, and that all consciousness communicates with itself is Pisces-derived. Examples are death, sleep, 'loss of self' or 'oneness' experiences, bi-location, remote viewing, distance heal-ing, psychic communication, past life memories, as well as offering one's experience for the greater good.

The Piscean Self-Identity is built around its relationship to the source of life (God) and how it lives and feels that in each moment. The innate conflict in this relationship – between self and its source – is central to understanding much of the Pisces archetype. How can we know God? Well, we can't, not directly anyway. The Mind of God is unknowable to the Mind of Human. The human consciousness initially requires intermediary symbols, pointers, or references in order to know God. This inevitable separation between seeker and sought is the source of Piscean illusion, the Buddhist notion of 'suffering' or the Existential 'pain of existence.' It is also the driving cause of the Soul's journey through incarnations. As humanity attains the capacity to communicate fully with and through its own DNA, it will organically draw closer to the Mind of God. Becoming more conscious of our totality through our own cellular instructions is a Pisces development.

If a self is understood to be an individuated aspect of total con-sciousness which naturally extends beyond the domain of normal human consciousness, then the self's initial awareness of its relationship to that totality will produce experiences or feelings of overwhelm, insignificance, threat, abandonment, betrayal, hopelessness, depression, and anger or rage. Later, the self learns to feel or know that its connection – its relationship to All That Is or total consciousness – is actually the source of its life and its happiness and, though much bigger than itself, that source is not threatening to it. It thus can release the egoic impulse to keep itself separate. No longer needing to be separate, the Soul can discover the inherent similarity it shares with all of life as a self. This in turn produces the ability to re-enter the world of appearances, of *maya*, and to be 'in but not of' the diversity it finds there.

But if Pisces never learns to develop *any* sense of difference, then it will not desire to form necessary boundaries between itself and others, the infamous 'lack of healthy boundaries' syndrome. An egoic 'oozing' will set in because of its weak self-structure and will be accompanied by a lack of desire to see mundane reality clearly. More accurately, it will be unable to do so just as weak arms are incapable of controlling 200 lbs. in a bench press. One might think one desires to become more realistic, pragmatic, and accurate, but the unwillingness to make the *deeper changes* in order to step more fully into a stronger Self-Identity will always dictate the level of attainable growth. What deeper changes? For one, to release the pattern of assuming energetic responsibility for all those one cares about or knows, or for all life itself. And in order to release this, Pisces will have to face (not deny) their strong emotions and loud inner voices accusing them of 'not caring', 'not being enough somehow to help,' or 'being selfish and insensitive.' These feelings are of course false as they arise from the delusional self-image of the savior or martyr archetype, the pattern of projecting one's subconscious issues of abandonment onto others and then 'saving' others to vicariously and temporarily allay one's own issues.

In Pisces is found a heightened sensitivity to the greater consciousness, and an intuitive knowing of life's inherent intimacy with itself. Pisces thus signifies the ability to be empathic, to feel the feelings of another, to be somewhat unaware or uninterested in the distinctions between things. This intimacy runs deeper than most non-Pisceans would be comfortable with. In fact, the intra-connection between life's infinite expressions is so deep that it actually undermines any separating- or differentiating-based reality one might cling to. In other words, life is innately an omnipresent oneness, a wholism or a unity which not only remains intact despite its infinite variations, but is in fact the *source of* those variations. And Pisces is the source of this reality and our knowing of it. In it we can understand the connection of the archetype of death to Pisces; death undermines *everything* that any individuated, definable, and phenomenal expression is created from. Death annihilates *difference*. It is known as the "great equalizer."

Ancient cosmologies around the world have addressed this quality of Pisces in various ways: 'It has been taught for thousands and thousands of years that Creation first occurred when the primordial One became Two, and further that the Two and their offspring the Many retain the inherent, core imprint of the One... The Chinese yin/yang symbol, the Kabbalist *Bahir*, the Mesoamerican Stone of the Suns, Alchemy's *prima materia*, the Australian Aboriginal Ancestors of the Dreaming, and the eternal dance of Lord Shiva and Shakti are ancient formulations of how the One becomes Two while maintaining Itself within the heart of all manifest creation.'[3]

From this, we see that in order to understand life's secret beyond the intellect – *that all truly is One* – we need a self-image that can allow for this to be true. There are two kinds of self-images that would allow this: a very weak one which observes this truth from a passive, naïve non-participation in life in which the ego has fallen backwards into meek acceptance of this fact to the degree that it does not threaten its safety; or an evolved one which has learned that individuality does not threaten one's connection or intimacy with one's source, that the existence of an unfathomably greater unknown is not threatening to oneself; and that one's expressed connection to one's own source does not overshadow another's connection with their source.

In Pisces, these lessons need to be learned and integrated specifically in those places which hold onto delusional beliefs, lazy acceptances or angry rebellions; in other words, where they emotionally hit home. It is very easy for shadow Pisces to lazily rely on its half-baked sense of universal oneness to avoid addressing its false beliefs about that oneness. We can see this is the popular aphorism, 'It's all good!' The implied core of this quip is that everything that happens, happens for a reason often unbeknownst to us, implying that all is at it should be. Yet what the phrase avoids is the personal responsibility required to consciously participate in strengthening our ability to be more present and know life to be 'all good.' The actual reality is, life is *not* all good. There is much pain, confusion and violence in the world and we are more often ignorant of our own patterns of self-abuse and manipulation of others than we are ready to admit. To deny this fact is to be living in illusion. Therefore, how conscious we walk through our lives will reveal how 'good' we are with life but *not* being 'all good.'

Underneath the laziness and fear which this phrase often cloaks lies a powerful, paradoxical truth waiting to be pierced open: individuality – the domain of subjective consciousness – is the only context or environment through which a true understanding of unity can actualize. This is one application of the alchemical opus. Individuals are the members, containers and discoverers of any bona fide collective reality. Undifferentiated mind requires differentiated consciousness to awaken itself to itself. This points directly to a Soul-level understanding of manifested reality, incarnational experiences and our Self-Identity; specifically, that the Soul requires Identity to evolve.

Because Pisces symbolizes Life itself and Consciousness in total, it is easy to see that it also represents final death – death of the self, or its return to its source.

"It is important that when Death finds you, Death finds you alive. To be alive is to be connected to the seeds of the thing growing [within and through you]. *"* [4]
(italics added)

Every Piscean resistance to one's authentic individuality (in the name of unity) as well as every individual who legitimately realizes a greater level of unity within their individuality symbolize consciousness itself striving to dissolve barriers between its Self and its Source. Thus any Piscean quality within us aspires to merge into and manifest itself as a greater understanding of the true nature of existence as an essential, ubiquitous oneness.

PISCES POLARITY: VIRGO

To balance, Pisces requires Virgo's practicality, frugality, realism, and self-defining qualities to ensure that it (Pisces) does not fall into the trap of egoically identifying with false egolessness. Virgo can also provide to Pisces a methodology to harmoniously bridge a greater *self*-awareness with a more accurate conception of life. In so doing, Pisces finds its center (as a self) which empowers its ability to know life more richly.

PISCES SHADOW

Delusional; fake innocence; emotionally manipulative; masochistic; passive; self-abnegating; addictive; weak; inconsistent; co-dependent;

illusion-prone; self-victimizing; self-martyring.

Resistance to separating from others; lack of appropriate boundaries with others; energetic parasite; passive acceptance of the status quo; directionless.

PISCES SELF-REALIZATION

The Piscean self-realization experience is most often described as the *samadhi* or *kensho* experience, in which there is a final release from the bounded nature of ego, of small mind, and of the I/me context. They and others like them are Piscean because the Pisces *concilio dominure* ('supreme result') is in fact the ending of the self.

♆ NEPTUNE

"The fish who is thirsty." [5]

"Saturn is the illusion that there is a reality, but Neptune is the truth that there isn't." [6]

Neptune[7] signifies the collective unconscious, the entirety of past and future human experience, or as Carl Jung has written, 'the pre-condition of each individual psyche, just as the sea is the carrier of the individual wave'. In other words, Neptune frames how all consciousness is inter-dependent and inter-responsive. It can reveal an individual's place within the soup of consciousness and also how that individual perpetuates its own consciousness. For this reason, Neptune embodies the idea of the collective unconscious, and will reveal an individual's ability or intent to experience the fluid nature of reality, to create art, to deeply care for others as symbols of life, to energetically merge or read the feelings of another, and to dream bigger than the current reality. It represents the individual's urge toward a state of bliss.

Neptune will also describe an individual's patterns of deluding itself because of the subconscious fear of becoming aware of its individuality or separating from (what it perceives to be) its source.

12TH HOUSE

The 12th House expresses in our relationship with our source and with unity consciousness; our personal or professional legacies; final death; our absolute existence and truth; our memories of the past (this or other lives); the collective expressions which we personally participate in; the results of our personal and collective efforts; our karmic and/or unconscious drives, motivations and compulsions; a wider, broader fame than in the 10th House; our completion of projects; our view of and relationship with God; and perhaps also our most recent incarnation.

The signs of the 12th House signify how we orient to the reality of God, or the oneness of life. They will thus reflect what we project or assume others' connection to a divine source or absolute truth should be and look like.

NOTES:

[1] I was first introduced to this association by the work of astrologer Jeffrey Wolf Green.

[2] From Maurice Fernandez' *Neptune, the 12th House and Pisces, The End of Hope the Beginning of Truth*.

[3] Excerpted from *Bridges of Union: the Archetypes of Masculine and Feminine Transformation*, Adam Gainsburg, to be published in 2006.

[4] James Hillman & Michael Meade.

[5] Sufi mystical poet, Kabir.

[6] Robert Hand, (unknown publication).

[7] For a comprehensive examination of the Pisces/Neptune/12th House archetype, the reader is encouraged to explore *The End of Hope, The Beginning of Truth* by astrologer Maurice Fernandez.

CHAPTER 5

THE ANGLES:
CONTAINERS FOR REALIZATION

INTRODUCTION

The horoscope Angles are different than any other plotted point in astrology. They are not planets, asteroids, other points, or intersections of planes. They do not describe cosmic events or movements of objects 'out there;' rather, their function is to *spatially and temporally frame our perception of those events.* Ultimately, Angles create a container or spatial context for our personal balance.

In the simplest way of saying, the four horoscope Angles create our 'personal east, west, north and south.' These 'personal directions' point to energetic qualities we find in ourselves, rather than to literal geographic directions.

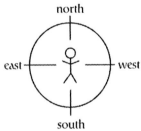

Figure 1: Each human being becomes oriented within time and space at the moment and place of birth. In astrology, this orientation is the result of the four horoscope Angles.

Where and when an individual is born will automatically create their personal energetic container or context for embodied growth. This is because each Angle is determined by a spatial and temporal context: the particular place and time of birth. This idea will be further explored in the sections that follow, but it is important to describe this idea a bit more here.

If we are peering out of our living room window at the apple tree in the yard, we will have a specific view of what is 'outside.' Yet if we then walk to the kitchen window and peer at the apple tree, we will have a different view of the same object or 'spatial event.' And if we were to remain in only one room for a long time, we may begin to forget that our visual perception of the tree is in fact still relative to our viewing position. The core dynamic and function of the Angles operate in much the same way. They determine our 'personal window of perceiving' through which we see ourselves and the world in a most primal and instinctual way. They orient us toward focusing on certain details, experiences, and realities and away from others. Thus knowing our Angular energies deeply supports our understanding of the person we are meant to become. The Angles are like 'framing devices' for our cellular relationship to space and time. As the signs on the Angles were the specific energies of 'east, west, north and south' at the place and moment of our first breath in life, they will remain so throughout our life. The four Angles are the Ascendant (AC), Descendant (DC), Midheaven (MC), and Lowheaven (IC).

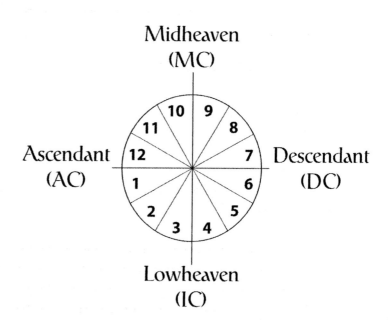

Figure 2: How the four Angles frame our view of the world, ourselves and our personal houses.

As we grow, we increasingly discover that those specific energies – both the specific Angular function *and* its sign energy – reveal our path of self-realization at ever greater levels. Once again, the location and time of our birth moment produces our personal cellular orientation to space, time and ultimately to ourselves throughout our life. Relative to the horoscope Angles, this orientation is cellularly imprinted into us by the sign energies of our personal east, west, north and south.

TECHNICALLY, WHAT ARE THEY?

Each horoscope Angle can also be understood to be an intersection of two of the three Earth-based planes or hoops responsible for the creation of astrological houses. The three hoops which combine to form the four Angles are: the visible horizon (the lowest visible point in any direction), the local meridian (the hoop formed from the highest (noon) and lowest position (midnight) of the Sun on a given day), and the ecliptic (the path the planets follow through our skies). These three hoops intersect in such a way as to create six points of intersection, four of which make up the standard horoscope Angles.

> *The Ascendant (AC) or rising sign is the intersection of the east horizon point and the ecliptic.*
> *The Descendant (DC) or setting sign is the intersection of the west horizon point and the ecliptic.*
> *The Midheaven (MC) or culminating sign is the intersection of the north meridian point and the ecliptic.*
> *The Lowheaven (IC) or anti-culminating sign is the intersection of the south meridian point and the ecliptic.*

It is perhaps useful to restate that these intersection points are entirely relative to the specific location on the Earth's surface and the specific point in time one is determining for. Thus, the eastern horizon point for New York City will be somewhere in the Atlantic Ocean, while that for Paris will be somewhere in middle to eastern France. This example hopefully supports your understanding that the Angles of astrology will likewise be different for different locations and times. Figure 3 shows how each of the four Angles are the product of the intersection of celestial planes or paths.

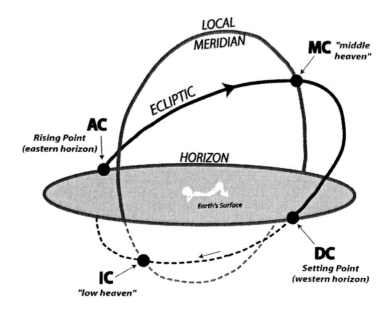

Figure 3 - Angles as intersections of planes or hoops.

Angles also orient us in time. The four Angles on our birth chart reveal what was up, what was down, what was rising and what was setting at the *time* of our birth. We might describe this as the view or picture of space from one location on Earth's surface which is produced by the rotational motion of the Earth around her axis. Or like we are sitting in a movie theatre as the film's mini-photographs (frames) are projected onto the screen in front of us. In a symbolic sense, our 'birth view' of space is the specific 'view of self' our Soul has chosen as its Self-Identity context, or that which frames our entire orientation to creation. With these ideas and orientations growing in us, we can begin to feel our location on Earth to be *below* that which is above us, *above* that which is below, to the *West* of that which is rising in the *East*, and to the East of that which is setting in the West. We come to know *where we are in space and time* by watching the movement of what is around us. This somatically 'locates' us on the surface of the Earth and in time. In this way, the Angles create for us our personal, moment-by-moment 'dimensional balance'. Once we develop a greater capacity to maintain a relationship with our outer space – with the outer sky – we are primed and ready to enter our interior space of *who we are*. The converse is also true. We come to feel 'lost' if we have no reference to anything familiar and so cannot determine *where we are*. And not knowing *where we are* points to the deeper issue of *who we are*.

ASPIRATIONS FOR REALIZATION

In my work, I see the Angles as those specific internal functions which create our ever-deepening and ever-expanding personal energetic context of who we are, how we interact with Other, and how we are meant to contribute to the world. This personal-identity context results from our relationship with Earth as physical context or 'home,' when we remember that each Angle is the product of certain planes or hoops around Earth intersecting with others in some fashion. To some degree, *every* point used to cast a chart like planets, asteroids, and nodes work toward the same goal. But it is the Angles which are the largest contributors to this effort, because only they are created entirely from an Earth-centric context which is homologous to a human-identity context. Indeed, it has been passed down for thousands of years across hundreds of cultures, that the human being and the Earth share a body. We can extend this beautiful image to suggest that we also share a personal-identity context as well. And what is a *context*? It is a time- or space-relative vehicle for understanding something. In the words of mythologist and storyteller Michael Meade, a context 'places knowledge within a particular view of the world to release meaning' (*Character & Destiny*, 1997.) Angles thus can be understood to *contextualize* our entire Earth experience because they are formed from an entirely Earth-centric context.

I refer to the Angles themselves (but not the sign energies *on* the Angles) as *personal aspirations* or *paths of self-realization*. They are *aspirations* for something not yet fully attained within, but they are also *realization paths* which lead us deeper into our Center and the mysteries there. In general, they are more unrealized early in life; as we grow, that potential becomes actualized and their latent energies are released for our use. Each Angle is a different process toward that aim. A thorough description of each horoscope Angle follows below.

The sign energies inhabiting our Angles tell us what those aspirations are (i.e., Leo is 'on' the Ascendant). The function of the Ascendant is for the individual to individuate themselves away from their known past through their unique self and views of the world. Leo is the domain of consciousness about personal actualization of creative potential in all ways. Thus, this signature (the combination of the function and the intended result of that function) suggests a drive to individuate oneself *as* Leo or *through* the Leo mysteries. The 'result' will be realization of one's Ascendant self as Leo. This applies to each of the remaining Angles with their different functions and the remaining 11 signs with their unique mysteries and expressions.

Each of the four Angles is clearly unique. What is to be embodied through one cannot occur through another. We require all four to catalyze their full potential. For example, to develop the sign energy on the Ascendant will necessitate work on the Descendant, its polarity. Thus the more I individuate myself (AC), the more I will interact with others in society and thus the more I will need to develop skills which help me successfully relate with others (DC). The same principle applies for the Midheaven and Lowheaven: the more I build a reputation or career (MC), the more I will need to root in my deeper Self-Identity (IC) so that I do not become a product of others' expectations or images of me. Self-realization and true centeredness can thus be seen to result only from work at *both ends* of our many polarities. Truly, Angles provide us with deep lessons in resolving conflicts from within: our sacred marriage.

Let's look at an example of how to 'read' the sign on an Angle operating through that Angle's function. The sign on the Angle symbolizes *which* energy the individual is meant to realize themselves *through*. So if a chart shows an 'IC in Taurus' ('Taurus is on the IC') then the Angular function involved is the Path of the Sacred Self, or the development of one's deep roots of Self-Identity (IC). The *goal* of that activity is Taurus. This individual will need to develop a deep Self-Identity as Taurus, or rooting in the qualities of inner stability, a clear sense of values, and an ability to manage one's resources. From this we can then infer that should this individual temporarily lose their stability or confidence in their ability to manage their resources, a very deep challenge to their Self-Identity will result. They may react to this challenge with receptivity and acceptance or anger, depression, or stubbornness. The same applies for any Angle and any sign.

THE RADIANT POTENTIAL OF THE ANGLES

Any conceivable planet, asteroid, Arabic part, Angle, or hypothetical point one may plot on a birth chart signifies some type of function within the human spiritual, electro-biological organism. They are each a unique *operation* of our being and thus share this commonality. They are quite different than, say, signs or houses or aspects. But if we look closer, their distinctions become quickly apparent.

Angles operate quite differently through our body-mind than do planets, nodes (lunar or otherwise), Arabic parts, or hypothetical planets. Describing the astrological differences between them is beyond the scope of this discussion. To the practicing astrologer or astrology student, their differences organically reveal themselves over time. Once we begin to work with astrology regularly, we naturally form impressions of each. The more we work, the more refined those impressions become.

Recall that Angles are not bodies which move through space, but orientational directions from our birth time and location. Angles tell us which sign energies – which domains of total consciousness – are our personal east, west, north and south. If you have previously participated in a ceremony in which the Four Directions were invoked, you will have a sense of this. Thus our Angles – our life-long, personal Four Directions – 'hold' the container for our entire self-experience, consciously, subconsciously and super-consciously.

An individual's natal Angular energies are their specific 'cellular possibilities' for centering themselves within themselves and in space and time. And what does *any* possibility or potential lead to? *Actualization!* A new possibility awaits the moment it comes into reality or form of any kind so that what has remained un-created can enter the world of creation, or the real. And this is the main difference between the Angles and all other chartable points. While the planets, etc. are the building blocks for the transformation of the psycho-spiritual self, the Angles symbolize how that greater self can increasingly orient to its literal and symbolic environments. More specifically, the Angles create a 'dimensional container' for sorting and applying one's planetary (somatic) functions. It is for this reason that SMA practices and teaches Angles as *aspirations* to be attained or *paths* to be traveled, and planets as specific intrinsic functions within the self.

Therefore, it is the Angles and *not* the planets (or other plotted points) which reveal an individual's deeper uniqueness. This is not in any way to say that planets, or aspect configurations between them, are not individualizing, or that the lessons symbolized by planets are 'easier' to learn than those of the Angles. Rather, it is to suggest that one's 'planet-lessons' can be seen to *serve* the 'Angle-lessons.' An electrician contracted to rewire a home (symbolizing planet-lessons) is one part of the larger effort to remodel the entire house (Angle-lessons). The rewiring operation is not the only one required to complete the job. Just as the electrical rewiring can be associated with a planetary function within us, the others such as plumbing, heating and structural changes would symbolize other planetary functions. Once the remodel of the home is complete, the owners will then 're-learn' or re-orient to their new *spatial* context (the house) in much the same way that an individual who successfully faces a challenging planetary position (a successful rewiring job) will quickly find themselves in an entirely new *identity*-context. And it is the Angles which astrologically symbolize the widest container or context of our Center.

It has been a source of wonderful insight and honoring the human design that in more than a few counseling sessions, I have intuitively 'seen' a client's Angular energy 'switch on' within them, and then 'wake up' throughout their being. In each instance, I received the impression the client was no longer 'sitting in the same room' as when the session began. Their personal, physio-energetic context – feeling themselves in their body, in the room, and in that situation – had transformed into a higher state of integration. There was observed more continuity or communication occurring at the subtle-energy levels, which always produces more peacefulness and an easier ability to receive, to allow and to be. Of course, my clients hadn't left the physical room, but they had left 'their old energetic room' behind for one of more radiance and presence. An Angular transformation in this way re-shapes their entire bio-electrical orientation to the present moment and to themselves. This result is always possible when assisting others to actualize their Angular energies.

THE FOUR ANGLES

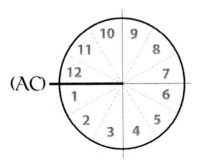

ASCENDANT (AC)

Begins: 1st House
Focus: Self
Self-Realization Path: Sacred Self
Aspiration: To engage oneself, others, and the world as the Ascendant Self

Celestially: The east-point intersection of the horizon and the ecliptic (see Figure 3).

Spatially: That which rises from and above the eastern horizon; the north node of the ecliptic on the horizon.

Archetypally: The impulse to individuate our unique, independent self expressed in the world.

Functions/Effects:

The first appearance of the inner self in an outward manner.

Where the self first emerges from the invisible into the visible.

Where the self is first known as an individual in the outer environment. 'It's coming out party'.

Will reveal any aspect of an individual which individuates him/her.

One's overall body shape and physical appearance, one's base personality, how one carries oneself.

Application: Look to the Ascendant to know how an individual is unique and is meant to individualize him/herself. It can answer the question 'If I give up my past patterns, who will I come out as?' The Ascendant is a powerful tool for leaving our known past patterns behind in a direct and self-supporting way.

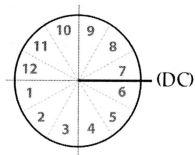

DESCENDANT (DC)

Begins: 7th House
Focus: Other
Self-Realization Path: Sacred Relationship
Aspiration: To relate to others as/through the Descendant Self

Celestially: The west-point intersection of the horizon and the ecliptic (see Figure 3)

Spatially: That which descends or sets into and below the western horizon; the south node of the ecliptic on the horizon.

Archetypally: The desire to know other in order to know self.

Functions/Effects:

How our individuality is expressed in relation to/with others.
The 'setting'[†] quality of the DC implies the disappearance of the solo individual living only from its own context. It suggests the individual's exposure to and engagement with others in a personally meaningful way.

The self becoming involved with others, which naturally changes the self's experience of itself. For example: how are my actions influencing others? How can I communicate with and successfully relate with others (who may have a different agenda)?

There are aspects of our being which only come out in relationships. 'There are lessons about ourselves only a close relationship can teach us.'

The way the self is meant to experience outside energies and relate with them successfully (give and take, compromise, good listening skills, balancing extremes, etc.)

Application: Look to the Descendant to identify an individual's 'relationship persona' and the type of relationships they are meant to create. The Descendant describes those qualities that arise in intimate, close or significant relationships, or who an individual progressively 'becomes' when involved in relationships. Because there is nothing a person does that is not in relation to others in some way, the Descendant is key to understanding the predisposed tendencies to project, to expect, to offer, to listen and to communicate with others: the whole domain of their relating.

† Planets at or near the Descendant have already or are about to disappear below the horizon in our western sky.

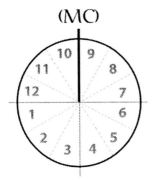

(MC)

MIDHEAVEN (MC)   MC = *medium coeli* or 'middle heaven'
Begins: 10th House
Focus: Outer
Self-Realization Path: Sacred Expression
Aspiration: To create and become known by others as Midheaven Self.

Celestially: The high-point ('north') intersection of the local meridian and the ecliptic (see Figure 3). Where the meridian crosses the ecliptic above the horizon.

Spatially: The highest (most visible) point in the sky the planets reach that day.

Archetypally: The most meaningful, aligned expression of one's role or place within (a) society; the desire to be known by others.

Functions/Effects:

One's activity within society in order to be 'placed,' known, and reputed among others.

The Self's position within the social environment (visible sky).

How and what one is seen or known as.

How one arranges or structures one's visibility or reputation.

The method (sign) and form of one's work.

Can be a career, but only as the vehicle or form of the creation and then the reputation/visibility earned from that creation.

Not a statement about the deep psyche per se.

Application: Look to the Midheaven to know what the individual can come to be known as – usually vocationally or in career, as well as their qualities to be developed in that effort. The Midheaven can reveal that famous 'reputation' which is said to 'precede' someone. If the individual is more identified with their reputation than their substance in this regard, then the Midheaven (sign) energy will tell us what the developmental intent should be and thus also what is out of balance.

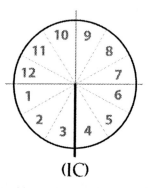

(IC)

LOWHEAVEN (IC)   IC = *imum coeli* or 'lowest heaven'

Begins: 4th House

Focus: Inner

Self-Realization Path: Sacred Identity

Aspiration: To self-identify as the IC Self.

Celestially: The low-point ('south') intersection of the local meridian and the ecliptic (see Figure 3). Where the meridian crosses the ecliptic below the horizon.

Spatially: The lowest (least visible) point in the sky the planets reach that day.

Archetypally: That which one desires to know, identify, and foundation oneself as.

Functions/Effects:

One's deepest knowing of oneself.

The psychological context and roots for Self-Identity.

Who/what we desire to feel ourselves as; who/what we tell ourselves we are.

How we feel most rooted to our origins; thus our emotional context.

The 'higher domain' of ego identity.

Relates to the subconscious level and its expressions.

Application: Look to the IC to determine the 'inner world' aspiration, or the most meaningful qualities one aspires to develop, embody and maintain within oneself. An imbalanced or undeveloped IC energy can reveal an individual 'stuck' in either an immature version of their authentic depth or an addiction to remaining internal (also immature), or it can signify an individual who strenuously avoids those domains altogether. The IC sign energy will tell us just what is 'going on in there' and so can reveal how to guide its greater embodiment.

THE ANGULAR AXIES

From an understanding of the Angles and their individual functions, we can now proceed to an examination of the *pairing* of Angles. As there are four Angels, there will be two pairings, or axies. Each axis forms a channel of energy intricately dependent on its polarity and highly unique to the individual. (For clarity, the plural of axis is axies.)

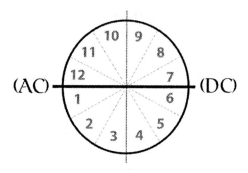

Ascendant-Descendant Axis – 'Self-Other Axis'

This axis is formed between the AC and DC. It bookends the sky at the extreme east and west points of our visible horizon, divides the sky into north and south hemispheres, and creates the distinction between visible (above the horizon) and invisible (below the horizon).

This Angular axis forms our entire cellular assumptions about ourself in relation with others. That which is above this axis is visible, known and social, both physically and on the astrological chart; that which is below is invisible, unknown and subconscious. This axis thus correlates with how we as individuals are meant to balance our attention between our necessary focus on ourselves and our equally important awareness of others, or how we are to balance the inherent stress of living within a relationship, family, society, nation or world. As we embody our AC energy (Self), we will more authentically interact and relate with others from our DC energy (Other). Likewise, as we create and engage in relationship with others (DC), we will inevitably come to redefine ourselves more meaningfully (AC).

In the human body, the Self-Other Axis symbolizes the synaptic communication between left-brain and right-brain activities, and all the related archetypes, expressions and physical conditions of each.

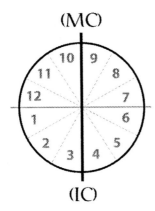

(MC)

(IC)

Lowheaven-Midheaven Axis – 'Inner-Outer Axis'

This axis is formed between the IC and MC. It marks the extreme north and south points of our viewing position on Earth, divides the sky into east and west hemispheres, and indicates the transition between rising or waxing movement up to the Midheaven and setting or waning movement down to the Lowheaven.

This Angular axis forms the entire energetic relationship between one's inner and outer spaces (however one defines them). That which is in the rising environment (to the east of this axis) is striving for expression and symbolizes the move toward singularness; that which is in the setting environment (to the west of the axis) is striving for completion and symbolizes the move toward unity. Thus it correlates to how we as individuals are meant to balance between our interior and exterior realities. As we root into our deep selves or IC energy (Inner), represented by the invisible environment below us and on the other side of the Earth, we will establish a social presence (reputation) through the MC energy (Outer) represented by the visible, common sky above us.

In the human body, the Inner-Outer Axis symbolizes the life-force channel (Sanskrit *susumna*) beginning at the base of the spine and continuing into and above the crown of the head, along with all the related chakra imagery.

Both axies operate – and can be understood – in several ways. Each is the unique *relationship* between two extremes: the energetic relationship between an individual's Self (AC) and relationship to Other (DC), and his/her Inner Self (IC) with their Outer expression of that Self (MC). And as they both form a relationship, we can take the position at either end of the axis in question and see what we see. If our observational view has us 'standing' at the Ascendant looking across at the Descendant, then our notion and experience of the Ascendant (what it is to actually *feel* that archetype – its energy) will be very different than if, say, we are seated at the Descendant looking across at the Ascendant. The same applies to the Midheaven-Lowheaven Axis as well. SMA strongly encourages its practitioners to intuit not only the *information* for the client's growth (accurate interpretation of the planetary signatures), but also which *perspective* to take in order to access that information. Surely, a thorough explanation of the AC/DC axis for one client may be just what the doctor ordered, but for another focusing on the DC function within them may be required.

For example, a client once came to discuss, or so she thought, how she should take the next step in the business she founded some years earlier. After answering some questions about standard Angular activities in life, it was clear that she had developed a moderate awareness of each individual Angle in herself (she didn't name it that to herself because astrology wasn't a focus in her life). In other words, she had embraced her Angular (sign) energies to a certain level. What was lacking however was the important *connectivity or communication between them*. From this perspective, there remained quite a bit of fear in doing so because for her it represented taking aspects of herself out of a protective box of beliefs and exposing them in potentially threatening situations. Of course, this was entirely the fear talking. In fact, at the beginning of the session, she described herself feeling 'quite fragmented.' In the sessions that followed, we devoted much time and energy to supportively challenging her to trust that her ideas of herself are only being limited by her own fear, and once she risks exposing otherwise protected facets of her being to the light at the other end of the tunnel (the opposite Angle) will a much greater clarity about her business come.

Each axis also divides the total space around an individual into hemispheres: the AC/DC axis creates above and below, the MC/IC axis creates east and west. If we examine the MC/IC axis creating east and west or left- and right-brain, a birth chart with most of its planets and points on one side may reveal either a strong emphasis or an imbalance in brain functioning. And the same certainly applies to the AC/DC axis revealing a potential imbalance between one's interior or subconscious functioning or one's external, social identity replacing one's autonomous Self-Identity.

Following these formulations comes our highest level of understanding the Angles: the Angular Cross. Before we explore the Cross (#3 below), let's review how we came to be here. Working with the Angles reveals three levels of operation within the psyche:

1. On the first level is the individual Angle (ie., Ascendant) and the sign there (ie., Cancer). This level determines precisely which energies are we meant to realize ourselves as. Each individual Angle represents a different self-realization path.

2. The second level is each of the two Angular axies, the AC/DC axis and the MC/IC axis. This second level determines the equilibrium or dynamic balance between the two Angles involved. It points to how the archetypal relationship between Self and its interaction with Other is most meant to be realized within (AC/DC), and how the archetypal relationship between one's Inner and Outer identity is most meant to be realized (IC/MC). 'Working on' an Angle on one axis will naturally produce new functioning awareness of the other. This level can be seen as the first step toward inner relationship, which we know as polarity.

3. The third level is our personal Angular Cross and is comprised of both axies in their relative relationship to each other. The Cross affirms how each axis is meant to relate and interact with the other.

When an individualembodies their Angular Cross more legitimately (in body, heart and mind), they are genetically setting the stage for a leap in consciousness to take place. Why is this? It is because when all four Angular energies are being 'walked with' through life, the individual's personal Center is now being held in power and alignment within greater amounts of internal space. Literally, there is 'more space' for the individual to realize him/herself within and into. Of course, this depends on the harmony or strength within each axis, which in turn depends on the level of embodiment of the individual Angles and their sign energies. Relative to the Cross, the term 'multidimensional' may be useful to describe its Angular energetics. However we think of the Angles, the axies, or the Cross, the Angular energies are truly a profound indicator for and path toward self-realization.

For a technique of tying each Angle to its natural 'fuel' energy in interpretive work, see Chapter 15, Essay V.

CHAPTER 6

HEMISPHERES & QUADRANTS:
SPACES OF SELF & OTHER

The practice of astrology asks the astrologer to divide the circle of the chart into twelve parts twice, once for signs and again but differently for houses. Yet there are also two other divisions of the chart which come before this twelve-fold division and create for us a wide and accurate *context* for understanding an individual's specific growth intents represented by the Signs. When we divide the chart into two equal parts, we have *hemispheres*; into four equal parts, we have *quadrants*.

The divisions which create the hemispheres and quadrants are the horoscope Angles, the AC, DC, MC, and IC (see chapter 5). Where one hemisphere comprises one-half ('hemi' and 'sphere') of the entire circle, one quadrant ('quad' is four) composes one-quarter of the circle. Each hemisphere is comprised of six houses; each quadrant three house. As you might expect, each hemisphere and quadrant exhibit unique characteristics. They naturally overlay each other and their combination creates a very useful understanding into the orientation of an individual's psyche. Before describing each hemisphere and quadrant, let's first examine this four-part circle as a whole.

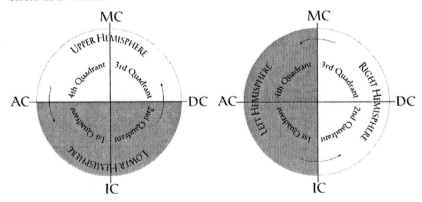

Figure 1- The four Angles create both hemispheres and quadrants.

If we understand the Ascendant to begin the circle, the 1st House to be the first movement away from that beginning point, the 2nd House to be the second, and so on in a counter-clockwise rotation, then we see that quadrants reveal a natural progression of development, just as signs, houses and aspects do. Recall that quadrants are determined by the two Angles which begin and end them on either side. We can also think of them as the six houses (hemispheres) or three houses (quadrants) which compose them. To understand what a hemisphere or quadrant relates to, we can look to the Angles which begin, culminate and complete them because it is the Angles which spatio-psychologically define them for us.

If Angles are the containers for *locating* our realization paths within our personal Identity (physicality on Earth) and for dimensionally centering us within our authentic Center, then hemispheres can be understood as modes of human consciousness and quadrants as regions of the human psyche through which we develop our personal path of evolution.

Just as in every cycle within Nature, each hemisphere and quadrant picks up the baton from its predecessor and continues development in and through its own activity. Watching the developmental growth through the hemispheres or quadrants, one may be struck by the strong similarity to developmental processes of the signs, houses and aspects. Such an observation would be accurate, as all things in Nature reflect the essence of that Nature. The main distinctions between the five developmental progressions are as follows:

Hemispheres describe the progression of distinct modes of human consciousness;

Quadrants describe the progression of distinct regions of the psyche;

Signs describe the progression of distinct domains of total consciousness;

Houses describe the progression of distinct areas of life; and

Aspects describe the progression of integrated relationship between the internal functions.

One last note before proceeding to the descriptions. Hemispheres and quadrants are most effectively used as 'framers' of our perception, rather than as acute descriptions of a psyche. To interpret a chart only by its hemispheric or quadrant emphases is both irresponsible and insufficient. But our understanding of both can greatly assist us in properly contextualizing the general area(s) of the psyche which are most actively being developed throughout life (indicated by the planets in signs and houses in aspect to other planets and points).

HEMISPHERES

Hemispheres describe entire modes of consciousness, such as subjective-objective and individual-relational (see Figure 1). Implied in hemispheric descriptions is the way the self orients to itself, to others and to its environment. As such, hemispheres are generalized domains, rather than specific descriptions.

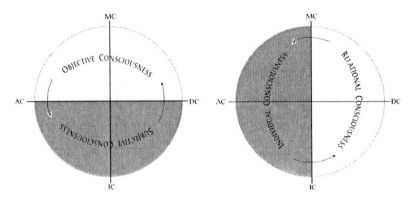

Figure 2 – The four hemispheres

'LOWER' HEMISPHERE – SUBJECTIVE CONSCIOUSNESS

Location: Below the astrological horizon (AC-DC axis)

Composed of: Quadrants 1 and 2; or Houses 1 thru 6.

Description: The invisible or hidden half of the sky at birth. This is the entire range of subjective, or I-centered consciousness within an individual. Planets, signs and houses here describe processes that usually operate underneath the normal range of conscious awareness. Phrases such as sub-conscious, unconscious, underworld, instinctuality, impulsiveness describe this hemisphere. Subjectivity describes a personal, inner, less conscious, insightful orientation to life.

Strengthen: One's internal (invisible) functions, such as one's psychological makeup, emotional nature and cognitive processes.

Growth: Begin with AC, culminate at IC, and complete at DC. The development of any subjective stance begins with the initial discovery of one's I-ness (AC). There is not a lot of consciousness here however. As this discovery leads to further and further explorations of self, the depth symbolized by the IC, is attained. This attainment and its resulting integration throughout the body-mind then aptly builds toward preparing one to interact meaningful with others (DC).

Shadow: Remaining ignorant of what one participates in and perhaps more importantly, why.

'UPPER' HEMISPHERE – OBJECTIVE CONSCIOUSNESS

Location: Above the astrological horizon (AC-DC axis)

Composed of: Quadrants 3 and 4; or Houses 7 thru 12.

Description: The visible sky at birth. This is the entire range of consciousness within an individual responsible for one's detachment or distance from one's personal, oft-hidden, opinion-based perspective; one requiring processes of discernment and consciousness. Planets, signs and houses here suggest those activities which have visible effects or which occur with others or in visible ways to others. Objectivity describes a broader, 'higher', outer, and visionary orientation to life.

Strengthen: One's socially-dependent functions, such as career, fame, relationships, and spiritual activities.

Growth: Begin with DC, culminate at MC, and complete at AC. The development of any objective stance begins with the initial experience of others and their realities, opinions and issues (DC). There is not a lot of knowledge or wisdom about others here. As experiences with others accumulate, the self widens to understand more and more about others which produces a more expanded Self-Identity. The self seeks to experience itself impacting others in a meaningful way, necessitating the creation of methods for doing that. A career or other long-term activity is chosen to serve as a marker for others to recognize the self through, so career, reputation, or social position symbolize the culmination of this hemisphere (MC). The longer and greater effort the self puts into building a social vehicle through which it can be known, the more it discovers that its greatest contribution and satisfaction ultimately derives from the social application of its own autonomous and highly individual characteristics (AC).

Shadow: Remaining in theory, ideas, the ideals; fundamentally disconnected from one's depth, and thus from others.

'LEFT' HEMISPHERE – INDIVIDUAL CONSCIOUSNESS

Location: To the left of the local meridian (IC-MC axis)

Composed of: Quadrants 4 and 1; or Houses 10 thru 3.

Description: The range of consciousness described by the self's independent operations and actions, which originate from or through oneself.

Strengthen: One's individual impetus, one's confidence in moving with one's inspirations and in trusting one's instincts and intuitions.

Growth: Begin with MC, culminate at AC, and complete at IC. The development of any individual or 'original-izing' awareness begins with the recognition of one's originality within a context of others (MC). This leads to continually refining one's unique vision or voice in order to make more significant, recognizable, and meaningful contributions from one's inherent originality, eventually culminating in an entirely new relationship with one's life intent and aliveness (AC). As the 'new individuality' continues to explore itself, it ultimately leads to and completes in a depth understanding of oneself and one's egoic, emotional and subconscious levels (IC). This symbolizes the natural evolution of individuality: 'in the end, we return, as we must, to ourselves.'

Shadow: Remaining isolated, uninterested, or superior to others because there is too strong a need to communicate, enforce, transfer one's own ideas onto others.

'RIGHT' HEMISPHERE – RELATIONAL CONSCIOUSNESS

Location: To the right of the local meridian (IC-MC axis)

Composed of: Quadrants 2 and 3; or Houses 4 thru 9.

Description: The range of consciousness described by all the self's relations with Other, including those which internally result from interactions with Other (2nd quadrant) and those which require an Other to trigger one's deeper experience (3rd quadrant).

Strengthen: One's social skills, self-stability with and acceptance of others, social flexibility and (ultimately) self-valuing.

Growth: Begin with IC, culminate at DC, and complete at MC. The development of any relational awareness begins with an exposure to one's own depths, feelings and mysterious nature (IC). This self-depth is gradually stoked to come out into the light of awareness and culminates through one's discovery of one's own unique ways of understanding and communicating with others meaningfully (DC). Without self-depth, there is no foundation on which to build a meaningful, balanced and conscious social life. As social experiences and learnings accumulate, the self gains wisdom about what others need on a larger scale and how one's social uniqueness might be parlayed into a successful career, reputation, or social creation (MC).

Shadow: Either remaining in social interactions to continually 'fill' the emotional and egoic lack in oneself or avoiding them altogether because of one's hypersensitivity to others' opinions.

HEMISPHERES AND ANGLES

An interesting correlation between the hemispheres and Angles arises. Recall the Angular axes are described like this:

Ascendant/Descendant Axis is named the **SELF-OTHER AXIS.**
Lowheaven/Midheaven Axis is named the **INNER-OUTER AXIS.**

If we then associate the hemispheres with these axes, we have:

Hemisphere	Defining Axis	Developmental Progression	Result
Lower Hemisphere	AC-DC	AC ➜ DC	DC, or Other
Upper Hemisphere	AC-DC	DC ➜ AC	AC, or Self
Left Hemisphere	MC-IC	MC ➜ IC	IC, or Inner
Right Hemisphere	MC-IC	IC ➜ MC	MC, or Outer

From this we can understand how deeply interdependent the hemispheres and horoscope Angles are. Yet if we had made this statement before exploring *how* they are connected, we may not have been able to make the connection, for the Angles are highly personalizing while the hemispheres are large areas of personal space providing at best general understandings. The same certainly applies to the quadrants.

QUADRANTS

Quadrants can be described as general regions of the human psyche or groupings of developmental intent and the associated styles or foci for realizing those intents.

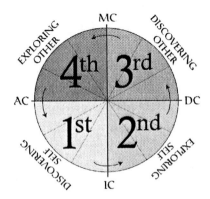

Figure 3 – The four quadrants

1ST QUADRANT – DISCOVERY OF SELF

Location:	Between the AC and IC
Composed of:	1st, 2nd, 3rd Houses
Description:	This region is the raw, eye-opening discovery of oneself as an alive, physically viable and cognitively capable singular self.
Strengthen:	One's aliveness, one's instincts and one's trust in them.
Growth:	Transition from an unexamined, reactive self-awareness into a more stabilized, well-rounded, and cognizant one. This requires substantial experience of existence-ness (athleticism, competition, financial stability, education, travel).

2ND QUADRANT – EXPLORATION OF SELF

Location: Between the IC and DC

Composed of: 4th, 5th, 6th Houses

Description: This region is the maturation of the Self-Identity: healthy, stable (not necessarily predictable) emotional life, resilient self-love, and compassionate self-acceptance. It intends to develop an appropriate ego structure and an accurate sense of one's gifts and challenges on one's own terms. It encompasses the maturation of subjective consciousness.

Strengthen: The *conscious* Self-Identity.

Growth: Transition from a pre-conscious self-image into an internally balanced, accurate Self-Identity. This requires internal investigations into one's psyche, emotions, or physicality (artistic expressions, healing, counseling, etc.)

3RD QUADRANT – DISCOVERY OF OTHER

Location: Between the DC and MC

Composed of: 7th, 8th, 9th Houses

Description: This region represents the self's first interaction with the social world – its first experiences and learnings which arise from the general process of socialization. The self-identity will necessarily be challenged, provoked and ultimately served by its interaction with all kinds of Other – people, places, opinions, fears, realities, etc.

Strengthen: The socially interactive Self-Identity.

Growth: Transition from either an exaggerated or diminished Self-Identity into a more 'worldly' or socially-proven Identity. This requires explicit explorations of one's personal desires in a social environment (spiritual, family, sexual, travel, etc.)

4TH QUADRANT – EXPLORATION OF OTHER

Location: Between the MC and AC

Composed of: 10th, 11th, 12th Houses

Description: This region represents the maturation of socialization. It encompasses those domains of consciousness constellating around social leadership, service, and objective consciousness;

in other words, the matured *application* of one's socially-learned skills.

Strengthen: The efficiency of one's socially-expressed leadership/service.

Growth: Transition from a subjective Self-Identity into an objective one. This requires explicit expressions of one's personal desires to contribute to the world in specific ways (group leadership, social revisioning, etc.)

APPLICATIONS

When a single planet or a grouping of planets appears in a hemisphere or quadrant, we can gain useful information about the psyche's structure in general. The populated sector will indicate the strength of that mode of consciousness or region of the psyche. If there are many planets located there, then that sector's focus comprises a majority statement about *how* those sign-infused planets will be building the psyche. It speaks specifically to this. For example, if there are six natal planets located in the Discovering Other quadrant (3rd), then those planetary functions in their signs and houses and involved in their aspects with other planets are all assisting the discovery of the individual's Identity of himself socially. Or if the grouping of planets is located in the Subjective Consciousness Hemisphere (lower), then they are assisting the development of the individual's deep and thorough experience of his/her own subjective standpoint.

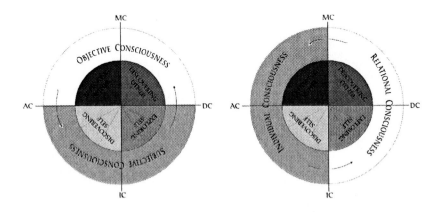

Figure 4 – Hemispheres and Quadrants overlayed on the astrological wheel.

This is very helpful to know in cases where the sign, planet, house and aspects give a combined picture of something *other* than the hemisphere or quadrant suggest. For example: let's place the Moon in Taurus squared by Pluto ('Hades Moon'). These are all very subjectively-oriented signatures. Yet if we now identify a 3rd Quadrant Moon (let's say in the 8th House), then we know that the Moon function (one's egoic identity) will be developed through regular experiences with others. It will in fact require these interactions to undergo the necessary transformations. Though we can certainly obtain similar observations from the House position alone (because Houses comprise both hemispheres and quadrants), the hemisphere or quadrant locale gives us an accurate, bigger picture with which to make our interpretations.

SMA sees work with hemispheres and quadrants most supportive of the astrologer's first examination of a new client's chart. By focusing our intuitive vision on just the hemispheres and quadrants first – before diving into planets in signs, houses, and aspects – we form a general idea of the structure and emphasis within the psyche, similar to a doctor asking questions of the patient and making physical observations of the body before receiving back the test results from the lab.

CHAPTER 7

ASTRO-ENERGETICS

MODALITIES

The astrological modalities or modes describe general qualities of energetic movement. Each describes *how consciousness is developing*, but not what is developing. Modes are a study in dynamics or process theory. They are not personal or specific descriptors for the signs or houses. They instead point to the movement-quality of their energy.

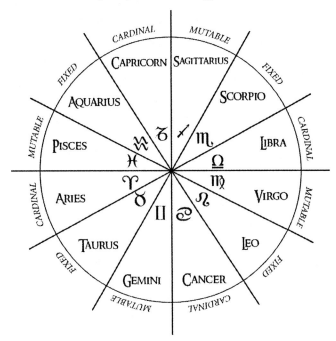

Figure 1 – Sign modalities.

Nearly every tradition on the planet has in part formulated its cosmology, religion or spiritual tradition based on the trinity, the three. In

Christianity, the Father, the Son, and the Holy Spirit. In Ayurveda are the three constitutions or *doshas: vata, pitta,* and *kapha.* And in alchemy are found salt, sulfur and mercury. In astrology, there are likewise three Modes: cardinal, fixed, and mutable. The progression – in standard astrological order – of one mode to the next and to the final is a study of *how things change.* If the classic Chinese *I Ching* or Book of Changes pops into our mind, then this is accurate to the domain Modes address.

The *I Ching* and the Mayan Sacred Calendar, the *Cholqi'j* or T'zolkin, describe the stages of creation from absolute beginning to final ending of the energy or intelligence within creative consciousness. This is the root of the ancient Indian assignments of the three great deities to what we in astrology know as Modalities: Vishnu (Cardinal), Brahman (Fixed), and Krishna (Mutable). In scientific theory, the Modalities correlate to the progression from *thesis (Cardinal), anti-thesis (Fixed), to synthesis (Mutable).*

The Modes are generally seen to describe sign energies only. There is a different yet related three-part division used to describe houses. As houses are created from the Angles (AC, DC, MC and IC), their 'Modes' are related to their Angular origins: angular (cardinal), succedent (fixed), and cadent (mutable). Thus where Cancer would be described as 'cardinal', the 4th House would be labeled 'angular.'

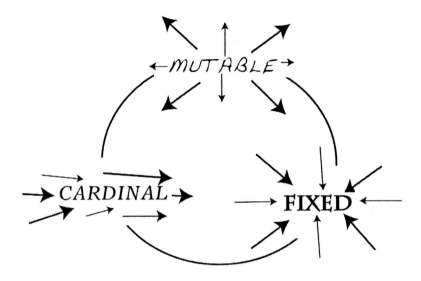

Figure 2 – Astrological modalities or qualities of movement.

Cardinal: *Context:* Life is a highway; life is active.

          Description: That which has been understood (as Mutable) is here acted on, moved with, activated, initiated or begun. Action is occurring in a direction or with energy. Something new is sought after. Each of the four Cardinal signs act as a bridge, for they connect the prior developments (prior quadrant) to the one they begin. 'Thesis'.

          Cardinal Signs: Aries, Cancer, Libra, Capricorn

          Cardinal Houses: 1st, 4th, 7th, 10th

Fixed: *Context:* Life is a mountain; life is productive.

          Description: That which is begun (as Cardinal) solidifies here through its application. Energy or consciousness here desires definition and stabilization. Fixed energy ultimately intends to be employed in some way. And through its employment, it becomes more structured and thus defined. Each of the four Fixed signs act as a 'producer', in that they put to effective use the energies prior to them in order to create forms that work. 'Anti-thesis'.

          Fixed Signs: Taurus, Leo, Scorpio, Aquarius

          Fixed Houses: 2nd, 5th, 8th, 11th

Mutable: *Context:* Life is hologram; life is inter-reflective.

That which has been utilized (as Fixed) is now contemplated, understood, learned from, thought about, integrated, and released through its applications. Each of the four Mutable signs intend to merge with their area of expertise and thus to bring it to perfection, or to seamlessly integrate into itself the domain of expertise. *'Synthesis'.*

Mutable Signs: Gemini, Virgo, Sagittarius, Pisces
Mutable Houses: 3rd, 6th, 9th, 12th

When learning astrology or interpreting a chart, the understanding of a sign or a house's Modality can often open an important observation as it describes its unique dynamism, its method of change. Nonetheless, you are invited to base your learning of the Modes – either of signs or houses – on *your experience of reading charts* rather than studying them as abstract principles. Certainly, familiarity with basic ideas and qualities of each Mode is the first step. And the more you familiarize yourself with how the sign, planet, and house energies inter-penetrate each other to give structure to consciousness within an individual, the more familiar you will become with their Modes.

ELEMENTS

The astrological Elements describe *qualities of energetic existence.* They have been seen for thousands of years as the *flavors* of existence. They do not speak to dimensionality or conspicuous domains of a large whole. Rather, they are inherent, intrinsic qualities of the is-ness of creation.

It is on the level of the Elements and perhaps also the Modalities which the scientific art known as the Great Work or alchemy operates. In fact, our notions of these distinct qualities of existence emanate out of ancient Egypt and Greece, also responsible for much alchemical knowledge.

There is no intrinsic *ordering* of Elemental energies and no 'normal' progression to them, as that would require them to be located within a context, be it spatial or otherwise. Rather, Elements describe entire regions of energetic nuance, or natures of existence. One Element can quite naturally flow into another, just as it can quite naturally resist another. There is no Elemental hierarchy. Perhaps the only frame for identifying the Elements we have at our disposal is our own consciousness, our unique perspective. It is for this reason that Elements will arise and express in infinite ways.

Astrology recognizes four elements, though there is a fifth, *aether*, which is the actual stuff of existence itself. *Aether* is the origin of the other four, or the blank canvas onto which the other four are painted in incomprehensible diversity to produce the nuances of existence.

The names themselves – Earth, Air, Water and Fire – do not refer to physical elements, but to those timeless qualities of existence-ness. It is also important to understand that each Element has contained within it each of the others. In my experience, this is the level of understanding which begins an advanced working with astrological Elements. For example, within the Earth element, there are specific sub-qualities of each of the four. Thus we have: the Air quality of Earth, the Fire quality of Earth, the Water quality of Earth, and the Earth quality of Earth.

The following descriptions of the Elements do not attempt to be comprehensive as there is a plethora of available literature on this subject. They do intend to pinpoint specific qualities which lend themselves well to the practice of SMA.

EARTH

The Earth element refers to and encompasses matter, form, stability, definition, containment, utility, ground, structure, dimensional balance, dependability, persistence, consistency, mass, body. Earth wants to concretize and foundation.

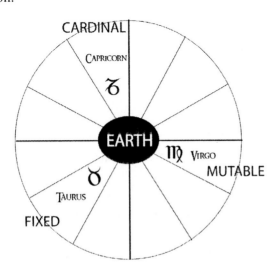

Fixed Earth (Taurus)- *'The earth that stabilizes.'*
Defining the form; putting to use our resources; holding fast to what we know; being reliable; establishing our lives in the physical.

Mutable Earth (Virgo)- *'The earth that understands (frees).'*
Seeking to fix[1]; locating purpose; striving for definition, form, perfection; understanding through form; freeing from within form.

Cardinal Earth (Capricorn)- *'The earth that coalesces form.'*
Moving in or toward a structure; being an agent of form; creating results; activating and supporting definitions; catalyzing activity or coherence in the direction of definition.

WATER

The Water element refers to and encompasses wisdom (through the feminine mode) or self-knowing, fluidity, flexibility, homogenizing, unifying, including, feeling, emotion, sensate experience, consideration, compassion, intuition. Water wants to flow and merge.

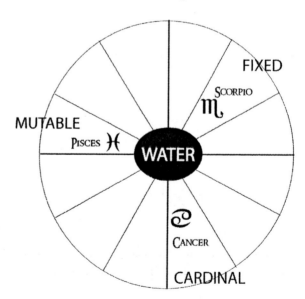

Cardinal Water (Cancer)- *'The water that flows.'*
Feeling into things; experiencing emotionally; identifying needs through sensitivity; caring for others in specific ways.

Fixed Water (Scorpio)- *'The water that cuts through rock.'*
Rooting in feelings (feeling deeply); containing[2] fluidity; utilizing depth; penetrating wisdom.

Mutable Water (Pices)- *'The water that is (in) All.'*
Merging diversity; 'cosmic water'; unifying through feelings; understanding empathically.

AIR

The Air element refers to and encompasses cognition, communication, relating, conceptualizing, balancing, harmony, expansiveness, ubiquity, objectivity, understanding, and relational balance. Air wants to expand and understand.

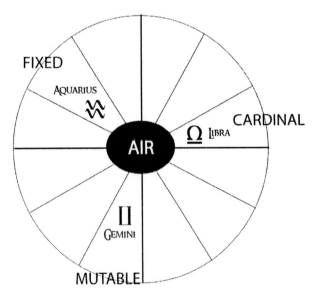

Mutable Air (Gemini)- *'The air that is free.'*
Understanding relatedness; unrestricted thinking and associating; omni-directional movement; objective exploration.

Cardinal Air (Libra)- *'The air that seeks.'*
Seeking relatedness; initiating understanding; interacting with/moving toward Other; the seed of objectivity.

Fixed Air (Aquarius)- *'The air that frees.'*
Stabilizing relatedness; forming our ideas; utilizing the resources of relatedness (connections); objective reality; containing[2] inspiration.

FIRE

The Fire element refers to and encompasses wisdom (through the masculine mode) or inspiration, prana or chi, excitability and eruptiveness, instinctuality and intuition, channeling of energies, strength, focus-able, subsuming resources, spirit, motivation, and enthusiasm. Fire wants to engage and radiate.

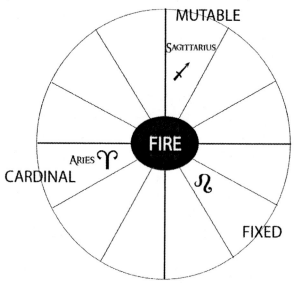

Cardinal Fire (Aries)- *'The fire that engages.'*
Initiating motivation; actively engaging; activating in life; moving with courage; inspiring activity.

Fixed Fire (Leo)- *'The fire that creates.'*
Magnetizing energy; attracting resources; stabilizing inspiration; subjective reality; creating; radiating life-force.

Mutable Fire (Sagitarius)- *'The fire that seeks.'*
Understanding origins; elevating knowing; following inspiration to understand; exchanging opinions for truths.

ASTROLOGICAL POLARITY[3]

To say two items are in a strong *polarity* with one another is to suggest a direct *relationship*, normally thought of as moving in opposite directions (contrary intentions). This also suggests the domain of relationship, requiring a self and an other to be distinguished.

In astrology, we can identify how a planet in a sign is meant first to balance and then evolve within the psyche by looking to its polarity sign. In general, one sign will reflect its polarity sign, its Other, and create a context or mirror off of which to bounce its experiences, ideas and behaviors. This energetic 'second opinion' creates a type of reservoir of individual traits to pick and learn from. The next step is its evolution, which occurs when the sign (or more specifically the planet in the sign) changes its base vibration to one which is more conscious and integrated. This shift can only result from the release of lower vibrations – in the form of fears, beliefs, and egoic orientations. In its role as evolutionary guide, polarity energies offer many qualities and an 'other' type of wisdom from which to draw on and progress toward. But it is important we do not make the mistake that every sign must then evolve into or be destined to become its polarity. This is simply not accurate. Rather, each sign evolves into *its own* higher expression and realization, which will naturally incorporate more and more of its polarity's qualities. Those qualities do not replace its own, but foster its fullness to come to fruition. It itself remains intact, albeit in a higher state of integration or consciousness.

Let's look at the Cancer/Capricorn axis for an example of this. Let's say the sign we are beginning with is Cancer. At this point, I will intentionally avoid including a planet in this sign to allow for a thorough understanding of the archetype of polarity itself, without additional factors. Cancer will naturally become caught or stuck in its subconscious needs for emotional security and a stable sense of its roots, internally and externally. If it feels without a home, or is under the influence of emotionally reactive patterns, it will be in its 'lower' expressions. Applying our notions of polarity described above, Cancer will need to first balance in itself by drawing on qualities of Capricorn, such as self-authority, perseverance, an inner knowing of its wisdom and autonomy among others, a desire to manage effectively and responsibly, and a drive to establish its social position. From any of these or other Capricorn qualities, Cancer will be able to reduce and eventually cease its subconscious needs for approval from others to ground itself emotionally, release the deeper belief that emotional security is crucial to its existence at all times, and accept its own emotional content as appropriate. Once our initially-unevolved Cancer does this and its balance returns, its ability to actually evolve will come into play. Once again, Cancer will look to Capricorn in its natural leadership abilities and wisdom to remind it that it can leave behind the comfortable waters of its emotionality (subconsciousness) and play an increasingly socially-impactful role. This will require that Cancer develop a thicker emotional skin and healthier boundaries with others, both of which will depend on Cancer's deeper and fuller self-acceptance. Once again, Cancer is not striving to *become* Capricorn, but to augment its natural abilities and qualities (and thus evolve) from its innate magnetic polarity with Capricorn.

POLARITY AS AN AXIS

Let's examine two polarized points. We can call them the 'point' and its 'polarity' or in more human terms, the self and the other. Whatever they shape as in our lives, they are in fact two expressions of the same *domain* or *space*. This domain expresses on astrological charts as a polarity line. The point and its polarity carry strong similarities with each other *not in how they express, but on the deeper level of their mutual origin*. To see how any sign, planet or individual invariably carries a strong relationship with its opposite (or enemy) is to understand how that sign, planet or individual can achieve greater balance by strengthening those qualities it is weak in. In general, any natal planet will become stronger or round itself out by developing the qualities of its polarity. This will occur relative to its specific qualities and not in a generic way. For example, what Capricorn gains by drawing on Cancer is very different than what Aquarius gains from Leo. For a human being, self-development *without* awareness of one's polarity is to ensure a pattern of false results and quick fixes as one never actually knows how thorough lessons have been cellularly integrated. If we do not have the strong mirror of our personal polarities, we are not actually engaged in the Mystery School called Earth. For example, a newly certified legal mediator (Libra) will be truly tested in their ability if they find themselves assigned to a dispute between two business entrepreneurs who are enemies (Aries)!

This notion – the integration of opposites – is the basis for the world's numerous alchemical teachings. Let's look at the Gemini-Sagittarius axis next. In order for Gemini to evolve, it will need to draw from the wisdom of (its polarity) Sagittarius. This will eventually produce the realization that self-knowledge (Gemini, the self) ultimately leads to truth (Sagittarius, the other). In another way of saying, without drawing on the qualities and wisdom of its opposite, Gemini will never learn that a rational understanding of the world (Gemini) is incapable of providing spiritual insight into a greater reality (Sagittarius) and thus its own evolution. Gemini will need to learn and assimilate some Sagittarian qualities within itself to truly grow. The truth is that *any sign or house* in which a planet natally exists *necessarily implies* a very strong relationship with its opposite sign and house. This way of working with polarity is essential to the power and magic of astrology.

AN ORIGINAL, PROMISING THEORY

An intriguing and original observation regarding astrological polarity is currently being explored in SMA counseling. This section attempts to describe it. As this theory has not been sufficiently tested before publication of this book, these ideas are offered as intriguing speculations and areas of inquiry at this time.

If we see each astrological planet as a unique human function within the psyche or body-mind, then it may prove to be that the specific energetic dynamic – the 'rules' of interaction – between it and its polarity position would likewise be unique to each pair. This would produce a picture of planetary polarity which might be summed up as 'Not all planetary polarities operate equally.' What we are describing here is *an expansion to the understanding of astrological polarity itself as well as its practical applications.*

And this is what it might look like: the *way* Mars energetically evolves through its interaction with and progress towards its polarity position (whichever sign that is) will be a fundamentally different archetype than the *way* Saturn interacts with its polarity position for its balancing and evolution. A note to those for whom this information is brand new: a planet's 'polarity position' is simply the identical degree in the opposite sign from the planet's natal position. Thus if our natal planet's position is 18° of Pisces, then our polarity position would be 18° of Virgo. There does not need to be an actual planet *at* 18° Virgo for these ideas to be tested because what we are addressing here is the *implied* energetic relationship between *any* point and its sign- and degree-specific polarity energy.

It seems plausible that any characteristic of a planet or other point (asteroid, hypothetical planet, etc.) could be utilized as a clue for understanding the nature of its relationship with its polarity. Some examples are:

1. The *magnetic orientation* of the planet (positive or negative) would reveal the orientation of its polarity (would be the opposite);

2. The *energetic quality* of the planet or point would reveal those of its polarity energy: active or receptive, inward or outward, self- or socially-focused, the quality of earth, water, air or fire, and other descriptors.

3. The sphere or *inter-related functions of body-mind organism* which the planet or point symbolizes may indicate what is needed by that planet to regulate or balance its related functions, both internally (*chakras, doshas,* and meridians) and externally (physiology). For example, Mercury symbolizes cognition, left-brain functioning and the nervous system; thus its polarity may point out what is needed to balance such processes.

There are other possible additions to this list which may grace our awareness as time goes on.

NOTES:

[1] In this context, 'fix' does not imply 'to correct.' It instead suggests 'to fix on something' and thus to define it or know it or give it identifiable qualities in order to know it.

[2] In this context, 'containing' suggests the idea of 'placing a container around' in order to hold it.

[3] A treatment of astrological polarity appears expanded in *The Soul's Desire & the Evolution of Identity* (SMA Communications, 2005), available at *www.SacredMarriageAstrology.com*

CHAPTER 8

ASPECTS: OUR PERSONAL WIRING

INTRODUCTION

Astrological Aspects are special, spatial relationships between two points plotted on a chart. They are 'special' because the distance between the two points in question reveals itself as a harmonic or energetic octave of the full 360° circle. Just as in other fields, the astrological circle used to create a chart symbolizes totality, completeness and also oneness. No matter how we divide the circle – in half, in quarters, into twelve signs or houses, or into 360°, it remains the symbol for wholeness. This is especially appropriate to astrological practice in that each time a chart is cast, it is examining the *entirety* of a person, a place or an event. As we will see, every aspect is a description of the *implicit relationship* between two individual parts within an *explicit totality* of the complete sky or consciousness.

WHAT THEY REVEAL

Aspects are the indicators of *relationship* between the many functions of the human body-mind. Each function is symbolized by a planet, an Angle, an asteroid, a midpoint or any other chartable point one works with. For example, where astrological Mercury symbolizes the function of cognition and communication, astrological Neptune indicates our Soul-level strategy for realizing a greater reality which we are a part of. These are simplified descriptions to say the least; for complete descriptions of the signs, planets and houses, see chapter 4.

Aspects describe *how two psyche-logical operations are wired together, how they function in relationship together, or the nature of how their independent operations affect one another.* They will indicate how an individual will be learning and growing into the destiny his/her Soul has chosen for that incarnation. For example, there are many ways to build a house. I might choose to pick out the trees, chop them down, size them to my plans' needs and then construct the house myself, while you may choose to hire contractors to achieve the same result. Aspects work in the same way. They tell us *how* the individual is meant to build their relationship between any two functions. If we remember that everyone ever born has *every* planet, asteroid and point *somewhere* on their chart (even if most of them aren't used by astrologers), then aspects are crucial components for revealing how the chosen planets and points are destined to build a unique relationship together. For this reason, aspects describe the most unique and individualizing facets of our psyche. They are very specific markers of our body-mind makeup.

On the level of the Soul, aspects reveal themselves in another way. The Soul exists within a profound wholeness, such that it only knows that which is engendered from union – qualities such as gratitude, love, and compassion.[1] Each incarnation a Soul chooses does not represent a beginning or end to the Soul itself, but rather a next step in its journey of return to that wholeness. It is therefore quite appropriate to use the sacred geometrical shape of *a circle* as the basis for an astrological chart (Vedic astrology charts notwithstanding) in that the wholeness which the Soul both *is* and *desires to return to*, is reflected accurately.

A Soul-level approach to working with aspects confirms this symbolism. It says that each aspect appearing on a birth chart reveals *the Soul's current state of evolutionary progress between the two planets or points creating the aspect*. This is a powerful understanding for it paves our way to apply our interpretation of aspects to the Soul. It seems to suggests that even the most unique qualities of an individual fall within a much larger, ordered and logical progression transcending the current incarnation! And it implies that the Soul has reached the point in its evolution where the current aspects appearing on the birth chart energetically represent its next lessons. Natal aspects reveal *intended alchemies of internal facets of the self in specific ways and for specific reasons*.

A third way to understand aspects is to frame them as alchemical processes. Through the lens of alchemy, we see each aspect as a specific method for creating a new resolution to an otherwise conflicting internal condition.[2] Though there are seven most recognized alchemical processes (*calcinatio, solutio, coagulatio, sublimatio, mortificatio, separatio, and coniunctio*); there are, in fact, many more known to the alchemist.[3] Each one is unique. With knowledge of each process, our insight into the unique dynamics of each aspect is expanded. For clarity, there is not a direct correlation between each of the processes and each aspect; rather, the qualities of the processes educate us about the nature of the transformation of consciousness which then inform our understanding of the aspect functions.

With our three lenses for understanding aspects (incarnational or Self-Identity, Soul or Self-Essence, and alchemical), we can now place aspects into the flowchart begun with signs, planets, and houses in chapter 4. Recall that *sign* energies infuse into the *planetary* functions (within us) which then get expressed most naturally into the *house* areas of life. Aspects are how each sign-infused and house-expressing planet interrelate with one another. Let's look at an example.

Say Uranus is in Cancer in the 9th House and it is producing a *sextile* to Venus in Virgo in the 12th House. We first interpret Cancer infusing into the Uranus function and expressing through the 9th House and then interpret Virgo infusing into the Venus function and expressing through the 12th House. Once we have a good feel for each signature on its own, we then relate one to another through the sextile aspect. To do this, first identify the core functions in each signature: Uranus is the striving to create new understandings separate from what has come before, while Venus is the nature of our femininity.

In this case, 9th House Uranus in Cancer can be interpreted as the drive to redefine one's self-image by opening to a broader understanding of reality beyond the worldly realm. The individual will gravitate toward alternative ways of doing this, which will produce a change in the way one cares for others. 12th House Venus in Virgo can be interpreted as the intent to develop one's femininity from an accurate self-definition and knowing of one's place within creation. The individual may experience periods of disenchantment, frustration and loss of self-control in order to force the release of egoic security enough to open new space for this balance to occur.

If we now relate these two together *through the sextile function*, we see that this individual's Uranus functioning will be trying to change Venus' familiar ways of receiving and self-stabilizing into more personally valid ways. Specifically, the sextile will create a relationship much like two people meeting each other for the first time who each feel a new friendship is possible with one another. To create a friendship, however, will require effort beyond the initial meeting. With Uranus and Venus in a sextile, the overall intent is to revolutionize (Uranus) one's femininity (Venus) through a more expanded idea of reality in order to create a greater, more realistic embodiment (Virgo) of actual reality (12th House).

TWO TYPES

SMA identifies two categories of aspects: *harmonizing* and *catalyzing*. These are general descriptions only, used to frame how the relationship between two astrological points (such as planets) will be formed and honed through life in a generalized way. These categories should not be used to replace the diligent and intuitive study of each aspect in its unique function. It may be that aspects are the astrological component requiring the most amount of experience with others and their charts to learn. If this is true, the following categories should be used in the proper context.

Harmonizing aspects are those relationships which occur in synchronistic ways. We might think of the harmonizing aspects as two functions working in parallel to form greater integration within the psyche total. This does not mean that harmonizing aspects do not have their challenges. They do! They require lots of effort from the individual to actualize their harmonious approach to the intended alchemy. So while they do imply a *harmonious* action between them, such harmony will only occur with intentional and devoted *effort*.

Catalyzing aspects are relationships of conflict and challenge. Each planet involved in a catalyzing aspect challenges the other by forcing it to adjust its otherwise unimpeded action. Catalyzing aspects approximate a competition, a battle, or a fusion reaction; their effect occurs through the resolution of some manner of conflict. These aspects will naturally create anxiety or stress in the psyche. As this is their natural mode, we can assume that there are appropriate reasons for a Soul to choose a life with many catalyzing aspects. In general, we might understand such a choice by first understanding that the condition of *conflict* is the natural milieu of evolution, creation and thus manifestation.[4] The Soul is thus choosing to familiarize and experience itself, as it were, amidst a storm of cross-currents.

In addition to the more specific psychological indicators for the Soul's growth found in the signs, planets, and houses, the dominant category of aspects – harmonizing or catalyzing – represented in the birth chart will indicate the dominant mode of forging new resolutions between the Identity's many internal functions.

WORKING WITH ASPECTS IN SMA

Let's introduce basic understandings of how aspects are formed and identified.

Elongation - The distance between two points is called *elongation* and is measured in degrees of arc or °. 1° is equal to 60' minutes of arc, and 1' is equal to 60 seconds of arc. If two planets are 152° apart from each other, they are said to share a 152° *elongation*. The term 'aspect' is usually reserved for special elongation amounts, such as 45°, 90°, 120°, etc. Obviously, all points plotted on a chart share an elongation with every other point on that chart; but this does not mean that all points are in aspect to one another. It is suggested this naming procedure is followed to maintain consistency.

Unidirectionality - In SMA, there are guidelines for determining which planet or point to begin from in calculating elongation. Any two points on the circumference of a circle have potentially two elongations: one determined by their clockwise distance from each other, the other from their counter-clockwise distance. In almost all cases, SMA uses the *counter-clockwise* elongation as the determinant for aspects because counter-clockwise is the forward direction on the chart. Counter-clockwise not only is forward movement on the chart, it also indicates progressive evolutionary movement or change as well. The only exception is working with the Nodes, either the Lunar Nodes or other planetary nodes. The reasons for this are explained in chapter 11.

Starting Planets - To determine which planet to begin from to determine elongation, there are three simple ideas to follow:
      ❧ Begin from the slower-moving planet and count degrees in a *counter-clockwise* direction until the second planet is reached.
      ❧ However, if the *Sun* is one of the planets in consideration, then *always* start with the Sun and proceed counter-clockwise until you reach the second planet.
      ❧ However, if a *Lunar Node* is one of the points in consideration, then *always* begin with the planet and proceed *clockwise* until you reach the

Node. The basic reason for this is that Nodes move backwards in our sky, so this must be accommodated for astrologically. For an explanation of the movement of the Nodes and how to work with them, see chapter 11.

Here are some examples: if Mercury and Pluto are the focus, begin with Pluto (because Pluto is exterior to Mercury). If Jupiter and Venus, begin with Jupiter (because Jupiter is exterior to Venus). If the Sun and Neptune, begin with the Sun (because the Sun is always the starting point when it is one of the planets involved). If the NorthNode or SouthNode and any planet is involved, begin with the planet *and move clockwise.*

Waning & Waxing - Once two planets' elongation is calculated, it can then be categorized as either a waxing or waning aspect. *Waxing* aspects are those that are 180° or less. Waxing aspects generally indicate the Soul-level intent to develop subjective consciousness. In this light, they are *building, forming, and stabilizing.* Waxing aspects signify a newer relationship in the Soul's incarnations than those of waning aspects. 'Newer' does not mean more free or more immature, but rather indicates an earlier stage of development *relative to the complete cycle of evolutionary development (the entire circle).*

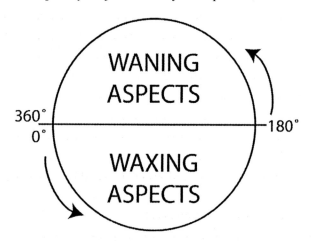

Figure 1 – Waxing and Waning elongations and aspects

Waning aspects are those sharing a 180° elongation or more. Waning aspects will indicate the Soul-level intent to develop objective consciousness through the two points' relationship. In this light, they are *dispersing, communicating, and releasing.* Waning aspects indicate a more developed relationship between the two planets than waxing aspects. However, 'more developed' does not mean easier or wiser within the individual, but rather focused on a later stage of development *relative to the complete cycle of evolutionary development (the entire circle).*

Determining the waxing or waning quality of an aspect helps to build the context for the specifics of the dynamic and should never replace the aspects' meanings themselves. Each aspect used in SMA is described in both its waxing and waning natures below.

Figure 1 shows how the aspect circle is identical to the progression of sign energies and house domains. Through lifetimes, a Soul will evolve around the Aspect Wheel as well as around the Sign Wheel (Aries to Pisces). In fact, the progression through each Aspect around the Aspect Wheel accurately mirrors that through the Signs. Not surprisingly, the degree of an aspect will determine 'where' it falls in the Sign Wheel and thus give the astrologer a flavor of its energy in that light. For example, a waxing semi-square, a 45° aspect, can be related to the 15th degree of Taurus: if we begin at 0° of Aries and travel 45° counter-clockwise, we will come to the middle of Taurus.

Orb - As astrology and specifically aspects show us, the universe is a precisely inexact system. Specificity can become the very obstacle to the attainment of truth when our search for it blinds us to the relative nature of manifest reality. It is from these ideas that orbs were devised to assist the astrologer in interpreting the relationship between two points.

An astrological orb is the amount of space allowance the astrologer grants *on either side* of an aspect's target degree. To use a statistical term, they are differentials or allowed margins of 'error.' Orbs effectively increase the amount of space in which aspects operate and influence the individual. The less the orb amount, the stronger the effect of the aspect; the greater the orb, the weaker the aspect's influence.

There are no strict rules for determining orb sizes. Astrologers have their opinions on how big an orb to allow for each aspect. These determinations will result from his/her interpretive experience and those applications and points used in practice. For example, if one planet is located at 7°, and the aspect involved includes a 6° orb, then that planet will 'feel' the aspect (no matter what it is) from 1° to 13° of that sign. See figure 2.

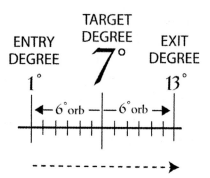

Applying and Separating Orbs - When the first planet's target degree lands *before* the degree position of the second (in astrologically forward, or counter-clockwise, direction), the aspect between the two is an *applying* aspect. When the target degree of the first planet lands *after* the position of the second, they are in a *separating* aspect.

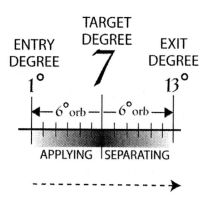

Figure 3 – Difference between applying and separating orbs

ASPECTS AS SACRED GEOMETRY

As described above, each aspect symbolizes a specific energetic dynamic existing between two objects. They point to *relationship* and are determined by spatial distance around the circumference of a circle. If we recall a circle symbolizes completeness, then each aspect is one part of that completeness. This basic idea is illuminated for us by a sacred geometry view of astrological aspects.

"Geometry is the study of *spatial order* through the measure and relationships of forms... The practice of geometry was an approach to the way in which the universe is ordered and sustained."[5]

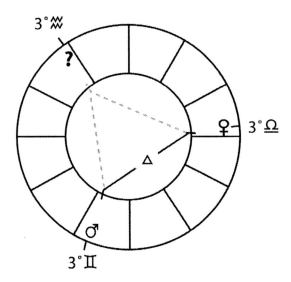

3° ♒

3° ♌

3° ♊

Figure 4 – One aspect line necessarily implies the others in the complete geometrical shape.

When we identify an aspect on a chart, we are pointing to a specific division of the circle into equal parts. In figure 4, locating a 120° trine (△) between Mars (♂) and Venus (♀) necessarily creates one side of a hypothetical equilateral triangle. Their trine implies its other two sides as well (dashed lines), *even if there is no planet or point in the third position.* The absence of a third planet or point in the correct position (at 3° ♒) to form the full triangle or 'grand trine' does not in any way diminish the trine that does exist between Mars and Venus. In interpreting aspects, only two points are needed to form an aspect. In our trine example, we see the trine connotes the complete equilateral triangle with all its symbolisms. A study of the triangle in sacred geometry would naturally deepen our understanding of the astrological trine. Finally, we observe that a trine effectively divides the circle into three equal parts.

"The significance [of an aspect] is to be found in the symbolism of the number by which the circle is divided." [6]

Each of the other aspects can be seen as equal divisions of the circle as well: The *opposition* (☍) divides the circle into two equal parts of 180° each; The *septile* (S) divides the circle into 7 equal parts of 51.25°;

The *sextile* (✶) divides the circle into 6 equal parts of 60° each; it can be seen as a sub-aspect of the trine;

The *quintile* (Q) divides the circle into 5 equal parts of 72° each;

The *square* (□) divides the circle into four equal parts of 90° each; it has two sub-aspects, the semi-square (∠, 45°) and the sesqui-square (⬜, 135°);

The *trine* (△) divides the circle into three equal parts of 120° each.

These aspects foundation any astrological practice or interest. There are a number of other aspects used by astrologers as well. Any of them may provide you with another tool in your interpretive tool belt.

ASPECTS IN PRACTICE

Following are the descriptions of aspects used in SMA. It is useful to remember that aspects describe how two objects or points relate, communicate, challenge or 'don't see' one another: *aspects are best learned by studying the energetic dynamics of systems and how things meet in order to bring about change.* These lessons will come to us more from our work with others and our study of human nature than through simple memorization of their definitions.

Often the same aspect will reveal itself in very different ways depending on the planets involved. For example, Mars and Venus will express their trine in different ways than will Pluto and Saturn. While Mars trine Venus and Pluto trine Saturn will indicate *the same general dynamic or relationship between each pair*, the similarity will not indicate how those unique relationships will manifest personally. The trine effect will create different results in each case. It is in fact the nature of the natural alchemy between two planets or points which to a large degree determines the aspect's effect for the individual. It is for this reason that SMA prioritizes a deep understanding of each sign, planet and house over strict memorization of aspect dynamics.

Aspects will also lend themselves to *more than one interpretative strategy*. For example, we can interpret a conjunction (0°) between Jupiter and the Moon in three ways. We can see:

- ❧ Jupiter as a major influence on the Moon;
- ❧ the Moon as a major influence on Jupiter; or
- ❧ the combined effect produces something new and perhaps unexpected.

With Jupiter as an influence on the Moon, we might see that the individual's egoic identity absolutely requires for its stability and comfort an ongoing education in greater reality, foreign cultures, or spiritual/religious activity. With the Moon as a major influence on Jupiter, we might see the individual's capacity for spiritual growth through one's own efforts absolutely requires integrating one's dreaming life in meaningful ways. In the third example, we might learn that the individual is on a path of creating a new spiritual practice which promotes the development of communication with one's ancestors as guides along one's path.

Finally, we can appreciate the messages being communicated to our conscious minds through our unique array of aspects if we see each and every one as an attempt to discover, develop and inhabit our center. If an aspect implies a geometric shape of awareness around us, then that shape's center must necessarily be *our center*. We can then use our aspects, our Soul-chosen intra-relationships, to locate that center.

PRACTICE WITH IDENTIFYING ASPECTS

The following graphic offers the ability to practice identifying aspects and their various characteristics.

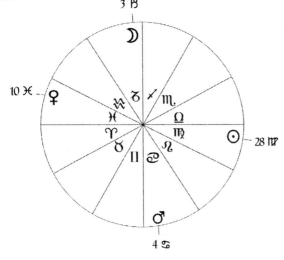

Figure 5 – Aspect identification practice

When calculating each aspect, remember to begin with the correct planet.

Aspect #1

What is the elongation between Venus (♀) and Mars (♂)?_____°

What aspect does this form? _____

Is it a waxing or waning version of this aspect? _____

What is the orb of this aspect? _____°

Is it an applying or separating aspect? _____

Aspect #2

What is the elongation between Mars (♂) and the Moon (☽)? ____°

What aspect does this form? _____

Is it a waxing or waning version of this aspect? _____

What is the orb of this aspect? _____°

Is it an applying or separating aspect? _____

Aspect #3

What is the elongation between the Sun (☉) and the Moon (☽)?_____°

What aspect does this form? _____

Is it a waxing or waning version of this aspect? _____

What is the orb of this aspect? _____°

Is it an applying or separating aspect? _____

Aspect #4

What is the elongation between Mars (♂) and the Sun (☉)?_____°

What aspect does this form? _____

Is it a waxing or waning version of this aspect? _____

What is the orb of this aspect? _____°

Is it an applying or separating aspect? _____

SMA Aspects

Astrology is an ever-expanding and collaborative field. Within its domain, aspect work seems to morph and offer new understanding into the psyche's dynamics more frequently than other spheres of astrological study. The following list of aspect descriptions results from much counseling experience and study of the work of other astrologers. Much gratitude is specifically expressed to astrologers John Addey, Charles M. Graham, Jeffrey Wolf Green, and Bil Tierney (listed alphabetically).

Examining figure 5 on the next page, we see the Conjunction at the 0° position (waxing conjunction) begins the journey. Each aspect in counter-clockwise order from that point represents a next step or further development of the astrological relationship between two planets or points. For example, the 90° waxing square will naturally pick up where the 72° waxing quintile left off. In this way, each aspect furthers the growth from its predecessor. The following descriptions of each aspect are presented in this context – *as a continuity.*[7]

You may notice that each aspect associates with a sign based on its position. If we overlay the standard Sign Wheel (with the beginning of Aries lining with the waxing conjunction (0°)), we can see the close correlation. Each aspect thus 'falls into' a sign area. Associating aspects with signs in this way for effective interpretation strongly requires that we do not make one-to-one correspondences between signs and aspects. Doing so is not only illogical but also irresponsible. We do not describe an apple strictly in terms of how an orange tastes... we describe it on its own terms, having developed a personal understanding of apple: the different varieties, the ripeness, the color, etc. In much the same way, aspects ask us to study them and feel their energetic dynamics on *their* own terms. Intuition, trust, intelligence and a good measure of investigative fun will assist your study of the aspects.

It continues to be born out by practicing Sacred Marriage Astrologers that the most effective and supportive interpretations and guidance to others – the most powerful use of astrology itself – comes first and foremost from the astrologer's intimacy with the astrological energies. The personal interaction between astrologer and client creates an energetic focus for 'magnetizing' the most appropriate information for the client. In this light, allow your understanding of aspects to develop over time. They more than any other component in astrology require patience and sufficient practical experience.

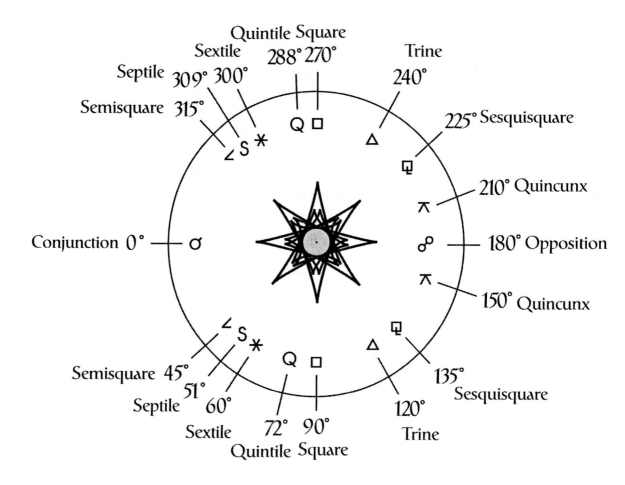

Figure 6 – SMA's Aspect Wheel

♂ **WAXING CONJUNCTION** - 0° *(both catalyzing and harmonizing)*
Start of a new alchemy, union, or resolution between two or more planets (aspects of the psyche). Two energies in random, unfocused relationship with each other. The individual may not be aware of the presence of two distinct energies and will instinctually orient to them as one. The intent is to merge together what would otherwise remain separate in order to create or begin something new. This aspect begins the cycle of subjective awareness of two points' relationship and operates primarily instinctually.
Suggested orb: 8°

∠ Waxing Semi-Square - 45° *(catalyzing)*

Conflict between one's instinctual desires for continued *external* active exploration and the nascent capacity for *internal* awareness and preliminary awareness. A sub-aspect of the square, the waxing semi-square will challenge the tendency to remain fixed in the familiar by blocking the individual in some way. Since the start of the relationship between two points (at their conjunction), the waxing semi-square is the first hint of discordant experience to the still-young subjective awareness. It can mark the *beginning* of the long process of maturing one's subjective consciousness (Identity-building) by *introducing* the concept of modification or flexibility. This seeds the later germination of preliminary self-awareness to an otherwise automatic ego-based orientation to life.

Suggested orb: 4°

S Waxing Septile - (51.25°) *(neither catalyzing nor harmonizing)*

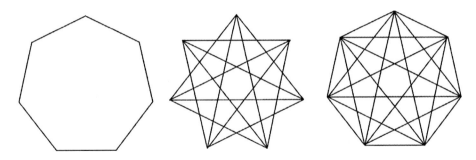

The waxing septile seems to invite further self-inquiry as to *the reasons for* the discord experienced in the waxing semi-square stage. Different types of questions begin to be formed, which represent an expanding consciousness. Interests in the occult ('hidden') explanations also form in consciousness, symbolizing one that is capable of seeking deeper than superficial under-standings. This septile specifically remains within a context of a strong, subjective, incomplete self-conscious awareness. The insights and conclusions gained are thus oriented to make personal sense of one's personal mystery in often pre-conscious ways (such as automatic writing).

Suggested orb: 2-3°

✳ WAXING SEXTILE - 60° *(harmonizing)*

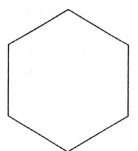
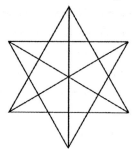
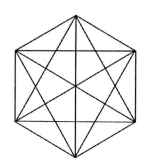

The first subjective experience of a harmonious interaction between the two planets or points which directly supports greater understanding of self. The insights gained from the waxing sextile here strive to be cognitively accessed and explored but only through specific effort exerted by the individual. As it is the first of its kind, this sextile can reveal an area of laziness, passivity or an assumption that growth or success will come easy. Cognitive processes must be turned into kinetic explorations in order to fully benefit from the harmony promised by this aspect. Such effort will occur within a context of subjective identity, which will cause many opinions, or personal cognitive orientations, to form. This sextile can also point to erratic patterns of thinking and opinion-forming because mental *focus* and clear sense of self is still developing. It may create experiences of relatively unchallenged learning if engaged in, or undisciplined, unfocused and assumptive stagnancy if not. *Suggested orb: 6°*

Q WAXING QUINTILE[8] - 72° *(neither catalyzing nor harmonizing)*

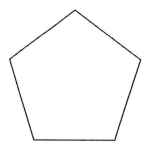

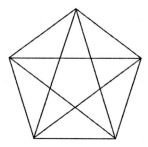

This aspect focuses on subjective explorations of the 'deeper forms' of life, or developing understanding of the underlying structures which give rise to manifestation. These structures exist etherically and cause innumerable expressions to phenomenally arise. In one sense, these 'structures' can be tied to the shapes of sacred geometry. They will express as thoughts, behaviors and visions, and also as art, projects and relationships. The waxing quintile develops one's ability to penetrate into the Mind of mind to discover how the unmanifest realm informs the manifest. This aspect can give rise to masterful creativity or aberrant, malevolent expressions if the core Identity is underdeveloped. For example, it can be used to rationalize an Identity's electrical imbalance and resulting behaviors. This quintile shows how to alter the use of the mind, relative to the subjective Identity, by tapping the archetypal power of one's deeper Mind.

□ WAXING SQUARE[10] - 90° *(catalyzing)*

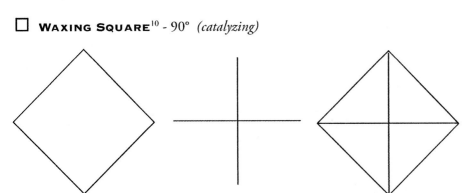

This aspect forces changes to the specific forms or patterns of Self-Identity which are preventing growth. From the waxing quintile, the waxing square will block any further development of the subjective awareness until the required change is made. The types of change this square demands are those to the Self-Identity, which include overly subjective ego-definitions and assumptions. In the geometrical image of two developments meeting at right angles, we see the absolute requirement for re-adjustment of *both*. This square will often seed the individual with the first explicit experience of their innate, latent creativity in that the strong obstruction forces the individual to 'create' a new solution to an otherwise impassable problem. The prior aspect can be seen as the etheric seed for this square's expression of just such a discovery. The waxing square will force into awareness where and what the inner resistances to change are. In other words, it will force the consciousness to, as it were, 'take the plunge' into matter more fully and with greater commitment.

Suggested orb: 8°

△ **WAXING TRINE** - 120° *(harmonizing)*

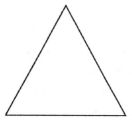 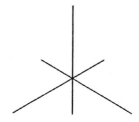 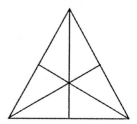

The waxing trine signifies the main integrative or harmonizing stage within subjective development (symbolized by the waxing aspects). This trine augments and fosters communication and education. It promotes one's ability to integrate personal vision with its implementation (albeit still in quite subjective terms). This trine fortifies the new identity within its environment and indicates a natural ease at finding a mutually beneficial outlet, solution, relationship. Similar to the sextile (one of the trine's sub-aspects), it requires effortful activity to actualize its potential, specifically in the sphere of rooting in one's Identity deeply. Thus it will promote the development of self-strength and solidity in order to 'hold' meaningful experiences and learnings from others. This trine supports balanced individuality – two individuals relating and honoring the other's individuality – which will attract or be noticed by others.

Suggested orb: 8°

 WAXING SESQUI-SQUARE - 135° *(catalyzing)*

After the waxing trine, the waxing sesqui-square roadblocks any selfishness, narcissism, or reactive behaviors. These excessive subjective traits are exposed with others, in more of a 'public' arena, than from a self-inquiring mode. Embarrassment is often an experience common to this aspect. In this light, the waxing sesqui-square counteracts much residual trine-related egotism or subconscious behaviors. Though its effect is different than the square in that it curbs excessiveness in order to balance (where the square blocks in order to redefine), the Self-Identity will be forced to choose other than its familiar self-based behaviors, and *for* more conscious, self-balanced ones. This will produce further modifications to its Identity (ie., learning not to take things personally, ceasing to self-identify in old ways, or opening

to the possibility of personal change).
Suggested orb: 4°

⟑ WAXING QUINCUNX[10] - 150° *(neither catalyzing nor harmonizing)*

The intent of the waxing quincunx is to separate in order to discipline, improve and make more accurate the Self-Identity. The quincunx separation is *not* the same as that of the following opposition aspect because its separating-impulse does not emanate from an exact polarity (with the magnetic implication that carries). And without the strong pull that opposites exert on one another, the quincunx effect is one of *disconnection*, or an absence of awareness of the other. From this view, the quincunx is more of a *psychological* separation than the opposition because the two points or planets here do not necessarily know about or desire communication with the other. This perhaps explains the quincunx's reputation as the aspect of 'no relationship.' The waxing quincunx will apply these core ideas in the domain of subjective awareness development as it is indeed a waxing aspect. It will create the inner experience of 'something missing' which can easily produce patterns of anger, guilt, depression, or hopelessness. These will be coupled with strong urges to *do something about* those feelings. At this stage however, much if not all the options available lead one to 'internalize in order to discipline.' Internalization here will create more awareness of what is and what is not true about oneself. With greater self-accuracy, greater awareness of *both* functions (planets) comes. This aspect can greatly assist the development of a personal humility.
Suggested orb: 4°

☍ WAXING & WANING OPPOSITIONS - 180° *(catalyzing)*

In general, the intent of an opposition is to create new awareness by becoming aware of Other. Here, 'Other' is not only other people and society, but also one's own Other self. It can include denied aspects, forgotten dreams, lost memories, even ancestors. The opposition is thus the birth of the subjective awareness of this Other. Oppositions create strongly divided relationships astrologically yet ones with equally strong magnetic ties to one another. It should not be assumed that an opposition suggests 'no relationship'. It is more accurate that they catalyze stronger relationship by exposing individual differences reflected by the other. This can result in a greater ability to see oneself as source of *both* sides of a polarity[11], argument, or conflicted decision.

Oppositions are created from magnetically opposite intentions which, as we know, create a *very strong attraction between them*. Two planets in opposition are trying to discover how they can individuate and thus foster stronger relationship between them. On the Soul-level, an opposition indicates the choice to polarize in order to increase mutual understanding. On the archetypal level, the opposition marks the change-over from subjectively-focused development to objective development. In SMA, oppositions are referred to as 'conjunctions in the opposite direction' to remind of their innate 'same but opposite' relationship to the effect of conjunction aspects.

Waxing Opposition - If the opposition formed is less than 180°, the intent of the Soul is to use the oppositional dynamics to complete its subjective development (in order to prepare for the birth of an objective orientation to life). In other words, the waxing opposition intends to prepare for the deeper reality of Other to be acknowledged in the immediate or longer future.

Waning Opposition - If the opposition formed is greater than 180°, the intent is to initiate many types of relationships in order to consciously explore one's Other, whether that be reflected by an individual, a business, a religion, a family, a nation or a universe. In waning opposition, there will be more of a focus on socially applying this awareness with Other in order to further develop Identity through social interactions.
Suggested orb: 8°

☓ **WANING QUINCUNX** - 210° *(neither catalyzing nor harmonizing)*
As in the waxing quincunx, the 'no relationship' quality here in the waning quincunx creates a disconnection between the two planets or points. But the effect here produces more of an external blockage (where the waning quincunx produced internal resistance). This quincunx can be extremely intense and has been occasionally tied to death experiences. The actual meaning of the aspect, however, must first be grasped in order to place this in a proper context. Following the waxing opposition, this aspect serves to disconnect those internal functions which, while left unaddressed, continue to create overly willful acts which do not take into account one's social climate. The disconnect-effect in this quincunx will thus produce an opportunity to become aware of how such overt, stubborn willfulness and

emotional aggression are still functioning deep in the psyche. The degree to which the individual acknowledges their disconnected relationship (between the two functions represented by the planets involved) will indicate how efficiently and thoroughly the individual can turn old patterns around. If effective, it will force a shift of the self-image in order to more effectively participate in life *with others*. In this way, it engenders a personal motivation to develop objective awareness. This aspect can greatly assist the development of a social humility.

Suggested orb: 4°

⬚ Waning Sesqui-Square - 225° *(catalyzing)*

This sesqui-square produces regular conflicts between the drive to exhibit or disperse our wisdom and skills and our underlying egoic reasons for doing so. It will place stubborn obstacles in our path until we shift into a deeper understanding of these egoic reasons we maintain under the surface. Once accessed, awareness of a deeper layer of self-serving motivations appears to us. We then have the opportunity to make different choices. Therefore, the two main intents of this aspect are to further refine our knowing of what we have to share, and to simultaneously create more awareness of what actually serves others in their development rather than forcing our lessons down their throats. Until both occur in significant ways, this aspect will produce broken friendships, unexplainable rage, and inner conflicts. It is designed to force the development of *self-accuracy* in a social context.

Suggested orb: 4°

△ Waning Trine - 240° *(harmonizing)*

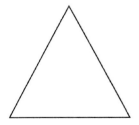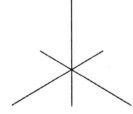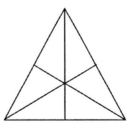

As in any trine, both individuals involved in the aspect are successfully individualized relative to each other; there is harmonious or balanced interaction. The waning trine perhaps represents the first harmonious interaction of self with Other. On a personal level, the individual has reconciled to adjust aberrant beliefs and behaviors to what is more socially effective. This symbolizes one level of balanced interaction: *self-image within social context.* On the social level, the individual interacts with Other in a mutually meaningful way representing a second type: being an *individual among many other individuals.* Through this aspect's influence, the person successfully disperses to others what is meaningful (to him/her) and also society recognizes that contribution as valuable. If engaged fully, this aspect will create a growing need to find other areas or domains of external life through which to spread its knowing. The individual will desire more experiences of him/herself like this and will search high and low for opportunities to do just that. Here the individual experiences being socially received or acknowledged, though the full depth of such an experience is still nascent at this stage.

Suggested orb: 8°

☐ WANING SQUARE[12] - 270° *(catalyzing)*

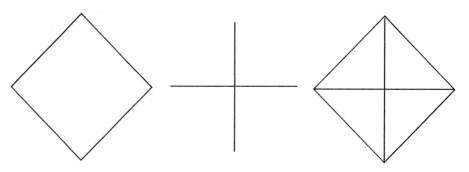

The waning square will return the individual to its need to change itself. Here, the needed changes must occur in one's subjective *context* of Identity, rather than on the specific Identity definitions themselves. There will be a forced release of one's subjective bias, or excluding of others, in order for an objective awareness to be more fully chosen and embodied. This square *may* address one's past social, religious, and cultural attachments or identifications. But it will *always* force one to address the social pressure to conform, to provide for self and family, and to responsibly meet the needs of daily life. This will create periods of internalization, such as depression or isolation, as the individual wonders how to continue amidst so many 'rules' or so much pressure to 'fit in.' Internalizing has the effect of separating oneself from others which through this aspect is a healthy sign. It affords the opportunity to examine one's stubborn egoic ideas about what it needs and what society doesn't provide. This square then catalyzes significant changes to one's Self-Identity which, interestingly, are brought about exclusively from *outside* of oneself – one's social involvements. As in all squares, there may be many crises produced by this aspect. Here the crisis will be oriented more towards one's future and one's perseverance in society (rather than towards one's Identity outside of a social context). It will cause a change to how one views oneself within one's environment, which will reveal one's unaddressed ego-based beliefs.

Suggested orb: 8°

Q **WANING QUINTILE**[13] - 288° *(neither catalyzing or harmonizing)*

With the newly refined, socially-aligned Identity (from the waning square), the waning quintile will assist the meaningful exposure to the creation principles underlying all life. At this stage, these understandings are quite new, yet they begin to point the individual into new directions and help to initially form those directions into tangible plans. The high creativity often found in the quintile (waxing or waning) can seed the eventual creation into form of fantastic things – art, organizations, teachings – particularly through this aspect. This is because the individual at this stage is beginning to cellularly change into a more evolved expression of its Soul's Desire, the quintessential intention for its incarnation.[14] This quintile may represent the developmental stage in which the initial 'download' for this evolutionary growth takes place. This will produce new ideas about what one's life is to be focused on or include.

NOTES

✳ WANING SEXTILE - 300° *(harmonizing)*

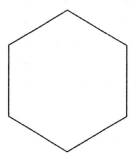 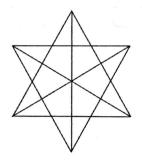 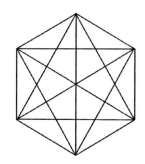

The intent here to foster a *refinement* of one's personal connection to others or society from the new awarenesses gained in the previous aspect. This intent receives support from the innate harmoniousness promised by any sextile but, once again, requires active effort to take advantage of its opportunities. Many circumstances may arise to provide opportunities for fleshing out one's life plan and underlying purpose (Soul's Desire). The general trend of objective consciousness development here is furthered by the refinement of a more personally-meaningful vision of (one's) life and reality. This will naturally occur in the social arena. Though the 'big picture' will usually not be fully formed at this point, there will be many experiments into which piece of that vision 'sticks' and what doesn't. 'Stickiness' will be determined by the amount of social success or harmony experienced. This aspect also indicates a strong drive to understand how groups work and how to improve them. One's objectivity is also strengthened here through one's relatively unchallenged ability to observe oneself and/in one's society. The waning sextile can produce experiences of feeling aligned with/hopeful about one's life purpose within society.
Suggested orb: 6°

S WANING SEPTILE – 309° *(neither catalyzing nor harmonizing)*

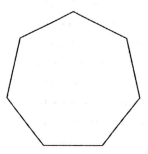 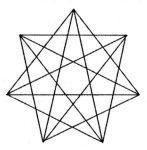 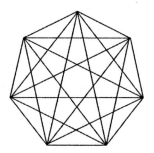

Whereas the previous aspect opens consciousness for understanding the underlying patterns of life, the waning septile opens it to augment its intuitive strength. This aspect will create specific circumstances in life to continue development of its objective consciousness by allowing the individual to rely on his/her intuition as a guide for discerning which directions to move in. The process of intuition, though personally experienced, is in fact an objective archetype in that listening to the intuitive voice requires stepping back from one's moment-to-moment mental activity. While the previous aspect collected lots of experiences with others to establish a broad base of understanding, this aspect then foments clarifying of direction through, once again, personal intuition. It will create the effect of feeling destined for something, yet the specific form of that feeling is not yet known, or will drive towards understanding the bigger picture in which it plays a part.
Suggested orb: 2-3°

∠ WANING SEMI-SQUARE - 315° *(catalyzing)*

This aspect reveals a conflict between adjusting to current conditions and relying on familiar relationships, methods or past successes in social or business activities to continue into the future. The waning semi-square can reveal ideological stubbornness through many failed attempts at implementing one's visions. It can also point to an impatience for the future visions to be received. This aspect contains a very strong objective orientation to life, and may even reveal patterns of psychological dissociation. If utilized effectively, it will produce a radiating-effect of individual consciousness, which will create a very expanded awareness – that of sensing the future and one's role in it.
Suggested orb: 4°

☌ WANING CONJUNCTION - 360° *(both catalyzing and harmonizing)*

This aspect completes the full cycle of development between the two planets or points. Two energies return back intimately together as a symbol in consciousness for completion, dissolution and death of their former relationship. This is to make space for their new journey together in the future. This aspect holds great wisdom locked away, and its key is, ultimately, a balanced subjective-objective Identity. If awareness can be brought to this conjunction, a deep wisdom is ready to be hatched. The waning conjunction's intended alchemy is to create a transcendent or transpersonal experience of the two planets' or points' quintessential oneness and timeless reflection of each other. Objective consciousness here maximizes beyond itself into the final completion, or 'death' of the entire developmental cycle. *Suggested orb: 8°*

NOTES:

[1] The ancient Egyptian conception of an individual's Soul is described similarly: it has no capacity for understanding or communicating anything but that which emanates from a profound non-duality or oneness. The Egyptian term for this component of each human being is his/her *Ba*.

[2] The human psyche is filled with conflicts. This idea is layed out in the astrological birth chart wherein we see each of our basic psychological operations in some type of conflict or resolution-in-the-making with every other operation. Thus, the term 'conflict' is chosen to describe *what is*, and not to add pejorative weight to the human condition.

[3] For explanations of these processes, *Anatomy of the Psyche* by Edward F. Edinger is recommended. For additional reading on alchemy, see the Bibliography.

[4] Philosopher Ken Wilbur states, "From the inside, evolution is like riding a psychotic horse toward a burning barn. Half of the [evolutionary] experience is a blissful pushing into newness, while the other half is a carpet burn from a death of the old."

[5] Robert Lawlor, <u>Sacred Geometry</u>, 1982.

[6] John Addey, <u>Harmonics in Astrology</u>, 1976.

[7] With this in mind, there are several variations or sub-aspects which are not included in this list, such as the semi-sextiles, the bi- and tri-quintiles and –septiles, the novile series, the decile series, the undecile series, and others.

[8] Quintiles in general form a pentacle, often yet erroneously associated with satanic origins. In fact, the pentacle was first identified in ancient Sumeria, in that culture's highly accurate tracking of the Venus cycle each 19 months as it disappeared below the eastern horizon and rose again over the western horizon.

Thus, the pentacle shape is related to all form, including the cognitive forms that give rise to explicit forms. In a large sense, the quintile refers to the feminine function as it can be known through human consciousness. For a complete examination of the Venus Journey and how it brings with it the pentacle shape, the upcoming book, *The Mars & Venus Journeys* by Adam Gainsburg, is suggested.

[9] The waxing square in astrology is homologous to the Crisis in Identity Phase in the Mars Journey. For those familiar with the Mars Journey and its phases, the waxing square speaks more to the individual human being. For those unfamiliar with the Journey's phases, the Crisis in Identity Phase addresses specific areas of consciousness which prevent accurate subjective awareness of one's masculine nature. The upcoming book, *The Mars & Venus Journeys* by Adam Gainsburg, addresses each Phase of each Journey in detail (2006).

[10] Technically, the term "inconjunct" refers to both aspects which constitute 180°: the quincunx (150°) and the semi-sextile (30°). The semi-sextile is not normally used in SMA.

[11] Astrological polarity is described extensively in chapter 7.

[12] The waning square in astrology is homologous to the Crisis in Destiny Phase in the Mars Journey. For those familiar with the Mars Journey and its Phases, the waning square speaks more to one's destiny as an embodiment of masculine consciousness. For those unfamiliar with the Journey's Phases, the Crisis in Destiny Phase of the Mars Journey addresses those areas of consciousness which prevent further objective embodiment of one's masculine nature. The upcoming book, *The Mars & Venus Journeys* by Adam Gainsburg, addresses each Phase of each Journey in detail (2006).

[13] see note 7.

[14] The Soul's Desire is explored in chapters 9-10.

CHAPTER 9

PLUTO: THE SOUL'S DESIRE, THE IDENTITY'S LACK

The information presented in this chapter and the next arises in part from the pioneering work of astrologer Jeffrey Wolf Green, founder of Evolutionary Astrology and author of two groundbreaking books on Pluto which are both recommended for the interested reader (see Bibliography). Evolutionary Astrology is taught in many countries and is, in my view, the most penetrating use of astrology which has reached a worldwide audience. Thanks to this and resulting efforts by many talented astrologers, there is now a methodology for tracking the actual Soul of an individual using nothing more than the natal chart. What follows is a shortened and perhaps simplified version of the complete method outlined by Mr. Green and utilized in Evolutionary Astrology. I am not a student of or certified in Evolutionary Astrology and thus the following should not be taken as a substitute, as it simply results from what I have found works best within an SMA context. A companion book now available, Pluto & the Lunar Nodes in Sacred Marriage Astrology *(SMA Communications) offers a more comprehensive explanation of how to work with Pluto and the Lunar Nodes in an SMA context.*

Be sure to read re-chapter 1 as an introduction to some of this chapter's material.

THE SOUL

To our minds, a Soul is many things. It is our essential energetic uniqueness, our unitary vibration of Divine Light/Love, the divine spark of God-light which we are, and our consistent, 'individuated' consciousness persisting through incarnations. In SMA classes, I teach the Soul as an individual's *Self-Essence*. Connecting the notion of *essence* to the Soul is a useful tool because the Soul is not fixed in time or to a certain incarnation which implies the idea of essential-ness, or beyond context. The Soul is self-originating and self-perpetuating as it emanates throughout space-time dimensions *simultaneously.* It is pure consciousness at a specific frequency or vibration. From the standpoint of undifferentiated consciousness (God), the Soul is an individuated expression of that unity, a light traveler guided only by its growth needs which get met through incarnational lessons. Throughout its experience in incarnation, the Soul retains its essential nature as one-with-God, regardless of how much its current Identity remembers of itself. The Soul remains the Soul. And as all Souls are whole, they forever remain whole. Souls emanate from the same source – God – and are thus synchronized in all times and dimensions with every other Soul. It can only be this way as there is nothing in existence which is not part of existence, or God. This contrasts greatly with the popular notion of 'the dark night of the Soul.'[1]

PLUTO

A human life results from a Soul's choice to further its growth. This is known in SMA as the *Soul's Desire*. In its full breadth, the Soul's Desire is more of a spectrum, or range, or axis within the totality of consciousness, than it is a specific definition of mundane goals. As we will see, the Soul's Desire arises from both the position of natal Pluto and its polarity.

The Soul's Desire is the Soul's growth *intent* for its current incarnation. It is its eveolutionary'guiding principle,' which is sourced in its karmic past, takes form as the current Identity within the current incarnation, and reveals a peculiar continuity of abiding intelligence from past to present. This intelligence is of course the Soul itself. The Soul which guides one's life is the same Soul which has chosen and guided the life of many past incarnations. The Soul carries this 'memory' from incarnation to incarnation in a sort of 'karmic momentum.' A newly beginning life is thus a threshold between all past incarnations and the current one, and the Soul's Desire is the woven, intelligent *pattern* of progression which the birth chart reveals.

This is essential to understand because it will foundation our understanding of astrological Pluto as the nucleus of incarnational choices and thus *all* experiences the self has through them. Pluto thus can be described as *that which reveals our karmic imperative for continuing our evolution.* The current incarnation is the product of the Soul's prior incarnations because it holds key opportunities for it to evolve in specific ways.

In Sacred Marriage Astrology, when we examine a chart to 'track the Soul,' we begin with natal Pluto. Pluto's natal position (sign and house) indicates precisely 'where' the individual's Soul or Self-Essence is on its evolutionary journey. It acts like a snapshot in time revealing *both* the evolutionary results of the past (what it previously intended to evolve toward in prior incarnations), *and* the starting point of the present (what it currently intends to evolve toward in the current incarnation). Pluto also speaks to a third level of meaning, that of 'lack' which is explored later in this chapter. In this way, natal Pluto is the full-range indicator for the Soul's Desire itself and can tell us much about how the current life is positioned to thread the past with the intended future. Let's describe natal Pluto first from *both* its Soul-level significations in order to build a foundation.

PLUTO AS PAST SOUL'S DESIRE

From the view of the karmic past (which implies either one or more prior incarnations), natal Pluto will reveal specifically the past Soul's Desire which produced the past incarnations. It can thus be used to reveal to us 'where' that Soul is coming from, or what the past lifetime(s) have intended as their highest attainment of consciousness. Think about this for a moment. I am suggesting that a planetary position on the *current-life* natal chart indicates a *past-life* characteristic (and a very important one at that!) To accept this, you will have to *feel* into natal Pluto's house and sign. The more familiar and intimate you become with the sign energies and the house assignments in general, the more fully will natal Pluto 'speak' to you about the individual's past. However, it is important to underscore here that this level of Pluto's symbolism – as indicator of the Soul's past Desire – is a generality and must remain so. This is because we are describing the *Soul's* intentions which cannot be defined or understood through any Identity-level manifestation, such as a career goal, philanthropic activity or spiritual practice. We are well-served by remembering always to seek understanding of the Soul on its own level, and *not* project our Identity-level on being onto it. As I share in my classes, the reason a Soul chooses an incarnation is never ultimately 'to save the world', 'to feed starving children', or 'to battle environmental injustice'. These are choices about *how to express or explore one's Soul's Desire* and thus deepen its experience of itself. In other words, the Soul's Desire exists *prior* to the incarnational experience and thus to any life choices one might make, and so is best understood as an overall spiritual intention or goal. Examples of why a Soul would choose to incarnate into a specific life might be 'to learn forgiveness' or 'to more fully explore the feminine or masculine aspects of itself'. Within the context of the karmic past, interpreting the Soul's Desire begins with Pluto's house and sign, and then with aspects of natal Pluto.

PLUTO AS CURRENT SOUL'S DESIRE

Let's shift to describing Pluto's current-life significations. With this lens on, we now see natal Pluto describes two domains: the 'starting blocks' or beginning point for the Soul's current life evolutionary growth, and as the Identity's unconscious beliefs in its own 'lack.' But how can Pluto signify something as grand and noble as our current Soul's Desire while at the same time pointing out our deepest beliefs in our own insufficiency?

An old Greek myth may hold the answer. One of the five Underworld Rivers in Greek mythology is said to be the River Lethe. It is this River which each Soul, just prior to incarnating, must drink from. Once it drinks from Lethe's waters, the Soul loses all knowing of who it really is as well as its intentions for its upcoming incarnation. It is as if a veil is raised between the Soul and its incarnational Identity; hence the popular notion of a 'veil between the worlds.' In Soul-focused astrology this symbol evocatively explains how the past Soul's Desire (the treasured goal of self-realization in the karmic past) can become, for the very same Soul, the place of its deepest lack and limitation. This occurs for every Soul ever born into a life. But why does this pattern exist in the first place? As many people come to question more than once during their paths of spiritual awakening, *why does it have to be like this?* It would seem that the shift from one dimensional reality to another – from the state of greatest union and unified intelligence as a Soul into a dualistic, separation-dominated reality as an Identity is responsible for the schism. It may also be the result of our own karma, as it manifests into our inner conflicts. In other words, because natal Pluto represents all we were trying to evolve toward in past incarnations, when a Soul drinks from the River Lethe, those same goals and any memory of their attainment will be removed from our conscious memory in this life, creating the Identity's *experience* of self-lack. This creates the evolutionarily-desired effect of cellularly motivating the Soul to continue its evolution toward wholeness once again, rather than remaining in a distant memory of faux unity. It is as if the natural law of Soul-forgetting is the prime catalyst for humanity to continue in the direction of its evolution toward Soul-remembering.

'LACK'

Let's now examine the 'other side' of Pluto's current-life symbols: an individual's perceived self-lack.

Signified astrologically by the sign and house of natal Pluto (in addition to its significations as the karmic Soul's Desire), this 'lack belief' is an unacknowledged, unaddressed assumption within the deeper layers of our consciousness which the conscious level has no initial awareness of. This idea of a subconscious belief pattern of self-lack should not be read as the individual is either normally aware (conscious) that such beliefs exist within them or that they will hide it from others, as one would a personal secret. *Rather, the pattern of 'lack' can most effectively be seen as just that: a subconscious pattern or overlay, influencing thought and behavior in specific ways eventually producing the awareness of a 'missing piece' in one's life or self-awareness.*

One's 'lack' issue is thus that which the individual carries into life (Pluto as past and present Soul's Desire) as one of the key components to transform yet perhaps the most difficult to identify (Scorpio). An astrological counselor's ability to interpret this level of Pluto's meaning will greatly augment the amount of support s/he can offer others who desire more self-awareness and authentic transformation.

Pluto's intent on the level of our psychological or body-mind functioning is to empower the self. This will organically occur through deeply challenging (traumatic) experiences. Each experience will in some way offer the opportunity to *consciously* inhabit, deeply embody, and fully embrace those aspects of self which the subconcious would argue it came into life without. This is courageous work and may signify some of the most transformative patterns in human consciousness. As many of us have learned, our conscious minds can believe one thing, while our unconscious (as yet un-integrated) selves may believe something quite the contrary. For example, if a woman is subconsciously believing she lacks the ability for intimacy, she may very well find herself in situations which ask of her nothing but to open herself vulnerably to another (intimacy). All of her projections, fears and issues will rise to the surface to prevent her from doing so initially. She may spend years of her life in the conviction that she is not interested in intimate relationships or alternately that she doesn't understand why all her relationships promise an intimate bond but never deliver. Her natal Pluto in Libra in the 8th House speaks directly to why this is, by revealing that her lack issue – intimacy – actually derives from a rather superficial knowledge of self and an over-dependence on (perhaps manipulating) other people to compensate for it.

FILLING THE 'LACK'

How then can we 'fill the lack' signified by natal Pluto? First, we must remember that the 'lack' here exists in the mind specifically, and in the Identity more generally. From the level of Soul, there would be seen no such insufficiency. Psychologically, through our subconsciously-held 'lack' beliefs will at first produce an equally subconscious reaction to seek outside of oneself to fill the absence. Wherever Pluto is, this will be proven out. We might look outside of ourselves to emotionally feel we're alright (Cancer/4th House), we might discover that we can never travel, pray, or practice enough (Sagittarius/9th House), or we might come to learn of our addictive dependence on constant streams of new information (Gemini/ 3rd House). Whichever external ideas, experiences or goals that we believe hold the key to our happiness and fulfillment, the Pluto lesson enforces on us the reminder that we are ultimately seeking a deeper, richer experience of *ourselves* which can only come from a broader, more honest awareness of *all* aspects of us.

NATAL PLUTO POLARITY

The remaining piece of the Pluto-as-Soul's Desire equation to be addressed is the current-life Desire; in other words, how Pluto reveals where we are evolutionarily headed through our efforts in the current life. As we've learned in chapter 7, astrology works most powerfully when we are cognizant of the *polarity* relationships between signs, planets and houses. Pluto as the Soul works in the same way.

The *Pluto polarity point*[2] is in fact the indicator for where the Soul intends to evolve toward. On the birth chart, Pluto's polarity position is simply the exact *opposite* point by sign and house from natal Pluto. For example, if natal Pluto is 4° of ♍ (Virgo), then we know that natal Pluto Polarity is 4° of ♓ (Pisces).

In SMA, each planet is understood to energetically interact with its implied polarity in ways particular to itself. The following descriptions of Pluto's polarity energy should not be applied to other planets' relationships with their polarity energies.

The Pluto polarity point indicates 'where' (within consciousness) the Soul is intending to evolve. It indicates an individual's life purpose in evolutionary terms – their destiny – and the object of their Soul's Desire. A useful way to understand the Pluto polarity is to see it as a well-spring of pertinent lessons and balancing characteristics for the individual. It represents all the qualities and aspects of consciousness which the Soul Desires to experience itself as within the lifetime. It is the holy grail of Soul growth. It also is too vast and undefined to be limited to any form or expression. In our example of the woman with natal Pluto in Libra in the 8th House, this would place her Pluto Polarity in Aries in the 2nd House. With this kind of instinctual-based emphasis (2nd house Aries), her Soul Desires to access the raw power of life and learn to stabilize herself within that experience through her own values, beliefs, and ways of engaging others. This is a radical departure from her co-dependent tendencies indicated by her natal Pluto (8th House Libra). As we can see here, if the qualities of an individual's Pluto polarity by house and sign can be accessed, learned, explored, and gradually embodied, a tremendous foundation for Soul-focused growth becomes catalyzed within the Identity. How does this work?

Remember, the individual's Soul is, as it were, *coming from* its natal Pluto position and intending to move ever deeper into or toward its Pluto polarity energies *through* the incarnation. The way this happens can be thought of as an 'exchange of ideas,' a 'learning about the other,' or an 'inter-penetrating dialogue'. As an individual becomes more aware of their self-lack beliefs from the past (natal Pluto), s/he will eventually be forced into choosing between continuing in the same vein of denial, or investigating new facets of themselves in some way. They will gradually discover within themselves the very qualities believed for so long to be absent. They will require time to adjust to the cellular shifting which results. They will see a radical shift in how they relate to themselves, their family, their career and their life. Their desires will shift to more closely align with their Desire.

The experience is one of a rebirth or a significant awakening to one's deeper nature: profound and life-changing. It results in an entirely new and more deeply honest self-image, a greater confidence, a stronger fortitude and self-reliance, and, interestingly, in most cases, a deeper humility. This evolutionary experience can only result from, for most of us, the most challenging experiences of our lives.

A case example of how to interpret the position of natal Pluto, its polarity energy as well as the Lunar Nodes (described in chapter 11) is offered in chapter 12.

NOTES:

[1] In an essay which will appear in an upcoming book, *Bridges of Union*, I suggest the current interpretation of the centuries-old phrase "dark night of the soul" is erroneous and outdated. For our post-modern times, I suggest a more accurate re-framing of the reference would be a "dark night of the ego."

[2] To my knowledge, astrologer Jeffrey Wolf Green is the originator of this practice in a western astrological context. Though SMA benefits from this deeply insightful technique, it makes no claims of originating it.

CHAPTER 10

PLUTO THROUGH
THE SIGNS & HOUSES

The following descriptions of Pluto focus on one of the three levels of Pluto described in the previous chapter, that of 'lack,' or that within the context of the Self-Identity.[1] They attempt to illuminate the psychological underpinnings of our repressed beliefs in our insufficiencies ('lack'). However, if we were to re-examine Pluto from the context of *Self-Essence*, we would discover entirely new expressions and meanings because our context for inquiry would be different. With this in mind, these recipe descriptions are offered to support a realistic or balanced approach to working with Pluto on this level.[2]

In each of the following placements:

෴ The *Lack* statements describe the domains of self which an individual subconsciously believes to be absent. It does not suggest in any way that the individual *is* in fact lacking them, only what the belief is.

෴ The *Pattern* statements describe the contexts, types of experiences, and intended evolutionary results inherent in each lack belief pattern.

PLUTO IN ARIES/1ST HOUSE

Lack of one's own power, autonomy, independence, self-assertion, intelligence, initiative, ability to enact changes and go for what one desires.

Pattern:

Entry into life with a non-self-assertive, 'group mind' assumption about one's activity/desire in life: unaware of the need or the method to take initiative.

This results in repeated situations which force these individuals to react, make choices, get angry, show initiative, and assert themselves in crucial ways.

These experiences are designed to produce a strong ability to effectively sustain and interact with others from their own standpoint and basis. They will also create within the individual a more conscious, courageous, and empowered sense of self.

PLUTO IN TAURUS/2ND HOUSE

Lack of an ability to create or feel for oneself, one's own stability, self-value, sexual safety and power, one's own resources, one's inherent substance to sustain oneself in the world, and one's knowing of how to utilize the outer to develop the inner.

Pattern:

Entry into life with an illusory over-dependence on others, one's own physicality, sexuality, and/or expectations of being taken care of by others.

This results in repeated experiences of being abandoned, unsupported, and lacking in the ability to care for oneself.

These experiences are designed to produce a new building of self-reliance, work ethic, survival instincts, internal self-sufficiency and stability. They will also reveal to the individual their deepest values in life.

PLUTO IN GEMINI/3RD HOUSE

Lack of enough knowledge, information, education about one's world. Lack of the ability to sufficiently communicate one's ideas, needs, and beliefs. Lack of knowing/learning enough in general.

Pattern:

Entry into life with a belief and ego investment in the superiority or sufficiency in one's knowledge/intelligence level.

This results in many situations in which one's knowledge is revealed to be insufficient or wrong which causes a breakdown in one's Self-Identity.

These experiences are designed to produce humility in relation to one's ego identity, and a broader base from which to foundation one's sense of stability within a larger and potentially threatening environment. This will occur through a re-orientation and re-definition of one's self within that environment.

PLUTO IN CANCER/4TH HOUSE

Lack of feeling, knowing, and trusting one's emotional experience to be legitimate, sufficient, and self-sustaining.

Pattern:

Entry into life with a pattern of perpetually externalizing one's source of emotional security and fulfillment.

This results in repeated experiences of emotional instability, co-dependence and projected abandonment which intend to broken down through revealing the false, misconstrued self-security needs.

These experiences are designed to produce within the individual a self-originating egoic identity not based in external sources but in the inherent stability of one's existence.

PLUTO IN LEO/5TH HOUSE

Lack of feeling seen and uniquely, creatively alive. Lack of an ability to express and creatively manifest oneself within one's social/familial circle or in life.

Pattern:

Entry into life with a disbelief in and fear of one's own vitality (aliveness) and power.

This results in a pattern of deeply suppressing one's unique radiance/aliveness, creative voice or expressivity which creates experiences of failing in the public eye, being rejected or unacknowledged by others, or self-sabotaging.

These experiences are designed to produce a re-creation/redefinition of oneself as unique, vital and powerful, as valued for one's creative uniqueness by others, and as the felt center of a circle.

PLUTO IN VIRGO/6TH HOUSE

Lack of control over themselves and their environment, lack of a meaningful function in life.

Pattern:

Entry into life with a pattern of manipulating one's body and physical space (perhaps including others) as a method to maintain control.

This results in experiences of chaos, self-destructing breakdowns of belief and familiar structures (i.e. body or job).

These experiences are designed to produce the attainment of an effective and accurate balance between one's sense of self and one's relationship to one's body and physical environment.

PLUTO IN LIBRA/7TH HOUSE

Lack of self-trust, self-definition and self-centeredness in relations with others. Lack of awareness of one's own relationship motivations.

Pattern:

Entry into life with a pattern of projecting one's Self-Identity definitions onto others resulting in an ego structure in which one looks to the other(s) to fulfill their needs or one avoids relationships altogether because of fear of rejection.

This results in repeated experiences of being abandoned, left behind, of one's ideals being betrayed by others, or of being used and manipulated by others.

These experiences are designed to produce the awareness of one's significant lack of self-esteem, unrealistic idealisms, and co-dependence. This awareness gradually engenders a heightened awareness of how to balance meaningful social interactions with self-value.

PLUTO IN SCORPIO/8TH HOUSE

Lack of knowing and feeling one's power and life-force.

Pattern:

Entry into life with an unconscious assumption of the seemingly insurmountable limitation of one's life-force and will power.

This results in repeated circumstances where one uncaringly attempts to draw from others that which one (unconsciously) believes one lacks: power, control and life-force. This necessarily produces experiences of betrayal, rejection, powerlessness – the very qualities one unconsciously fears are one's own.

These experiences are designed to produce the lesson that what one seeks – a significant depth of emotional experience, intimacy and self-power – can only be found in the absence of the need to control others or the process.

PLUTO IN SAGITTARIUS/9TH HOUSE

Lack of one's connection to, capacity to trust, and ability to know spirit or higher reality (natural law). Feeling deeply abandoned by spirit and one's spiritual wisdom or truth.

Pattern:

Entry into life with a belief that one already knows the truth about the most important things in life without needing to legitimately look further or examine those assumptions.

This results in experiences of spiritual alienation in order to confront one's false assumptions and limitations of one's own beliefs (about what God is and one's connection to God).

These experiences are designed to produce a deeper faith in one's timeless connection to spirit and truth which transcends rational proof, a growing humility that all paths to spirit and truth are potentially valid, and the cessation of the 'spiritual superiority' of the early-life assumptions.

PLUTO IN CAPRICORN/10TH HOUSE

Lack of ability to sustain dominion over one's life direction, to maintain self-authority, to know what to do (in life), and to have (and earn) teachers or predecessors to learn from.

Pattern:

Entry into life with an inability to make choices based on one's personal needs (outside of the group's needs) and establish healthy boundaries with authority figures outside of cultural pressures and projections.

This results in experiences of tremendous overwhelm (from one's false and excessive assumption of responsibility), being ignored, used or manipulated by authority figures, and deeply feeling unacknowledged, underappreciated and forgotten.

These experiences are designed to produce the development of one's 'inner compass' in work, with others, and in life, which naturally builds confidence and feelings of self-authority and develops one's capacity to administer and manage within a group or in the world.

PLUTO IN AQUARIUS/11TH HOUSE

Lack of access to one's freedom, creative expression and vision. Lack of the ability or originality to implement real change and be seen as an individual. Lack of like-minded individuals and/or community to foment and be supported by.

Pattern:

Entry into life feeling socially isolated, limited by family or society to change things and surrounded by conformity.

This results in habitual behavior of seperating oneself from the group either explicitly or implicity, *and* for usually inappropriate or fear-sourced reasons (such as that of being boxed in). This is due to the subconcious fear that others – individually or collectively – do not understand or will control oneself.

These experiences are designed to produce a strongly developed balance within the human experience (emotional and physical life matching the intellectual prowess) in order to fuel one's envisioning/innovation/ushering in a new world and vision.

PLUTO IN PISCES/12TH HOUSE

Lack of connection or oneness with source/God (deep fear of being inherently separate from source). Lack of desire to know oneself as unique and distinct. Lack of the ability to manage one's life and to make choices based on one's own self-centric needs.

Pattern:

Entry into life with an unconscious belief that one's own individuality, strong ego and personal preferences will keep one separate from source.

This results in a defeated ability to deal with life's inherent unpredictability and pain (Buddhist: suffering), which causes many experiences of inner overwhelming chaos through which one's lack of awareness and false beliefs are revealed.

These experiences are designed to produce a more accurate and conscious knowledge of the necessity of one's uniqueness and individuality within the totality or oneness of all creation.

NOTES:

[1] Aleathe Morrill was instrumental in the formation of this chapter's descriptions. Aleathe is a Sacred Marriage Astrologer and shamanic counselor. Visit her at www.aleathe.com.

[2] Pluto's symbolisms through the Signs and Houses are addressed in more depth and comprehension in the companion book now available *Pluto & the Lunar Nodes in Sacred Marriage Astrology.* Vist www.sacredmarriageastrology.com for more information.

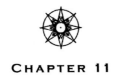

CHAPTER 11

THE LUNAR NODES: THE SOUL'S VEHICLE

WHAT'S A 'NODE'?

NOTES

The etymology of the word 'node' reveals its origin to be what we know today as a 'knot.' It implies a crossing or an intersection of two paths, flows or directions. It's related to the French *denouement* as an 'unraveling' or 'revealing.' This chapter is devoted to the Nodes of our Moon, both celestially and astrologically. To understand how to work with the Lunar Nodes are, we first need to understand some basics about the celestial mechanics of the Nodes. This requires we learn what our solar system's 'ecliptic' is.

THE ECLIPTIC

The ecliptic of our solar system is technically the plane in space formed by the mean orbits of the planets around the Sun. For a visual depiction of the ecliptic, see Figures 1 through 3 (*below and the following page)*. Psychologically, the ecliptic represents that which is collectively known or shared by all. It is what all planets share: their spatial plane or orientation around the Sun, or the Center. On the level of Soul however, the ecliptic suggests something else: the collective forward movement of consciousness or the agreed-upon 'forward' evolutionary progression of consciousness within our solar system.

Figure 1 - Top view:
Actual planetary orbits

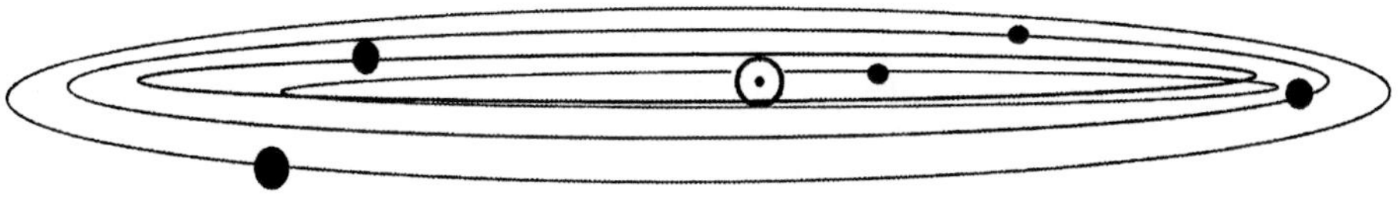

Figure 2 - Side view:
Actual planetary orbits

Figure 3 - Side view:
Mean orbit = Ecliptic

Figures 1 – 3 views of our solar system's ecliptic plane.

Where a planetary body, such as a planet, an asteroid or a moon, intersects the ecliptic is known generally as that planet's node. Planets, moons or other physical bodies circling the Sun have their own nodes. As the orbits of planets and the ecliptic itself are round, there will be two *nodes* of each planet because the planet's movement around the Sun will cross the ecliptic twice, once from interior to exterior and once from exterior to interior of the ecliptic. We can think of this as two hula hoops which cross each other twice. See Figure 4.

Figure 4 – When two circles cross each other, they form two intersections or 'nodes.'

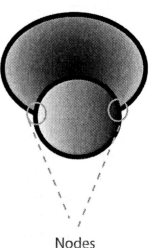

Nodes

The Nodes of a planetary body will signify within consciousness 'how' or 'where' that individual planet's function (represented by its orbit) will intersect, interact, influence and be influenced by the collective consciousness of the solar system (represented by the ecliptic). In other words, how and where the individual (planet, moon, etc.) enters and exits from the collective (ecliptic) within consciousness energetically locates it between a prior crossing and a future crossing of the ecliptic. Once again, each crossing is a node. When these ideas are applied to our Moon, the pair of Nodes formed create an exact 180° axis or a track through the plane of the ecliptic, and bound by the lunar orbit from one Node to the other. Let's examine more thoroughly the implications of a planetary body crossing into and out of the ecliptic.

ENTRY & EXIT POINTS

Every planet and moon in our solar system has their own pair of nodes, which are generally categorized as the 'north' and 'south' nodes of that planet or body. A 'south' node will indicate that it is the intersection created by the planet or body moving *interior* or entering to the ecliptic. A 'north' node is the intersection created by the planet or body moving *exterior* to or exiting the ecliptic. See Figure 5. When we focus on our Moon's nodes, we see that they mark the two intersections created between the orbital path the Moon tracks around the Earth and the ecliptic plane.

It is important to know that the Nodes are not physical bodies as planets are. They are *intersections* of spatial planes and therefore can be *located* in physical space. For thousands of years in many cultures around the world, the Lunar Nodes have been interpreted as the source and destination of the individual human life, the solar system, the galaxy, and even existence itself. As stated above, any Nodal pair implies directionality or progression, *from* the SouthNode *toward* the NorthNode.

The Lunar Nodes can be seen from two perspectives. Determining which node is the starting point and which is the ending point rests on one's subjective choice. If our perspective is from within the *individual or physical life* (as a human being on Earth studying human consciousness or the stars for example) then naturally we will see the 'entry' point as that (node) which brings us into life (our physical or Identity context), just as we normally see our physical birth to be the beginning or entry point into life. And of course we will see our death as our 'exit' point from this life. In this perspective, we have the SouthNode as the entry and the NorthNode as the exit node. This is the most popular orientation to the Lunar Nodes.

But if we switch our perspective to the *collective or energetic life* – the view that de-emphasizes individuation and personal identity and sees individuals as vehicles for collective evolution – then our 'entry' point will naturally be the Node which brings us into that collective union: oneness with all things, which we might call physical death. And it follows then that our 'exit' point would be the departure from this oneness into physicality and individual identity, which we might call birth. In this perspective, we have the NorthNode as the entry and the SouthNode as the exit node. This view was generally introduced by the originators of what we now know as astrology, the sages in ancient India and the alchemists in ancient Egypt through the Pharaonic tradition. It is clearly the less popular of the two. Taking time to reflect, practice and feel these orientations can be very valuable in building your cognitive dexterity.

There is no preferred perspective of the Nodes in SMA. Each is useful in its own way. As we progress in our astrological understanding, we will discover which is more useful for us at which times. In general, the individual context will prevail for most our work with natal charts, and the collective context for higher-octave studies of consciousness, such as that found in the Mayan sacred calendar and the Tarot's major arcana. While the collective context can also be used with natal charts and can, in

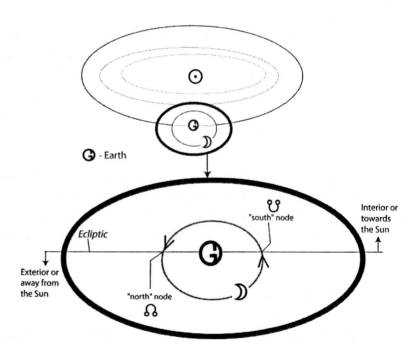

Figure 5 – The Lunar Nodes are intersections of the Moon's orbit with the ecliptic.

some cases, greatly support a rich, Soul-focused understanding, *we should always begin our Nodal education with the individual context* – the South-Node as entry point and NorthNode as exit point. As this chapter strives to illuminate, very often beginning astrologers face a significant challenge in opening their psyche to truly grasp the multi-dimensionality of the Lunar Nodes. *Any references to the Lunar Nodes in this chapter arises from the physicality/Identity/individual context.*

Therefore, our 'entry' point will bethe Node which brings us *into (physical) Life*. This is the SouthNode of the Moon or the South Lunar Node (☋). And the 'exit' point will be its polarity, or that which brings us away from physical life, toward an unknown future or destiny. This point is the NorthNode of the Moon or the North Lunar Node (☊). It is important to point out that the terms 'south' and 'north' within this context are not geographical directions in any way.[1] They do not refer to anything directionally on the surface of the Earth.

MOVEMENT OF THE NODES

Due to the orbital movement of the Earth around the Sun in relation to the ecliptic, the Moon's orbit around the Earth in relation to the ecliptic changes moment by moment. This of course creates the 'movement' of the position of the Lunar Nodes as perceived from Earth. This movement appears to us as the phenomenon of 'stutter-steps' or a Geiger counter pattern of mini-backward and mini-forward micro-movements. Yet there is without doubt a definite *mean movement* of the Lunar Nodes: *the Lunar Nodes move in the opposite direction as the planets, angles and other points do*. Thus, because the normal movement of signs, planets and houses is in a counter-clockwise, or astrologically-forward motion on the chart, then the normal motion of the Nodes are clockwise on the chart. In other words and just to be clear, *the normal, 'forward' motion of the Nodes is clockwise.*

LUNAR NODES IN ASTROLOGY

Astrologically, the Nodes symbolize a fundamentally different function within individual consciousness than that of the planets. It is as if the Nodal axis – the straight line formed by the exact opposition of the SouthNode and NorthNode which cuts the Moon's orbit into two equal halves – has one nodal foot on the ground of Identity, or the known past, and the other foot reaching toward the sky and the realms of Soul, destiny and the unknown future. The nodal axis' clockwise or astrologically backwards motion reminds us that the choice to live from our Soul intelligence and our love *requires* that we look into invisible places, outside the box and in non-ordinary realities. Mythologically, the image of something moving backwards symbolizes one's intuition, one's Feminine nature, one's sub-conscious, as well as something hidden, internal, in the 'other' world, and in the realm of our ancestors.[2] The Nodes are our personal ladder out from the safety, stagnancy and addictions of the past and into the unknown magic and majesty of our destiny realized.

The Lunar Nodes are the Soul's *tools, vehicles, or means of expression.* They represent *how* the Soul is to participate in physicality, in duality and within a limited ego context. They are the vehicles the Soul has chosen. *The Nodes are not the Soul itself.* If we return for a moment to the idea that any node is the entry or exit point of a particular individual function into or out of the collective evolutionary progression, then the Lunar Nodes can be understood accurately. As the planetary body from which the Lunar Nodes are formulated, the Moon astrologically represents the egoic component of personal Identity (see 'Moon' under the 'Cancer' section in chapter 4). Therefore, the Moon's *Nodes* are that Identity's entry and exit points into dimensionality, into the inherent separateness of duality, and into a human context. In my view, there is no other planet which more directly correlates to the archetype of an egoic individual-ness than the Moon, so the nodes of the Moon must correlate to *how, from where, and to where* that individual Identity – the human being – is evolving or moving. Take time to absorb these ideas not only in a rational manner but in other ways as well, such as feeling-wise and intuitively.

The Lunar Nodes thus bridge the Self-Essence (Soul) with the realized Self-Identity. Without the Nodes, we would never be able to actualize our Soul's Desire, that enigmatic, ethereal and primary motivation for our current life. Actualization can only occur *through* the vehicle of Identity, which necessarily includes the ideas of ourselves as individuals. Heaven *requires* Earth to be made known, does it not? Once again, here is another way to frame the all-important *hieros gamos* or holy union of opposites.

This is quite important to understand before proceeding further with the Lunar Nodes. The Soul needs a vehicle to inhabit, get behind the driver's wheel of, and live its life *as*. It needs a defined context. In astrology, this vehicle is the Lunar Nodal axis; in psychology, it is our Self-Identity.

SELF-ESSENCE & SELF-IDENTITY

In SMA, the position of the Lunar SouthNode on the birth chart indicates the Soul's past Identity or vehicle for accomplishing or realizing its goal in that incarnation. But specifically, *what is a Soul's past 'vehicle' and how is its function seminal to the realization of the Soul's Desire?* I use the terms 'vehicle' or 'vessel' because they are accurate images for the energetic dynamic between the SouthNode and Pluto. Just as the SouthNode is the vehicle for Pluto, the NorthNode is the vehicle for the Pluto polarity point (see below, and chapter 9). Let's look at the relationship of Soul (essence) and Identity (vehicle) from a broader and deeper standpoint.

The players we are discussing here – the actual Soul intent for the life (Pluto) and the incarnational means to that intent (Nodes) – are in fact very powerful amalgams of energies existing and energetically wired throughout an individual's many levels of being. Both the Soul's Desire and its Vehicle are in fact the evolutionary contexts for the way the psyche is structured. Our conscious minds require images or symbols to refer to them, their structure, how they function, and how they relate with one another on any level. Understanding how the Soul level of being informs the Identity level of being can be a complicated process. The terms 'Soul's Desire,' 'vehicle' or 'vessel', and 'evolutionary intent' or 'goal' are some of the words and phrases used in SMA to describe this enigmatic subject. They can be replaced with others more resonant to each person.

The human ego[3] might be considered to be the quasi-'root chakra' of Self-Identity. As stated earlier, the Self-Identity is comprised of other components in addition to the ego, such as the persona, the unique electric wiring of the body-mind and the physical body. But the ego is the component responsible for managing the survival of not only the body but of the larger 'self' as well. The ego's function is to keep the Identity primally alive by alerting it to any perceived threat to its inner or outer security. As described in the essay, "The Nature of Ego, the Function of the Moon" (chapter 15), the ego's job is keep the self *separate* (and thus safe) from encroachment by Other. In order to perform its function, it requires access to any record of past hurt or joy. This includes experiences pre-dating the current life. The current ego structure thus results from a unique alchemy between the karmic past, the current life and intended future.

As we know, each human life has a particular, unique intent to accomplish during its course. Much literature refers to this as one's destiny or life purpose. This intent cannot be defined by an outer accomplishment, such as building a successful business, raising a family, or saving the world. These are all simply *phenomena* in that they describe an outer form created by deeper impulses. This is very important to remember. For example, though we will experience tremendous satisfaction when engaged in our most meaningful work in the world, the actual source of our satisfaction and feelings of connection emanate not from outer results or forms of our work but from the integrity or *depth of alignment* our work shares with our very Soul. In other words, if our most meaningful work and contribution in the world is to be an astrologer and we one day in the future find ourself doing that successfully, the inner knowing that we are doing what we are meant to do will not be emanating from our astrological practice per se, but from our Soul recognizing itself *through* our practice of astrology within our incarnation as an Identity. Ultimately, Soul alignment emanates from the Soul, and not from the world of form and success.

Yet the intent of any human life is in fact to realize this *inner* drive of Soul through one's unique human nature, predilections, karma and context. Therefore, if human *phenomenal* existence – that which arises as the world of matter and which occurs in a body, in the world and with others – serves the evolutionary purpose of actualizing one's unknown, mysterious destiny (the Soul's Desire), then that same phenomenal realm must also be seen as the only path one can walk to reach personal destiny. The same idea is expressed in the popular notion that, "we cannot live someone else's life nor live up to others' expectations of us and expect to be satisfied; we must live our own life and walk our own path." In other words, the way we

inwardly and outwardly is the means through which we realize

egitimately 'walking our own path' can bring us equally

ion as much as a socially-rich one. Indeed, our

means to our noumenal end (see chapter 16,

Self-Identity – both implicitly and explic-

ence or Soul-embodiment within that

tive of our human

would not be

our pain

and our joy would be met with a clearer mind, a more open heart and a cleaner body.

LUNAR SOUTHNODE AS KARMIC SELF-IDENTITY

Let's now address both levels of the SouthNode. If we understand a Soul to be a timeless, limitless aspect of divine consciousness, then it seems reasonable that the Soul would need some sort of container to inhabit in order to operate within the structured realm of physicality (as a human being). The container the Soul inhabits is in fact the human being. Specifically, it is the human's Self-Identity. I teach the first level of understanding the SouthNode to be the *karmic Self-Identity* formed in one or more previous incarnations. Because it psychically resides within the individual's karmic past, it is deeply familiar, and therefore *safe*. It signifies an individual's prior egoic patterns, resistances, preferences and orientations to life.[4] To understand how important this is, think of the normal function of an ego in the current life: to catagorize each experience into those that fit one's self-definition and those that do not. The approved are then acknowledged, identified and processed by the self. The rejects are cast off, avoided, or suppressed into the sub-conscious. Thus the ego's function is to maintain and protect its (sense of) security and safety. If we combine this idea with the notion that the SouthNode represents the *past safety mechanisms of Identity,* then we can appreciate how strongly attractive it is for an individual to remain in familiar patterns of their karmic past (even when these patterns repeatedly produce pain, alienation or frustration). The SouthNode serves up exactly what the current-life ego identity needs: a consistent, known set of criteria to filter every experience through in order to remain (feeling) secure and keep from admitting that its self-definitions are temporary.

An individual's karmic ego identity signified by the SouthNode also points to which aspects of consciousness s/he would have gravitated toward and excelled at in the past. It indicates the entire range of previous Identity uniqueness – personality traits, particular skills or abilities, chosen professions, life goals. We can then infer which aspects of consciousness the Soul would have avoided or perhaps strongly resisted and denied.[5]

Perhaps it is most important to understand how the SouthNode operates within the psyche. The sign, house and aspects of the SouthNode will describe our 'warm blanket' of Self-Identity; that is, it represents something so known and so familiar that we are very often unaware of how thorough we re-perpetuate its patterns in our current life. This, combined with the notion that our karmic past remains hidden behind a veil of forgetting (the infamous 'veil between the worlds'), produces our mass unawareness of ourselves and why we do the things we do. We are, in a sense, surrounded by our (old) selves and cannot see beyond those definitions and assumptions. The words 'karmically stuck' might apply here. As such, the SouthNode connotes much of what we will naturally and sub-consciously resist letting go of. It determines 'where' within consciousness we return to for ego safety.

SOUTHNODE AS SPRINGBOARD FOR CURRENT EGO IDENTITY

As the symbol for the karmic (past) Identity pattern, any work with the SouthNode will reveal information about our past incarnations. Yet the SouthNode function itself remains within the context of *the current life.* In other words, though we will not be working with the chart of an individual's prior incarnation, if our interpretive and intuitive skills are functioning, this system of SouthNode interpretation obviates the need for it... we can determine much about a karmic past from the current life chart because *the past is framed within the current life developmental goals.* This avoids the common trap of seeking out specific details of one's past lives as a way of *avoiding* current-life responsibility for why they are they way they are and behave the way they do. While SMA clearly supports individuals learn about their karmic patterns of thought and action, it will downplay them to those individuals whose patterns include an avoidance of present reality and a seeking of non-embodied answers to superficial questions.

We can also work with the natal SouthNode as the *springboard* for the current-life Identity, or *the context for the new Self-Identity-to-be.* It will signify 'what' the current Identity is developing out of and learning to gradually leave behind as a self-definition. As it does so, it will naturally come to find roots in the natal Moon position. We can create begin a flowchart of Identity progression and fill in the first two steps: *from* the SouthNode and *toward* the Moon. To astrologically apply these ideas, identify the sign, house and aspects of the SouthNode as the karmic Identity, compare this picture of self with the Moon's sign, house and aspects and discern the differences, similarities and opportunities for growth implied in this progression.

Yet this is not the full story for an individual's identity development as it does not address the NorthNode. The NorthNode's function is described below and completes the developmental flow of Self-Identity. See Figure 6.

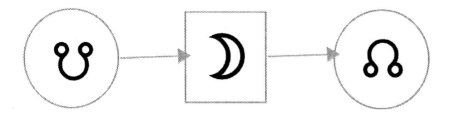

Figure 6 – The full progression of Self-Identity development begins with the SouthNode (☋), roots or foundations in the Moon (☽) and moves ever toward the NorthNode (☊).

   * NOTE: Figure 6 notwithstanding, it should never be assumed that this simple formula is all one needs to accurately interpret an individual's Identity; to assume so is irresponsible and unprofessional. Embedded in any SMA practice is the knowledge that a complete formulation of an Identity must include the entire chart because only the entire chart reveals to us how each facet of self plays into, influences, strengthens or detracts from every other facet. So-called 'outer planets' may be particularly influential on the Identity formation for one person and quite under-emphasized in that of another.

   As a beginning to understanding how to 'read' an Identity, I teach that the current-life Self-Identity can be interpreted from the relevant sign, house and aspects of the personal planets and the Angles. This equates to: the Sun, the Moon, Mercury, Venus, Mars, Jupiter, the AC, the DC, the MC, and the IC (see chapters 4 and 5), with each in their appropriate domain and seen in their respective function. With this as the first step, then the remainder of the chart can be brought into the Self-Identity equation. For a description of how to frame the entire chart from the twelve spheres of conciousness (where Self-Identity is one), see chapter 16, 'Sign/Planet/House Formulae'.

LUNAR NORTHNODE

   By sign, house and aspects, the Lunar NorthNode reveals the tools or the vehicle which the Soul intends to move ever toward as its Identity.

NOTES

The NorthNode is the *intended vehicle to bring the Soul to greater experiences of itself in greater numbers of ways*. In the NorthNode we have the answer to the questions, 'Where am I headed?' and 'What am I meant to *learn myself to be* in this life?' The NorthNode represents the polar opposite of what we have known ourselves to be in the past. The NorthNode energy is quite unfamiliar to us initially. Because it is not only unknown but also the polar opposite of the very familiar SouthNode, the NorthNode will initially be ignored or resisted. This is natural and represents the primal survival instinct, played out on the level of Identity. How long the resistance lasts and what circumstances are needed to break the resisting or ignoring pattern is a complex issue. As a generality, we first glean the nature of the NorthNode energies themselves (sign, house and aspects). We then investigate how 'far' the individual has come in developing them for themselves in the current life by asking questions and intuiting the client's level of embodiment of them.[6] We then can emphasize areas of life or qualities of self which the client (we) would be well-served to be aware of. We can provide insightful and poignant guidance about where they (we) need to be looking or moving toward for their (our) greater embodied alignment with the Soul's Desire.

To complete the flowchart begun in the last section, the North Node is the higher attainment of the individual's ego identity (Moon) because it represents where the individual is evolving toward. See Figure 6. The NorthNode indicates perhaps the richest source of personal self-discoveries, those experiences of discovering a new love of art, or sailing, or care-taking, or business, or relationships which we never would have guessed we possessed. And as many learn, to fully investigate these awaiting gems, usually courage, risk-taking and surrender are required in some amount. We need to be willing to let go and accept what is true about ourselves. The NorthNode thus symbolizes *both* the toad we initially don't want to kiss *and* the beautiful yet hidden prince/ss awaiting a life destiny together.

TWO VILLAGES AND A SEA

To picture the entire process of progressive Identity development, imagine there is very large sea with two villages at opposite shores. A woman in one port desires to 'expand her horizons' and decides to visit the other village, its people and its culture. She's only heard rumors about what lies waiting there. In order to get there, she hires a boat to take her across the sea. Let's pause here and relate these images to the developmental flow of Identity. If her starting village – where she was raised – is the SouthNode, the boat she hires to take her across the sea to her destination is the Moon, and the unknown village enthralling her imagination is the NorthNode, then as she moves further away from her origin, she will grow closer to her destination. She never leaves the boat because she doesn't yet know how to swim. Along the way there is unexpected weather, maybe a mutiny, and some significant leaks in the boat. She must respond in some way to each challenge because this boat is her way of reaching her destination. Thus she grows to know that boat – her Self-Identity vehicle – *intimately*. She learns ways to withstand the weather, defend or hide from the violent mutineers, and plug the leaking holes. She comes to know the inners and outers of the boat and in so doing, she has redirected much of her energy away from maintaining her Identity in her home village and into the development of her current-life Identity or vehicle. *Only* on the boat can she attain the new, unknown destination. Only by fully inhabiting her current vehicle can she reach her destiny.

Let's paint this story with a happy completion. She finally reaches the new village and discovers strange foods, peculiar people and different customs than she's ever known. In her first few weeks there, she notes to herself that had the boat ride gone more smoothly and expectedly, she probably would have a harder time with all the newness. But the difficulties and challenges presented to her on the boat forced her to release her notions of 'how things should be', 'how others should treat her,' or 'who she needs to be and what things she must always defend about herself.' The release of self-definitions (formed in her former home village) simply won't work here. As the months and then years pass, she finds increasing interest in people and activities of various kinds which she would never have considered in the past. She discovers herself anew and in so doing she awakens to her deeper nature, or Soul's Desire.

The following chapter presents an example of how to interpret Pluto, the SouthNode, the Pluto polarity, and the NorthNode.

NOTES:
   [1] Perhaps better monikers for the nodes would be, for the technically minded, 'interior' and 'exterior', or 'foundational' and 'possible', 'origin' and 'destiny', or 'feminine' and 'masculine.' Whatever we name them, the important point to

remember is that there is directionality or a progression implied *from* SouthNode *to* NorthNode. As SMA is evolution-focused, this directionality is evolution-minded, that the SouthNode is our karmic origins and the NorthNode is our implied destiny.

[2] Mythologist and storyteller Michael Meade is quite eloquent in his description of backward-moving or backward-facing symbolic images.

[3] For a complete description of the ego's function and its astrological correlation, refer to 'The Nature of Ego, The Function of the Moon' in chapter 15.

[4] This is the main reason the SouthNode represents a deep reservoir of emotional security and explains why, as a general rule, we humans will consistently choose known misery over unknown happiness. We would rather remain in the known than risk our security on something unknown. We humans are creatures of habit at the level of (perceived) self-preservation.

[5] I suggest the SouthNode identity is more familiar to the Soul than that of the Moon because the SouthNode's origin is *our karmic past*, whereas the Moon originates in the current life, as its ego identity-in-the-making. The generally assumed connection between the Moon, the sub-conscious and the individual's karmic past or memory, while accurate, is inaccurately explained in most of the literature. In short, the Moon's function is as a bridge between the subconscious level of the psyche and conscious self-awareness level. Thus, it has its feet in both worlds.

[6] For example, if we ask our NorthNode in Pisces in the 7th House client, "How are you doing in your relationships? Are they meaningful for you? Do you choose partners who share your desire for intimate relationship?" and their answer is "I'm doing fine", then the fact that their last four relationships have ended either because they got cold feet when love showed up or the pressure of intimacy pushed their self-doubt buttons, should clue us into the fact that our client has quite some way to go to more fully *embody themselves as their NorthNode Identity*. But this does not mean that their next relationship won't be the one through which they make a major step into their NorthNode qualities. How many of us have realized that only *because* of the same, repeated mistakes we've made have we learned not to make them again? In the same vein, how honestly do we admit that our successes are based in our past failures? And how willing are we to laugh at ourselves in humility, fun and self-love?

CHAPTER 12

THE SOUL'S DESIRE &
VEHICLE CASE STUDY

The following chart example can assist you in understanding how the information presented in the preceeding chapters fuels astrological interpretation.

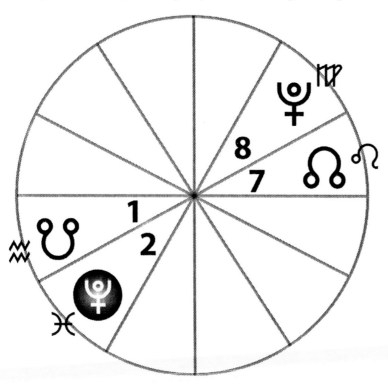

Chart Example – male

Note: The following interpretation is drawn from the chart above. It does not make reference to the rest of the planets, such as the Sun and Uranus, rulers of the Nodes. The complete chart would reveal other important information and more detail.

THE SOUL'S DESIRE FROM THE PAST

With Pluto in Virgo in the 8th House, the Soul's Desire in prior incarnations was the development of an accurate sense of self and a healthy relationship with one's physicality – one's body and one's environment. To the degree these intents were achieved, they would have occurred through typical 8th House domains: transformations ('little deaths') of this man's pattern of taking responsibility for everything around him and confrontations to his deep beliefs in his insufficiencies and 'wrong-ness' and need to be in control. There may have manifested behaviors of utilizing other people's resources (8th House) for his own purposes (appropriately or inappropriately), and becoming involved with those who he perceived possessed qualities he sought for himself, for example, personal power. As he interacted with that quality in another, he would come to know it in himself though his existing orientation to self-criticism (Virgo) may have blocked his ability to integrate the lesson. Thus the main issues or inner conflicts between Desire and Identity would have been his pattern of self-guilting; repressed anger or resentment at others for not being up to the task or not meeting him at his level (which reflects his beliefs in his insubstantial capacities), and ignorance around the true source of his power.

With SouthNode in Aquarius, he would have had a natural affinity with technology (which probably would continue into this life), an original intelligence, and would have been most motivated by his attraction to and skill in improving things in a unique way. He would have been highly intelligent, would have known it and utilized it, would have been impatient with others' perceived ignorance or consensus-thinking, and may have been quite the pioneer in his field. Plus, a driving motivation to always 'make things better' through courageous inventiveness, a strong need to follow his inspirations at all times, and an instinctual, impulsive approach to most situations in life (1st House) would have combined to form an Identity requiring an absence of restrictions to his creative flow. It appears his Soul chose this Self-Identity to strengthen his subjective self-image and orientation to life, and to provide an experience of himself as an original individual, with a unique vision or a unique connection to higher information. This would have catalyzed his Soul's Desire by showing him that he is unique and gifted in his own right and thus has the ability to improve or transform himself despite the voice of criticism. *In this incarnation, this Soul is now intending to change its focus of growth.*

THE LACK ISSUE

Now as the current life indicator of his self-lack issue and the 'starting blocks' for his evolutionary efforts in this life, Pluto in Virgo says he comes into this life with a hidden belief that he lacks the capacity to control and manage his physicality and his personal domain in a sufficiently cared-for or sacred way. And because of this, he does not deserve love and cannot receive it from others. He will thus choose relationships and subconsciously create experiences in which this is played out. Pluto in the 8th House says he will need to feel both his own power and his limitation. He will enter jobs and relationships to 'relive' these karmic patterns in the first part of life. He will work very hard to make them work and this feeds the need to feel 'in control' to allow the evolutionary shift from the past identity into the future to occur. His early bosses will recognize him as an intelligent, committed, hard worker and he probably will move up the ladder into leadership roles (NorthNode in Leo). For the first part of life, however long that may be for him, he will naturally resort to his Aquarius past Identity (SouthNode) to offset the encroaching lack beliefs. This will take the form of periodic, sudden departures from responsibility and side projects that consume his time. Of course, when he returns from his excursions, he will then be faced with the guilt of leaving the job (Pluto in Virgo). It may then happen that this type of behavior will for him cause a breakdown or blow-up in his professional or personal life. This then may cause him to (hopefully) see that he is not always able to keep things together in his life. He will then 'be asked' by his own nature to surrender the need for control, the pattern to take responsibility automatically, and open to who he may be *without* these patterns running some part of his interior show. If he can be more preemptively aware of his patterns, he may be able to avoid dramatic circumstances such as these and choose differently. Scorpio and Aquarius can be good balancers for each other: they both ultimately move toward growth (Scorpio internalizes and Aquarius externalizes). The combination might also exaggerate an imbalance: both tend to stick to known ways of operating (fixed signs).

THE SOUL'S DESIRE IN THE CURRENT LIFE

This man's current Soul's Desire – the intended destination of his realization – is derived from Pluto's polarity energy: 2nd House Pisces.

In regard to Pisces, his entire life is ultimately designed to promote his increasing embodiment of the Pisces mysteries (Pluto's polarity). Thus his personal destiny is to learn absolute trust in life *as it actually is*, rather than sourcing his actions and thoughts from the unconscious assumption that *he* has to control life (Pluto in Virgo). The more he resists learning these lessons when they show up whether in the form of subtle or overt experiences, the more harsh the lessons will become for him. He is also learning *how* to know God, and how to approve of himself *as he is*. Thus, acceptance, allowance and compassion are keynotes in this life, specifically in terms of his karmic pattern of controlling, assuming and denying. With Pluto's polarity in the 2nd House, the more he can internally rely on his own feelings about things and make decisions from his own needs (rather than relying on what he finds in other people to ratify his self-image), the more he will be able to solidify himself in the world (where in the past he would have been incessantly focused on improving himself by strictly controlling the process and himself). This greater substantiality may take the form of inner directives to leave those positions and relationships which require his old version of himself. On a deeper level, these directives are emanating from his Soul's Desire and may also be understood to extract him from the whole explicit pattern of 'interacting with Other in order to determine self-value.' He is trying to cement his current values based on a more autonomous Identity and set of desires.

How he is most meant to realize the lessons of 2nd House Pluto in Pisces is determined by his NorthNode in Leo in the 7th House. Creative ways to be in relationship which he feels himself to be at the center and/or creating his relationship to be a center-pole for others – perhaps in his work life – will create for him the new Identity roles. In Leo, the North-Node is gearing him towards a deeper Identity and self-love which naturally arises from his own creativity (rather than his prior identity arising from his unique ability to be ahead of the idea-pack). He is trying to learn how it can be that he himself is the source of his love. He will experience others' being drawn to his interesting and charismatic ways only if he allows himself to *radiate* it through everything he does, rather than dictate or 'do' it. In other words, the more personally creative he can allow himself to be – without the restrictions of guilt or social function – the more happy he will be. This will require him to explore all kinds of avenues of his creative impulses, such as art, children, sex, and entertainment. In the 7th House, the North-

Node will be most activated when he is regularly involved with all kinds of people and in some way is organizing them or being organized among them to create something together which any individual acting alone would be unable to realize or manifest.

CHAPTER 13

RETROGRADATION: FORGING UNIQUENESS

PLANETS MOVE 'BACKWARDS'?

When we gaze up into the sky at night or at the Sun during the day, we notice that the planets move from east to west. Astrologers call this a planet's 'forward motion.' Yet this perceived movement across our sky is actually the result of the Earth's rotation. There are other times when planets appear to be moving *backwards* in the sky, or from west to east. The appearance of planets moving 'backwards' in the sky is known astrologically as *retrogradation* or *retrogression*. This phenomenon is the result of planetary bodies in concentric orbits (sharing the same center) appearing to 'lap' one another due to the varying speeds at which they travel around that common center (the Sun). Figures 1 and 2, on the following pages, show the celestial picture.

For us on Earth the *inner planets (Mercury and Venus)* appear to move in retrograde motion in an entirely different way than the *outer planets (Mars to Pluto)*. Because retrogression is based on the concentricity of orbits, there are two planetary bodies which never appear to retrograde: the Sun and the Moon. The Sun cannot be retrograde because it itself is not in orbit around another body... it *is* the center. And the Moon cannot because it doesn't share the same concentric center with the Earth: the Earth is its center. The Moon will never appear to us to move backwards in our skies.

Retrogression has been seen in many ways by many astrologers and astrology schools. I do not believe there is just one way to astrologically interpret retrogression, either natally, by transit or by progression. There are, however, some basic understandings which SMA purports.

STRUCTURE OF A RETROGRADE

Whether a planet's orbit is interior or exterior to that of Earth distinguishes the two general types of retrogression. The celestial mechanics of *inner* planet retrogression and *outer* planet are different. But from the perspective of the retrograde process as its own pattern, there is consistency. The following is presented as a starting point for your own further research and exploration.

Inner Planet Retrograde

By 'inner planet' we mean *celestially interior* to Earth's orbit: Mercury and Venus only. For clarification, astrology in general will recognize Mars, Jupiter and sometimes Saturn as one's inner or 'personal' planets as well.

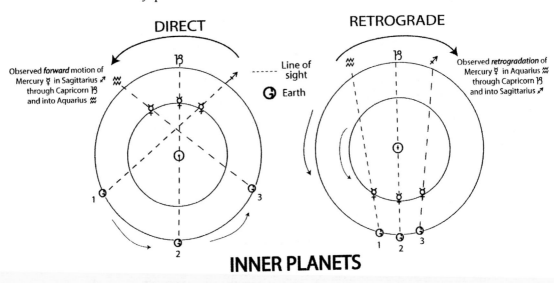

INNER PLANETS

Figure 1 – Stages of inner-planet retrograde cycle

The inner planet will:
1. Station retrograde (Rx): appears to stop its forward movement and move 'backward' in our skies.
2. Conjunct the Sun (while Rx).
3. Reach its maximum retrograde speed, then begin to slow in speed.

4. Station Direct (stops retrograde movement and begins moving 'forward').

5. Reach maximum distance from the Sun (maximum morning-sky elongation).

6. Conjunct Sun (while direct).

7. Reach maximum distance from the Sun (maximum night-sky elongation).

.... (repeat)

Outer Planet Retrograde

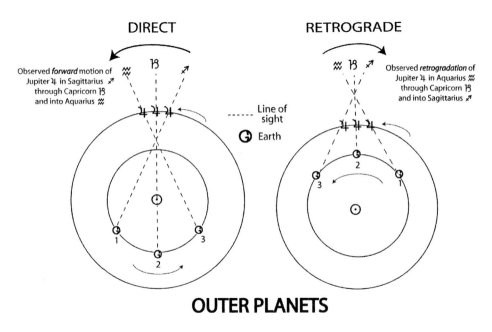

OUTER PLANETS

Figure 2 – Stages of outer-planet retrogradation cycle

There are no consistent patterns for *all* 'outer' planets. By 'outer' we mean all planets whose orbits are exterior to that of Earth. There is one general rule which we can see to tie together all outer planet retrograde archetypes. An outer planet will only be retrograde when it is *relatively opposite the Sun*. The orb for each planet varies widely and is based on the elliptical eccentricity of the planet's orbit as well as the position of Earth at the time of the relative opposition. Here are minimum distances (known as 'elongations') which each planet must reach to be retrograde.

Each amount applies in both directions from the Sun, clockwise and counter-clockwise.

Planet	Minimum distance to Sun to reach retrogradation (in either direction)
Mars	137*
Jupiter	117
Saturn	109
Chiron	100*
Uranus	102
Neptune	101
Pluto	99

From Retrograde Planets, *by Erin Sullivan, 2000, except * my calculations.*

RETROGRADATION IN SMA

In SMA, natal retrograde planets, asteroids or other bodies indicate two general meanings:

1. The retrograde planet is seen as a statement that something (karmic) from the past is attempting to be resolved or moved further towards resolution in the current life.

2. The retrograde planet's function within the psyche operates in a manner fundamentally different than if the planet were direct. It is a *personalizing* factor of the individual's psychological functioning.

SMA sees three ways to understand this distinguishing characteristic:

1. A heightened or *intensified internal functioning* of the planet (that function of the psyche). This might also be described as an inward-redirecting of that part of the psyche. Depending on the 'normal' function of the planet, this internalizing can intensify what is already internally operating or can conflict with an otherwise externally-dependent process.

2. A *sensitivity to stimuli* – people, experiences, places, energies – which are resonant with or emanate from the natal retrograde sign, planet, and house energies.

3. The attempt of the Soul to *individually identify* those aspects of itself represented by the retrograde planet.

These conceptual frames then give rise to a plethora of possible expressions. For example, if outgoing, aggressive Mars or Aries is involved (i.e. natal Mars retrograde or several retrograde planets in Aries), the individual might subconsciously resist the retrograde's natural internalizing effect (as they try to maintain their outward, aggressive impulses). This creates a pattern of anger, frustration, outbursts, etc. The intent of the Soul, however, is to re-source one's relationship to one's own authentic Aries/Mars energies. The blockage to an otherwise free-flowing Masculine nature is the setup to accomplish this. Once accomplished, the individual has established a *unique trait* about themselves formed in *one's unique way* through a deeper *internal process*. On the other side of the spectrum, if Venus and Taurus are involved in a natal retrograde, the retrograde effect may cement the feminine function into a pre-existing (karmic) pattern and thereby require a tremendous amount of motivation to 'break out' of one's stubbornness or reliance on remaining internally protected and on familiar ground.

Here are some other general descriptions of the retrograde archetype. These can help structure a larger understanding of the planet's retrograde in order to function.

1. More facility in accessing past incarnations, experiences and memories, possibly resulting in more confusion in the present.
2. Greater likelihood for mental or emotional repeated-pattern syndromes.
3. Both disorientation and multi-dimensional awareness are heightened.

THE SOUL CONTEXT FOR RETROGRADATION

What follows intends to provide a *Soul-level understanding* of the retrograde archetype through each of the planets. The information is presented as a starting point from which to build your own understanding of each archetype, rather than an all-inclusive recipe to categorize all individuals into. The nature of each retrograde archetype will largely depend on the nature of the planet itself. If a planet tends to be internally experienced and developed, its retrograde version will intensify or alter that internalizing. If a planet is naturally expressive, its retrograde version will force a greater inner awareness relative to its domain.

I teach and emphasize that a Soul-level context – that the Soul is the persistent consciousness and evolutionary intent inhabiting succeeding incarnations – is the most powerful strategy for astrological work. This certainly applies to retrogression. A retrograde planet on the natal chart indicates a unique strategy for developing its function in the current life precisely because it also implies a unique condition of development (relative to that planet's function) in the past, either hypertrophically or atrophically.

> *"The more we inhabit the present, the more*
> *we know the past, and the more we see the future."*
> —AG

Each planetary body in its retrograde mode is described from the perspective of *what the Soul is developing*. Following most of the descriptions are two scenarios describing a karmic over-emphasis and under-emphasis from past incarnations. Indeed, a retrograde planet on a birth chart can point to either scenario being true.

How can we determine which one applies to an individual? While there are no strict guidelines or formulas, the basic idea is to determine the level and quality of interaction with the rest of the chart that *that planet, its related sign and its related house plays*. For example, if Jupiter retrograde is being scrutinized, look to Sagittarius and the 9th house in addition to Jupiter to determine this. The more the themes and evolutionary intents of the planet, its sign and house are emphasized (perhaps through many aspects to that planet, or through several planets in that sign or in that house) the more emphasis has been placed on that function in the (individual's) karmic past. In short, the more a sign-planet-house energy influences the *overall picture* of the chart, the stronger the case for a karmically over-emphasized development. I hope to produce and make available a comprehensive explanation or quasi-formula of how to determine an individual's karmic under- or over-emphasis of natally retrograde planets. To my knowledge, there is nothing covering this domain of astrology available. In the meantime, utilize your understanding of the signs, planets and houses and formulate your own intuitively-based opinion or feel for an individual's karmic pattern, relative to that planet.

RETROGRADE SIGNS AND HOUSES

As final guidance for interpreting natal retrograde planets, let's look at retrogression from the perspective of a retrograde planet *in a sign* and *in a house.* These are general descriptions and should be applied to specific applications on an individual's birth, transit or composite chart.

Signs

When a sign is being occupied by a retrograde planet, the Soul intends to balance what is imbalanced within that planet's function *through* the sign energy. The Soul is seeking balance through the current life because either there has been a past imbalance in that area or the current-life demands for growth require this deep change to occur.

Houses

When a house is being occupied by a retrograde planet, that house's domain of the individual's life (children, family, work, sex, money, etc.) is to be the predominant terrain for working through the issues involved. More specifically, the dynamic created by the *combination* of the retrograde-function of the planet and its sign will determine how much resistance or ease is experienced in that domain (house) of one's life. For example, if Venus is retrograde in Cancer in the 7th House, then the individual's feminine function (Venus) is balancing itself relative to its karmic past through the Cancer energies in the current life, while the process will most catalyze through relationships of all types (7th House).

CHAPTER 14

THE RETROGRADE PLANETS

☿ ℞ MERCURY RETROGRADE

When Mercury is retrograde natally, the Soul is attempting to root the cognitive processes (rational thinking, mental processing, conclusion-making, communication) within the self more than has been done or allowed for in the (karmic) past; that is, make them more *implicitly functioning*. The Soul may be attempting to evolve into more of an independent Self-Identity through an individualistic, unique (and usually internally-based) way of cognizing itself and the world. The Soul may be attempting to build a more sovereign mental life – that is, develop its cognitive autonomy – due to karmic experiences in which it was significantly *not rooted* in its own reality, but in the reality of others. In general however, the Soul will be attempting to bring 'in house' – *into itself* – its left-brain and communication functions in order to more fully form its Self-Identity.

If the Mercury function has been karmically underdeveloped, the current-life Mercury retrograde signature will reveal the need to strengthen that function for itself in the current life. This will occur through experiences of being convinced or coerced by others (for good or ill), or through breaking the pattern of cognitive laziness or meek acceptance of the status quo which will catalyze the lesson to 'stand up for what one believes'. This requires that the individual know what they believe in the first place which itself will require facing its karmic (entrenched) pattern of avoiding thinking for oneself.

If the Mercury function has been karmically overdeveloped, the current-life Mercury retrograde signature may be revealing a Soul-intent to develop a non-ordinary reality awareness and/or to be able to communicate that – to oneself and to the world. This would ask its past expertise to be applied in a new manner of inquiry and self-inquiry. Otherwise, Mercury retrograde may reveal the intent to switch directions in terms of its cognitive development. For example, if the Soul in past incarnations has been an outspoken, brilliant, independent thinker, then the current-life Mercury retrograde may indicate the Soul's current-life intent to apply its advanced cognition (from its past) to matters of a less phenomenal nature and more of a spiritual or intuitive nature, one that is less physically observable or less logically arguable.

For more about Mercury, see 'Gemini' in chapter 4.

♀ ℞ VENUS RETROGRADE

With natal Venus retrograde, the Soul is attempting to experientially (re-)discover its uniquely Feminine nature. This transcends the question of gender and any traits attributed to men or women. After all, gender is largely perceived and assigned individual traits based on the values, beliefs and reality of the relevant culture. Over time, these change. What remains is Femininity (and Masculinity) itself, outside of definitions. And as the quintessential, universal quality of Soul likewise does not change, the Venus retrograde archetype is indicative of a Soul looking to redefine for itself its own Feminine nature. This can be focused on any one of the many Feminine assignations: one's body, one's receptivity, one's ease in relationships of any kind, or one's intimacy, sensuality, relationship to money and other types of resources, etc. The implication is that in the karmic past, the individual has become either out of balance or in denial of their Feminine nature. With the current-life retrograde appearing on the natal chart (being chosen by the Soul), the individual will have *an intensely internal experience of self as well as their relationship with the outside world and those in it.* This will inevitably produce the effect of the Soul turning inward on itself in order to – at the level of evolution – directly experience its 'innerness'; in other words, to experience itself as an interior being distinct and separate from what appears outside of self. As the Venutian function in the psyche is already an internalizing, self-stabilizing and self-protecting function, this forced or intensified internalizing effect of the retrograde creates disproportionate amounts of needing to feel safe, to be validated, or to exaggerate difficult experiences in order to engender emotional succor.

If the Venus function has been karmically underdeveloped, the current-life Venus retrograde signature will signify a sort of forced internalization of experience. These individuals will feel on some level distrusting of opening to others, which in fact reflects their distrust of their own inner lives and feelings. Because Femininity is naturally internally experienced, the karmic pattern for these individuals (signified by the current-life Venus retrograde) has been to avoid, resist, suppress or somehow obstruct the Feminine either in themselves or in others. Thus, the current life intent is to open the channels to one's own Feminine functioning which will naturally create an ability to witness and appreciate the same in others.

If the Venus function has been karmically overdeveloped, the current-life Venus retrograde will signify the Soul's intent to return to a more authentic, 'cleaner' relationship with one's Feminine nature. The evolutionary dynamic here can be imagined to be similar to the homeopathic process of healing: like cures like. By introducing a minute quantity of the very substance causing the disease or imbalance, the body is triggered to acknowledge its presence and then fight back (if a disease) or balance itself (if an imbalance). Because Femininity is naturally internally experienced, the karmic pattern for these individuals relative to their Venus functioning has been to remain in a Feminine-dominant (and quite familiar) energy. This might have looked like patterns of 'remaining in misery', needing financial, familial or social control, emotional self-delusion, sexual manipulation, or many others. Through Venus retrograde in their *current life*, they are intending reveal to themselves the types and levels of Feminine imbalance or dysfunction that are requiring healing and integration. This will occur through an active internal, feeling life, a revisited examination of one's stable relationship with one's source, and specific attractions to Femininity in all its myriad expressions and forms.

For more about Venus, see 'Taurus' and 'Libra' in chapter 4.

♂ ℞ MARS RETROGRADE

Mars retrograde on the natal chart indicates a Soul attempting to develop its Masculine nature specifically through working on its relationship with its Desire. This growth is intending to occur in a unique way relative to Masculinity's otherwise outward-moving nature. It intends to develop a greater *inner awareness* of the Desire function, of its vitality in expressing its Desire, and of itself as an affecting, initiating vessel for Desire to express itself through. Because Mars is the primary symbol for our self-assertion and instinctual actions in life (which intend to develop the self's autonomy and confidence), the retrograde Mars will innately create a pattern of deep inner frustration as one's ability to move, express and act on one's impulses is blocked from within. The frustration will find release in periodic outbursts of anger, rage, or violence. This pattern will continue until the individual comes to examine the source of their anger and inconsistent emotions. They will then become aware of the pattern and what causes it. Over time, the individual will learn to identify the *actual* source of their anger: *themselves* and their repressed beliefs or denied assumptions about their own deficiencies and/or that of the world in which they exist, which is itself an out-pictured projection from the same source.

If the Mars function has been karmically underdeveloped, the current-life Mars retrograde will force the individual to look for the source of their frustration or atrophied Masculine function. This may take longer in him/her than it will in others because the entire Masculine functioning has not been sufficiently explored in the karmic past. Thus, to these individuals Masculinity represents something foreign and potentially threatening. At the same time however, their inner frustration, impatience, periodic angry outbursts or repeated experiences of disempowerment from blocked efforts all point the individual to the very source of the 'problem': their own deep-seeded assumptions.

If the Mars function has been karmically overdeveloped, the current-life Mars retrograde will categorically block any attempt to act in the old Masculine ways. This block can appear internally – through an inner frustration from subconscious self-doubt – or externally – through many, overwhelming obstructions to one's initiatives and outer expressions being successfully accomplished. The anger that arises from either mode is the energetic signature pointing them to examine their assumption that they can continue to rely on their Karmically-familiar Masculine expressions, which of course they cannot. Thus, these individuals are attempting to effect a significant balancing to their Masculine energy.

For more about Mars, see 'Aries' in chapter 4.

♃ ℞ Jupiter Retrograde

When Jupiter is retrograde natally, the Soul is attempting to karmically 're-think' its connection to spiritual reality (the level of 'law' or order beyond human definition which governs Nature herself). The Soul has karmically developed within itself a relationship to this higher order which now needs to be re-rooted within the self. The core meaning of this archetype is to internalize one's higher connection in order to effectively strengthen it. One's relationship with higher order reality is meant to be *deepened into and absorbed* rather than *externally attained*. This will occur through the *direct experience of it* rather than coming into the connection purely as a result of outer accomplishments. These individuals will 'receive' intuitive information and 'know things' in very non-traditional ways which may be as mysterious to them as to others. Again, the intent with Jupiter retrograde is to *internalize* the method of connecting and knowing information beyond one's immediate or familiar domain which certainly includes the intuitive (right-brain) function. If Jupiter is naturally seeking greater understanding of the higher order nature of reality in which it exists, then the predominant methods for doing so will be externally, through teachers, books, travel experiences, spiritual awakenings. And when Jupiter is retrograde, there is a natural redirection of energies away from these external sources in order to develop more of one's *internally-originating* intuitive function.

If the Jupiter function has been karmically underdeveloped, the current-life Jupiter retrograde signature reveals that the individual has either disproportionately relied on others – spiritual teachers or teachings, religion or religious leaders, mentors, etc. – for their spiritual beliefs or religious affiliation, or has avoided the entire question of spirituality and one's unique place within a greater existence. In either case, the need is to develop one's own unique and *actual* intuitive nature which will organically produce the familiarity and intimacy with the greater reality.

If the Jupiter function has been karmically overdeveloped, the current-life Jupiter retrograde naturally creates a block to the over-confident assumptions and blind spots which are present in the individual (as a result of the past overdevelopment). The individual can no longer rely on what s/he has previously known because their intuitive function in the current life doesn't work in the same way as in the past. The Soul is now exploring a unique version of the right-brain function which will naturally (and in fact is designed to) cause the individual to deeply question how they know what they think they know. The intended result of course is for the individual to redefine this for themselves.

For more about Jupiter, see 'Sagittarius' in chapter 4.

♄ ℞ SATURN RETROGRADE

The signature of Saturn retrograde at birth indicates a Soul looking to re-identify for itself how it operates within the necessary limitations of its current incarnation: linear time and physical space. This can apply to one's position within society or one's family, one's relationship with one's own physical structure, or *how one operates in life within societal rules.* As Saturn is a natural structurer-strengthener-manager, its retrograde archetype creates an individual who evolutionarily intends to internally change his/her relationship to this inner drive through a hyper-awareness of how one structures oneself given the limitations of physical/societal life. This can produce an intensity of inner pressure because the individual is not only subject to the cultural pressure to conform to society's rules, but also the added personal pressure (through the retrograde dynamic) to reconcile or deal with their subconscious suspicion that they are not conforming or ordering themselves well enough. In other words, Saturn retrograde compounds the issue of conformity by making the individual both the voice of authority *and* its subjugated citizenry. In a sense, the individual's psyche is the entire courtroom: judge, jury, *and* defendant.

The 'way out' of this intense conundrum is for the individual to 'back up' from the many assumptions they make about themselves and others, and work to clearly identify his/her own patterns of self-criticism, depression and unexpressed frustration due to unrealistic self-pressure. The retrograde quality of *interiorizing* is perfectly suited to this task. As this occurs, individuals will be able to establish their own rules for themselves with no other justification other than *that they are the best authority for themselves.* This wisdom will last if the lessons underlying it truly have been absorbed. The entire pattern will transform because they will have 'pulled the plug' on the originating, assumptive and subconscious basis for it, which runs something like 'the responsibility is on my shoulders and I must not fail!' They will become powerful examples of how to self-define (retrograde) one's rules for living within a greater societal structure with its own rules (Saturn).

For more about Saturn, see 'Capricorn' in chapter 4.

♅ ℞ Uranus Retrograde

Natal Uranus retrograde indicates a Soul intending to deeply examine the ways it feels socially and creatively restricted in order to experience itself as a 'community of one.' In the current life, the Soul is investigating what needs to be internally changed in order that its individuality and unique vision can be reconciled, supported and integrated with that of others, for the improvement or advancement of society/the world. There is also the implication that, in the karmic past, the Soul has over-relied on its exclusivity, subjugated others in the name of one's vision, community or art, significantly repressed one's contribution to a better world, or blindly followed one's plans for social upheaval creating results that were less than optimal or even traumatic. These descriptions give rise to many possible expressions and experiences. The evolutionary intent of Uranus retrograde will catalyze the individual to self-discover the uniqueness of one's own intelligence and ideas, the manner in which one keeps oneself separate from and feels isolated by (what one perceives to be) the consensus, as well as one's subconscious patterns of avoiding one's emotional responses to outer stimuli. The retrograde quality here forces the realization that their perception of reality is in fact being filtered through these protection-based avoidances. These and many other self-insights are possible with Uranus retrograde.

The Uranus retrograde signature warps and bends the outwardly-focused Uranian energies back into one's interior self, forcing the individual to come to terms with how they themselves are perpetuating their felt disconnection (in any way) from others/society. It is precisely these karmic patterns of avoidance which will produce at times intense anger and frustration for not being understood, appreciated or followed. But the retrograde Uranus archetype produces a second wave of frustration. When Uranus is natally direct, the natural, reactive anger and frustration at not being acknowledged (a pervasive Aquarius emotional dynamic), often propels individuals to seek out others (or small groups) with which they can intellectually, artistically, or socially identify. These connections provide welcome solace and justification for the Uranus-direct individual's rebellious qualities. But the Uranus retrograde individuals will be prevented from finding the same level of meaning and solace because, again, the retrogradation intends that the individual find answers within themselves. If these individuals begin to focus here, then by all means fomenting a community of like-mindeds will provide necessary connection and feedback.

If the evolutionary cues through life are followed, the Uranus retrograde individual will become a *model for the future* for they will be embracing the full gamut of their humanity – *physically and emotionally* as well as intellectually and spiritually. This retrograde archetype is a good example of *interiorizing to produce individuality.*

For more about Uranus, see 'Aquarius' in chapter 4.

♆ ℞ NEPTUNE RETROGRADE

The Soul choosing Neptune retrograde at birth is intending to more fully and adequately identify for itself its source, the underlying truth in creation, or the divine continuity which permeates all of life. The Soul has chosen this retrograde signature in the current life because in past incarnations the Soul has inaccurately and painfully followed others' connections to God/source in order to know their own, and in such ways or to such degrees which were illusory and false (not true, therefore not God). In other words, there has been a past pattern of, in some manner, *externalizing the divine source of oneself* (God, divine creation, etc.) onto a religion, a set of ideas, a loved one, or a deity. Therefore, the current-life retrograde assists the individual to effectively go beyond (a Pisces move) their illusions, but not in the direction one would expect of a 'move beyond', toward the sky and the cosmos, upwards and outwards. Rather, retrograde Neptune challenges the Pisces blind spot which readily accepts the notion that truth and God exist in all things 'out there' while conveniently failing to include oneself in that group. Thus, retrograde Neptune actually transcends this false belief in a uni-directional expansiveness – that truth and God exist in all things *out there*, away from the egoic self – by focalizing the psyche in the opposite direction: toward one's interior and the *inner* reaches of one's cosmos. This impulse, however it expresses in one's life and impresses in one's psyche, will naturally challenge the individual as it pushes him/her closer and closer to the very thing they fear the most and perhaps have suppressed into the subconscious: being abandoned and forsaken by God, life, the beloved, or 'losing the knowing certainty of one's connection.' The unrelenting *interiorizing* of the retrograde here is pulling these individuals *into* the vortex within themselves to show them the very beliefs which are merely justifying their unacknowledged, regressive behavior. Thus, the evolutionary intent within Neptune retrograde is to first reveal and then dismantle those falsities in order to validly *self*-substantiate one's timelessness and divinity. Once dismantled, the individual is internally freed to rediscover the beauty, connection and oneness of life *everywhere*, even under one's psychic impasses, imbalances and ego obstructions.

♇ ℞ PLUTO RETROGRADE

When the Soul chooses Pluto retrograde, it is intending to catalyze a conscious recognition of itself *as timeless – as a Soul – within the human embodiment.* This occurs through the increasing recognition of one's humanity. Pluto retrograde forces the individual deeply into what it is to be human, in order to discover for themselves those qualities of self which are in fact larger than earthbound humanity. And much of what it is to be human is the steady movement toward understanding one's weaknesses, denials and fears. Therefore, the Soul of the retrograde Pluto individual will more deeply internalize or will look inward more often to understand why intense and/or repeated experiences of being afraid, overwhelmed, manipulated or disempowered have occurred or are occuring. The Soul intends to uncover the Pluto lesson that *we ourselves* are the origin of any obstructions to realizing ourself as a Soul in a personally unique way. For much more about working with Pluto to ascertain the deep-seeded issue of lack, please see chapters 9-10.

Because Pluto's nature is to catalyze the deepest aspects of ourselves to the surface, these individuals struggle to understand the *how* and *why* of their crises through a uniquely personal psychological process which operates *on their own terms.* They come to find aspects within themselves which are at the root of the 'problem' of intense and/or repeated crises happening to them. *How* they come to identify these aspects and *what* these aspects are will be are different for each individual, but generally result from the internal recognition of their dysfunctional reactions or patterns. An important point to keep in mind about counseling those with Pluto retrograde is that most individuals with this signature do not attempt to bring the subconscious information into the conscious awareness. In fact, a little less than half the world's population has natal Pluto retrograde and a vast majority of these individuals follow this trend. Depending on Pluto's involvement in the whole chart picture, those who do 'go there' will come to understand and embody that they are both a Soul (timeless) and also perpetuate resistance to and rejection of themselves as that Soul *at the same time.*

The current-life retrograde signature also indicates a karmic pattern of either denying one's deep interior or of manipulating, coercing or disempowering others in some way. The intent in the current-life is to balance this karmic imbalance.

Pluto retrograde individuals are 'wired' with less of a drive to rely on others as the source of their power and empowerment. Often, psychological therapy can assist them to understand the motivations and patterns blocking them. The *internal work* is to discover the meaning for themselves – autonomously and auto-temporally. These individuals are striving to realize themselves as self-empowered *beyond personality and the limitation of ego.*

CHAPTER 15

ESSAYS

This chapter presents seven individual essays on various topics. They are presented to further catalyze your Soul-focused astrological education and work.

I
INTIMACY:
A RESOLUTION OF PRIMAL URGES

Intimacy as a dynamic symbolizes the experience and desire to be authentically seen and received for one's inherent uniqueness. (in-ti-ma-cy = *in to me you see*). As an archetype, the function of intimacy is thus to unify these quintessential urges within the Soul[1] through deep self-acknowledgement and acceptance of Other. In this, what we know as 'intimacy' closely approximates a true understanding of what we call Eros and the erotic: the re-unifying of source not through homogeneity, but through diversified unity. Within the human psyche, there is simultaneously the need to discover and explore our individualized Self – indicating a departure from Source – as well as the need to explore and merge with Other/All – indicating a return back into Source.

The first urge symbolizes the masculine[2], or yang principle[3]. Within this urge, we are seen for who we are, in our naked, raw, genetic, and shining individuality. We are exposed and accepted as worthy/lovable/powerful/good. This is the experience of being made a part of Nature and ultimately all Creation without compromise or adjustment of our inherent uniqueness. It is a cellular and ecstatic *unforgetting* of our unworthiness, insufficiency, and self-negating realities. We thus birth the capacity to both dissolve our false requirements for love (anger, helplessness, and indifference) and release our false ideas of security. These falsities are created early in life when we first experience separation from Mother, signaling that consciousness has been birthed within us. They are known as our *sacred wounds*; to heartfully progress through our lives integrating or 'walking with' our sacred wounds is an act of profound courage, and exposing entire vistas of the self, as if for the first time. This is the realization of the masculine impulse of the Soul, *to emerge boldly and be received in our boldness*.

Within the second archetype – to merge or return back into Source – we emotionally open to Other and allow Other to move into our inner protected places. We might think of this as the feminine urge[4], which provides equally ample opportunities to address any sacred wounds to our feminine functioning. We experience the threatening 'foreigner' now as the 'entrusted'. Our ability to connect with another no longer depends *on* the Other and therefore we choose more wisely those with whom we can grow. Our joining together harmonizes us into the broader identity of the union, one woven from individuals. We find that our thoughts become enhanced, our feelings vitalized and our past-obsessed concerns diminished. Over time and with practice, this merging ceases to not threaten our Self-Identity (ego); rather, it *redefines* it, re-positioning us as the center of a larger, more inclusive field or circle. This is the second Soul impulse satisfied, the desire *to be absorbed back into Source.*

With both impulses now fulfilled, a type of *alchemy* can occur wherein the Lover and the Loved transcend their human hosts. They are observed for what they actually are: divine confluences of merged intelligence(s) inhabiting the human electro-biological vessel. Each human vessel becomes a conduit for Love itself, whether s/he is in the role of giver or receiver of that Love. The fearful need to know 'who I am', 'what is happening' or 'what I should do' drops away. The individual's consciousness, or sphere of awareness, releases from the constricting tightness of ego definition. It instead resides as if in a cresting wave of movement, motivated not by him/herself but by the Greater Mind/Unified Heart of the couple. In this way, true intimacy breeds a supra-personal experience formed from the laws of matter (physical vessel) but no longer bound by them (greater realized heart).

It is interesting to note that the wounds we carry are the very soil and seeds of our wisdom. Reconciling to our life situations – the trauma and conditioning of our past – with compassion and without denial or victimization, forges new space for our hidden longing to arise. The ancient Jewish, African, Egyptian, Essene, Celtic, Christian and Sufi masters poeticized this longing. Today, it can become for us an ongoing resource of connection and truth. Indeed, it is in this longing that the urges of the Soul are reconciled.

ASTROLOGICAL PATHS OF INTIMACY

With astrology, we are able to understand the many paths of intimacy by understanding the sign energies. The astrological signs are primary to existence. Whatever name or system we use to identify them – and thus to understand them – is in fact secondary to their primacy in creation. Relative to the domain of human intimacy, signs show us 'the way in' as well as 'the fruits of' our authentic intimacies. Cultivating our ability to be intimate with all of external life is symbolic of our intimacy with our own Soul.

'Intimacy' can be defined as a merging of the boundaries between self and other, and a letting go of the rigidified ego definitions. This leads to an experience of Oneness. Each astrological sign has certain requirements that must be met for its human host to enter into intimacy with the Other (both inner and outer). Once these needs are met and intimacy is established, there is a particular quality that arises within the individual during intimacy.

"Moment to moment the unseen world offers itself, yet we only find it when we are willing to suffer the conflicts and wounds that permeate the times to which we are born. Since humans are the psychic ground on which the split in the world becomes conscious, there must be human ways through which healing, wholeness and unity can be found." —Michael Meade

The following table presents the 12 astrological paths to intimacy. Each path is described by a *Requirement* and an *Emerging Quality*. The Requirement describes what an individual must feel from another in order to 'let down their guard', to open to their partner in an intimate and vulnerable way. It is what they feel they need to be met by or in. The Emerging Quality describes what happens when that magical space of intimacy is entered – the alchemical shift naturally occurring within the body-mind.

SIGN	REQUIREMENT	EMERGING QUALITY
♈ ARIES	Partner to match or accept its level of energetic engagement/ intelligence/ spark/ fire/power.	An easefulness; a slowing down; letting go into joy of being together without need to compete; being met.

♉ TAURUS	Partner to entrust and rely on; who can love and be loved deeply.	Experience of giving/receiving coming through one, rather than originating from self.
♊ GEMINI	Partner who can play in and enjoy freedom; *logos*-lover; who is not attached.	A settling occurs; staying in present moment (not needing to jump to next touch, next situation, next laugh); possibility of true commitment.
♋ CANCER	Partner who can receive nurturing and love; who can affirm one's emotional security.	A depth of emotion and acceptance of self arises; self-empowerment occurs through emotional (Identity) richness; accesses its ability to be nurtured itself.
♌ LEO	Partner who adores them (indicating the partner is loving him/herself).	Two equal powers meeting; not being threatened by or needy of other.
♍ VIRGO	Partner honors the sanctity of the bond, suggesting a quality of perfection of self.	Coming together of whole presence of each partner (other realms/realities are present); accesses broader understanding of union.
♎ LIBRA	Partner commits to the relationship; honors, trusts, respects and listens; equality.	Full immersion into the loving power of a mutual bond, beyond normal reality.

♏ **SCORPIO**	Partner who meets or challenges one's passion, strength and desire (ie., not boring in bed!).	Magic; tantric experiences; alchemy; empowerment.
♐ **SAGITTARIUS**	Partner equally devoted to seeking spiritual/higher reality or adventure.	Magical illumination; spiritual realm comes in; bond based in being together on a mutual quest.
♑ **CAPRICORN**	Partner authentically sees/honors/ respects one's wisdom, experience and counsel; can hold space for one's secret desires to be explored in trust and honoring.	Both empowering and returning to innocence (place of non ego attachment); energy widens to include its full depth and becomes transparent.
♒ **AQUARIUS**	Partner able to contain/track/fly with one's vision (not limit one).	Ability to center/love/ act from heart (instead of only head); its personal humanity drops in.
♓ **PISCES**	Partner who honors, understands and meets its empathic nature, visions, idealism.	Discovers own center of Identity and 'self-ness' (as distinct from others' wants and desires); 'the child grows up'.

NOTES:

[1] The Soul celestially magnetizes the etheric, astral, mental, emotional and physical characteristics of the individual into a complex and interrelated system of manifestations, tendencies, references, and contexts. It is the only true rutter of an individual's incarnational experience that maintains alignment with the personal destiny. It guides and steers the individual to create and re-create the required

experiences in the right timing for its eventual arising and supplanting the ego as the 'captain of the ship'. As this transition occurs, the Self-Identity is increasingly sublimated to the will of the Soul until that will is acknowledged and entrusted to guide the life consciously in all matters.

[2] For more on Masculinity, see chapter 1. Also, www.SacredMarriageAstrology.com offers several ways to learn about and engage your own authentic Masculine.

[3] Use of 'masculine' and 'feminine' do not imply gender, but the spiritual impulses co-animating all life.

[4] For more on Femininity, see chapter 1. Also, www.SacredMarriageAstrology.com offers several ways to learn about and engage your own authentic Feminine.

11
SACRED MARRIAGES
IN THE ASTROLOGICAL SKY

As there are traditionally 12 signs, 10 planets, 12 houses, four angles, and a host of asteroids, planetoids, Uranians and fixed stars, there is a nearly limitless number of opportunities for an individual to harmonize his/her various aspects. Each astrological point represents a particular function within his/her psyche or body-mind.

Thus any two celestial objects considered astrologically may also indicate a potential conflict. Whether two functions harmonize or contrast with each other will be determined by many factors. Some are more obviously parallel, others are more subtly conflictual. Any imaginable impulse within us – say that of asserting ourselves – will find usually several antagonistic impulses resisting its otherwise unabated influence on our thoughts, words and deeds – say that of compromising with another. Indeed, the human psyche is a virtual battlefield of intersecting, interpenetrating desires, beliefs, impulses, attachments and identifications. Even the smallest effort to increase one's self-awareness is a step in the right evolutionary direction.

All astrological resolutions ultimately occur through the fundamental understanding of the sign energies. With a thorough *and* open-minded foundation in the sign qualities, an astrologer can bring great assistance to any client, not necessarily in prediction, superficial matchmaking, or geographical relocation, but in the essential work of the human life: to maximize awareness of and then cellularly embody one's inherent qualities as an individual (which includes releasing old or false qualities not inherent to the self) and then to devote this fuller 'self' to its own unique and authentic life purpose.

What do we mean by 'resolution'? Does it imply a return to a familiar emotional security, or some type of implied contract between our inner child and outer adult stipulating not to act out or be irresponsible or rude Monday through Friday? Is it the intellectual understanding that excessive sex is no good for us?

Within Sacred Marriage Astrology, a 'resolution' does not truly begin until there is the deep acknowledgement and exploration of one's inner arguments and their causes. If the conflicting urges causing the 'argument' can be contacted through one's direct experience or self-inquiry, only then does true resolution become viable. In this context, 'resolution' requires an 'alchemy' of sorts. This notion of alchemy suggests an inner alchemy intended to transmute our base, unconscious reactions and patterns into consciously-woven threads stitched together to form one's Soul-aligned cloak of identity. Sacred Marriage Alchemy teaches that this cloak of 'Self-Identity' (that which contains) is genetically blueprinted to foster the flowering of 'Self-Essence' (that which is contained).

SIGNS

The signs are in fact the source of all other astrological symbols. They gives rise to planetary symbolisms (i.e. Leo ➔ Sun), the house assignations (Sagittarius ➔ 9th house), the angular meanings (Capricorn ➔ Midheaven), the nature of aspects (Virgo ➔ inconjunct) and even the natural evolutionary flow of consciousness (Aries *to* Taurus ➔ instinctual individuation *to* grounded self-stabilizing). It is of prime importance to first foundation one's efforts toward the Sacred Marriage principles on the bedrock of an intimacy with the sign energies.

The most obvious pairing of sign energies in Sacred Marriage work occurs from any pair of polarities (oppositionals): Aries and Libra, Taurus and Scorpio, Gemini and Sagittarius, Cancer and Capricorn, Leo and Aquarius, or Virgo and Pisces. Perhaps just as equally obvious is the succeeding pairs: Aries and Taurus, Gemini and Cancer, Leo and Virgo, Libra and Scorpio, Sagittarius and Capricorn, and Aquarius and Pisces. Not as obvious are all the dyadic combinations of signs arranged by angular relationship: sextiles (ie., Libra and Sagittarius), squares (ie., Aries and Cancer), trines (ie., Virgo and Capricorn), and any other aspecting relationship.

To distinguish a superficial agreement from an actual evolution between any two signs, the actual qualities or natures of the signs themselves must be observed. When this occurs, the sign energies reveal themselves in their primal nature as entire domains of consciousness. They come alive for us. When this occurs, they can 'speak' to and through us, they can go underground in us until we're ready to evolve those aspects of us, and they can grace our efforts with enriching insight and accurate intuitive abilities.

PLANETS

The traditional planetary pairs certainly apply to this model of Sacred Marriage-as-resolution: Venus and Mars, Sun and Moon, Jupiter and Saturn, Venus and Neptune, Mars and Pluto, Mercury and Aquarius, Jupiter and Neptune, Venus and Moon, etc.

As the planets reflect our psychological functioning, any Sacred Marriage work using the planetary energies can be profoundly helpful. For example, learning how to resolve the Saturnian influence with the Jupiterian necessitates leaving behind rational understanding of 'how' it should occur. It requires instead a courage to move into and through a darkened landscape without sure landmarks or familiar experiences. The fulcrumatic question, in this case, becomes: *how can I expand during times of necessary contraction?, or how can I bring into my mundane life my ever-expanding visions?*

ANGLES

The core concept of this 'Sacred Marriage of opposites' is most apparent in the angular axies: Ascendant-Descendant and Midheaven-Lowheaven. Everyone has the Ascendant (AC) opposite the Descendant (DC) and the Midheaven (MC) opposite the Lowheaven (IC). Thus, these two pairs are the most potentized opportunities for a lasting inner resolution. This potential is increased if we remember that an individual's angular energies (the signs on the Angles) require the planetary energies for full activation of this potential (see Chapter 5). Therefore, on any natal map, the IC and MC naturally form a heated argument within the psyche: where the IC wants to draw energy to foundation and root deeper and deeper into the conscious Self-Identity, the MC wants to increasingly move towards expression of Self-Essence outward, with others, into the outer environment, and ultimately to be noticed. A similar dynamic exists between the AC and DC. Within this light, Sacred Marriage Astrology places high importance on cultivating the client's awareness of their angular energies.

CONCLUSION

I have observed a consistent energetic quality presents itself in a therapeutic space when a sacred marriage (cellular re-wiring) is occurring. I am referring to a guided meditation I have formed to bring clients to *create for themselves* their experience of their Sacred Marriage, known as The Sacred Marriage Alchemy Meditation. Their experience during the meditation bears resemblance to a heightened, intensified awareness of oneself and one's surroundings, similar to the experience of traveling through unknown woods at night without certainty one is moving in the 'right' direction. It feels as if one is in the middle of an intense lightning storm: a powerful presence with highly focused energy. In this rarefied space, clients seem to lose their tracking of time, but remain very present and without the need to leave the body, to 'check out' or regress to familiar methods of escapism. Clients engaged at this level of transformation – in an actual process of inner alchemy or cellular resolution of conflictual impulses – seem to express at least one of the following traits: they will experience themselves in a way they have not known in this life or have forgotten since childhood; they will exhibit a notable absence of fear or cynicism about 'losing' the sacred marriage experience and 'reverting' to their previous state after the session; and they will naturally exude a peculiar evenness of temperament and solidity of self-acceptance. As you might imagine, it continues to be an honor to assist individuals and couples in these ways and to witness the profound capacity of the human being to realize itself at greater levels.

III
THE NATURE OF EGO,
THE FUNCTION OF THE MOON

Ego as a structure within the psyche has a primal function: to identify and evaluate subjective experience. In order to perform its identifying and evaluative functions, it requires a database of information with which to compare, identify, order and then process its *current* experience. The only resource the ego has to do this is what we call the Past. The ego, in its nature, is inexorably rooted in the past because the past is identifiable and is therefore dependable as a resource for performing its function.

The ego requires full access to all past experiences, which it uses to contextualize new experiences. It is a 'managing' engine in the fullest sense – never tiring, always on the lookout for new experiences to identify, associate, categorize and store. The ego is that essential human function which keeps alive the entire frame of experiential reference we call Past.

Therefore, to push our awareness past the limitations of the known – the egoic realm – requires a significant amount of energy (momentum) and strong, persistent desire. If the barrier can be surpassed, a previously undiscovered world is breached, a world of danger and depth, of profanity and reverence, death and life – indeed a *legendary world* filled with great risk – a world in all ways contrary to that which the ego is responsible for and invested in maintaining.

Ego now can be undressed to its deeper function: to create adequate barriers to the cellular discovery of this *legendary world* until such time as the Soul is sufficiently crystallized/integrated/blended into the egoic frame or structure of subjective identity. This framework is comprised of personality and physio-electrical structures or matrices, each of which themselves are created from more specialized components within the psyche in total.

Until such a time as the legendary world is accessed, the strength, stubbornness and fixity of the ego in a given individual reveals the egoic need to define and order his/her reality based on known quantities or successful strategies from its past, a personal reality structure that refuses the existence of such a world due to the perceived costs (to the ego) of greater fear, impending chaos and ultimately annihilation. However, an ego's degree of fixity also directly speaks to the magnitude of potential power laying in the dark currents of the personal subconscious waiting to be tapped.

To use imagery, we can picture the ego as a large boulder in the middle of a small brook as the Soul consciousness at the beginning of its journey through incarnations. The brook gradually grows into a creek, digging deeper into the ground around the boulder and widening its own shores. The creek becomes a small river eroding the boulder over time and increasing its capacity to channel greater amounts of water by further extending its borders and changing its overall shape. The small river turns into a large river that regularly tumbles the once-immovable boulder with each faster current. It is through change that evolution occurs, that life grows, and not through the desperate gripping onto boulders of identity.

THE MOON

In astrological interpretation, the ego is correlated with the Moon, 4th House, and Cancer. As the Moon is a physical body in space, it indeed symbolizes the current-life egoic identity structure, just as all other physical bodies (planets) reflect an aspect of the *current-life* psyche, and not an a *priori* reference to our past. This error results from interpreting the astrological Moon from the level of its qualitative expression, rather than its essential function within the psyche. The nature of our natal Moon energy, just like the nature of ego in general, is to be a *bridge between* the known and the hidden, the safe and the unsafe, and between our experience of 'me' from 'you'. It is the self which has the experiences and that moves through life with relative self-acknowledgement. In the view of SMA, it does not correlate with our genetic or karmic past as its primary function.

Because the Moon's domain is in fact this intermediary threshold, it connects to *both* the subconscious or past and the conscious or present. The Moon-as-past needs to be first understood as an *oblique* symbolism. The nature of the subconscious is to be literally 'beneath consciousness', or under the surface of our self-awareness. As such, the Moon potently symbolizes ways in which we act subconsciously, or 'below ourselves' in our subconsciously-motivated thoughts, actions and words. We almost always remain unaware of where these motivations are sourced from. But this should not always be seen as an indicator of our karmic, genetic history if we are discussing the Moon's domain. It is actually the *current-life* indicator of our self-structuring requirements – our ego.

The Moon's authority as our conscious or present ego is just as important to work with as its subconscious symbolism. As the present-life Self-Identity, the Moon reveals a fantastic opportunity to rediscover self. When an individual has treaded the path of courageously, authentically coming to terms with past obsessions, aggressions, patterns of inward- or outward-violence, or its stubborn insistence on remaining in familiar territory, there is new space opened within the psyche. This new space is filled – indeed can only be filled – by the freed-up Self-Identity, now unbound by the subconscious need to maintain familiar security at all costs. The experience is one of re-discovering oneself, as if for the first time, which in a manner of speaking, it is.

With the Moon symbolizing *both* the subconscious and the conscious self as a result of its unique bridging function, we can see any interpretation which leaves out either to be only half the picture. The exclusive association of the Moon with the subconscious/past results from seeing only the manifestation and not the essence of the Moon's function. In other words, *how* we express our Moon energy, rather than *what* the Moon actually is within our psyche. Again, this is in error. If we remain only in the former, we keep our blinders on snug and tight. If only in the latter, we idealize a person to the point of unrealistic goals. To describe an individual's natal Moon (sign, house and aspects) as the fundamental indicator of their karmic past and that which they need to release or move beyond in a majority way, is to mislead and aberrate the understanding of the healthy ego-development intent in the current life. It is only in the accurate and balanced comprehension of the actual nature and function of the Moon that its gifts of self-insight and growth are revealed.

IV
'PHACES' OF THE MOON:
THE NATURE & RESISTANCE OF IDENTITY

The following Moon descriptions are the product of a collaboration between Sacred Marriage Astrologer Aleathe Morrill and the author.

Once we become familiar and proficient in 'reading' the Soul's Desire (Pluto) and its Vehicle (Nodal axis), one avenue which opens to us next is to examine the Moon position. The natal Moon by sign, house and aspects will tell us the current-life ego definition the Soul has chosen to develop, inhabit and make conscious. Thus the natal Moon is the current-life vehicle for Self-Identity (see 'Two Villages and a Sea' in chapter 11). This does not mean however that most attain an 'evolved' relationship with their Moon energies. The reasons for this are quite understandable and have to do with the nature of the Moon's function, rather than the stubbornness of humanity (though this certainly plays a part). In essence, the Moon has one foot in the subconscious waters and one on the known ground of awareness. It plays a bridging role between the two. In addition to the nature of the human ego as a component of the psyche, this is the basis from which to explore the Moon's function and expressions because it will properly con-textualize the descriptions about each.

Each Moon position can be understood as a current-life choice on behalf of the Soul and not as a carry-over from the past. Because the astrological Moon within the human psyche is in part a bridging function between the sub-conscious and the conscious awareness in the current incarnation, each Moon description below necessarily implies specific areas which it denies and would otherwise like to keep 'hidden' in the wateriness of the sub-conscious. For more on this idea, see the article 'The Function of Ego, the Nature of the Moon' in this section.

When one becomes too attached to their Moon, too strongly identified with their ego identity, or too invested in their expectations, it is as if they are trying to subconsciously force or recreate what is cellularly familiar. In each of the following Moon descriptions:

🕊 *Ego-identity/Self-definition* describes the qualities around which one will default to defining themselves through (feeling secure in);

🕊 *Light* describes its progressive or self-affirming expressions;

🕊 *Shadow* describes its regressive or self-negating expressions; and

🕊 *Resistance around* describes that which the ego will naturally resist; those qualities or experiences which will energetically vibrate to the ego as a threat, limitation, or questioning of itself and its validity; and those qualities that are unfamiliar and thus un-trusted. (Remember, the ego's purpose is to secure the self through emotional stability and mental certainty).

The following descriptions are not comprehensive. Rather, they intend to suggest or evoke a core understanding of the lunar qualities of each Sign/House signature. If approached in this light, they can trigger more specific and relevant expressions for each chart you are working with.

ARIES MOON/MOON IN THE 1ST HOUSE

Ego-identity/Self-definition: Ability to be mobile (in many ways), independent, free, and strong. Needs to perpetually engage in its own areas of interest and to remain active. Will orient to itself and the world instinctually.

Light: Competitive; playful; dualistic; child-like; innocent; raw power.

Shadow: Shallow; defensive; immature; naïve; brash; aggressive; anger; quick to react; violence; must be right or number one; doesn't see compromise.

Resistance around: Any suppression or limitation to a wide open space in which to insert and experience oneself.

TAURUS MOON/MOON IN THE 2ND HOUSE

Ego-identity/Self-definition: Ability to be stable, responsible, rooted, persistent. Needs to feel connected to the physical and its own physicality through food, sensuality, and comfortable surroundings. Will orient to itself and the world sensually (through the senses).

Light: Persistent; dependable; dedicated; pragmatic; sensual; homey; strong values; independent; selectively intimate.

Shadow: Stubborn; dualistic; lazy; intractable; myopic; materialistic; close-minded; inflexible.

Resistance around: Any attempt to force them out of their familiar environs, the foundation they've developed, or materially or socially, their current value system.

GEMINI MOON/MOON IN THE 3RD HOUSE

Ego-identity/Self-definition: Ability to know the workings of its world, environment, social circle, habitat, country, or chosen field of expertise or hobbies. Needs to feel knowledgeable. Will orient to itself and the world cognitively.

Light: Intelligent; fun; funny; light-hearted; youthful; and dedicated to learning; quick; flexible; diverse; freedom loving.

Shadow: Noncommittal; impersonal; impatient; immature; shallow; uncaring; flighty; fickle.

Resistance around: 'Getting their hands dirty'; long-term commitments or anything that they perceive would restrict or infringe on their need to be free, available, or mobile.

CANCER MOON/MOON IN THE 4TH HOUSE

Ego-identity/Self-definition: Ability to create and maintain emotional security. Needs to feel effective in its nurturing abilities. Will orient to itself and the world emotionally.

Light: Deeply caring; self-nurturing; loving; giving; emotionally aware; stable; mature; responsible; sensitivity to others; intuitive; compassionate; communicative.

Shadow: Co-dependent; projecting; insensitive to others actual feelings; self-obsessed; over-processing.

Resistance around: The dislocation of their familiar experience of emotional security or the sources of that security.

LEO MOON/MOON IN THE 5TH HOUSE

Ego-identity/Self-definition: Ability to feel seen, acknowledged and centered around. Needs to feel unique, creative and special through interactions with others. Will orient to the world subjectively, or strongly from its own perspective and perceived needs.

Light: Radiate warmth and confidence; charismatic; personable; energetic; attractive; engendering self-love and comfortability; regal; standard of excellence.

Shadow: Self-obsessed; arrogant; narcissistic; insecure; stubborn; myopic;

ego-centric; blind to their own ego-centeredness.

Resistance around: Any threat to perpetuating their experience of self-grandeur.

VIRGO MOON/MOON IN THE 6TH HOUSE

Ego-identity/Self-definition: Ability to control and maintain the physical domain (one's body, home, work). Needs to feel it has excelled, that it has significantly contributed. Will orient to itself and the world critically and analytically.

Light: Organizationally excellent; devoted; pragmatic; helpful; high standards; caring; detail-oriented; service-oriented; team player; attuned to earth cycles.

Shadow: Emotion-less; controlling; eruptible; guilty; self-critical; nitpicky; lacking vision; harshly opinionated; judgmental.

Resistance around: Anything that upsets their ability to maintain self-control.

LIBRA MOON/MOON IN THE 7TH HOUSE

Ego-identity/Self-definition: Ability to be proper, kind, understanding and respectful. Needs to feel accepted by others. Will orient to itself and the world equaniminously.

Light: Good listener; gracious; understanding; fair; supportive; intelligent; mediating; 'people' person; team player; helpful; caring; equaniminous.

Shadow: Extremist; over-idealistic; unrealistic; naïve; co-dependent; incapable of deep intimacy.

Resistance around: Any change that creates a negative opinion of them.

SCORPIO MOON/MOON IN THE 8TH HOUSE

Ego-identity/Self-definition: Ability to be in control (of self and/or others). Needs to experience depth or feeling viscerally alive, and more powerful than challenges to itself. Will orient to itself and the world intensely.

Light: Sexual; seductive; intense; powerful; intuitive; intelligent; thrill-seeking; transformative; deep; mysterious.

Shadow: Manipulative; serious; dark; secretive; controlling; stubborn; vengeful; envious; angry; mean; violent.

Resistance around: Any experience that intimates their weakness, insignificance, superficiality, or that threatens the self-perception of being in control (of themselves or others).

SAGITTARIUS MOON/MOON IN THE 9TH HOUSE

Ego-identity/Self-definition: Ability to seek and know truth or higher understanding. Needs to (pursue and) understand larger meanings in life. Will orient to itself and the world philosophically.

Light: Intelligent; wise; intuitive; knowledgeable; honest; visionary; truth-seeking.

Shadow: Disconnected; know-it-all; rude; insensitive; exclusionary; dissociated.

Resistance around: Any challenge or disagreement to what they believe, or obstruction to their seeking.

CAPRICORN MOON/MOON IN THE 10TH HOUSE

Ego-identity/Self-definition: Ability to be recognized and treated as an authority. Needs to feel socially known, respected and responsible. Will orient to itself and the world dutifully.

Light: Responsible; far-seeing; good leader; wise; concern for others; passionate; sensual; deeply feeling; critical analysis; honoring of tradition; careful; righteous.

Shadow: Stubborn; elitist; impersonal; controlling; bossy; intense; manipulative; condescending; slow moving; depressive; serious.

Resistance around: Any challenge or change to their (perceived) position as an authority figure.

AQUARIUS MOON/MOON IN THE 11TH HOUSE

Ego-identity/Self-definition: Ability to envision or implement difference or unique changes. Needs to feel different than the consensus. Will orient to itself and the world innovatively.

Light: Creative; visionary; intelligent; original thinker; revolutionary; inventive; objective; detached; futuristic.

Shadow: Unfeeling; insensitive; denying; disassociated; fear of intimacy; unrealistically idealistic; harsh.

Resistance around: Being grouped into a consensus; being 'weighed down' by base concerns, such as emotionality, group rules, or the politics of relationships.

PISCES MOON/MOON IN THE 12TH HOUSE

Ego-identity/Self-definition: Ability to resonate with one's energetic environment (subtle or gross). Needs to feel at one with others. Will orient to itself and the world empathically.

Light: Compassionate; caring; psychic; mystical; creative; child-like; innocent; vulnerable; nurturing.

Shadow: Disconnected from own feelings; delusional; naïve; co-dependent; addictive; escapist; depressive; lethargic; manipulative; irresponsible; indecisive.

Resistance around: Creating 'space' or distinctions between self and other.

V
ANGLES & THEIR FUELS

What follows is an original formulation for deepening the Sacred Marriage Astrologer's interpretive skill with the Angles. If you are new to working with the Angles, I suggest you spend sufficient time learning the Angles as they are presented in chapter 5 before proceeding to learn this material.

In SMA, the Horoscope Angles are of fundamental importance. They symbolize the 'end goal' of all the workings of the psyche, represented by the planets. They are not finish lines waiting to be crossed, but 'potentialities' waiting to be actualized within each person. When actualized at the cellular level, our Angular energies open the door to a profound unification of self-knowledge and life purpose. It is in this light the following method is offered. Again, knowledge of the Angles on their own is a precursor to using this method effectively.

BACKGROUND

As you might find or may already have found, the sign on an Angle is a very personal statement about an individual. This is backed up by the speed at which the Angles change: approximately every 2 hours depending on the size of the house. However, you may have also found an Angle's sign is simply that... a sign. It is not as precise as, say, an aspect between the Angle and a planet. To say both you and your friend have Sagittarius Rising may have completely different meanings for each of you. Angles are made more specific to a person if there are planets conjunct them. (These are called 'angular planets', or planets on an angle). But without these and other types of distinguishing factors, an individual's natal Angles may remain 'like an empty room' with nothing 'inside' to give the astrologer a lead on *how* that Angle is specific and personal to that person. For example, you know you have Sagittarius Rising, but you may not know – simply from

257

the sign of Sagittarius – *how and through which function of your psyche* that Angle is being fueled. In other words, one Midheaven will naturally be more interactive and 'conversant' with a certain sign than with others. Yet that sign may not indicate its unique connection with the Midheaven by normal astrological techniques.

I have hit upon a way to precisely correlate an Angle with its personally relevant Fuel sign. An Angle's 'Fuel' is that sign energy which directly and highly personally supports the individual to 'realize' or attain an experience of their Angular sign energy. The analogy of an engine requiring fuel to run is accurate to our discussion here. Without fuel, the engine lays dormant, even if we have the key to ignite its activity. An engine requires the liquid fuel in order to function according to its design. The same goes for an Angle. It will lay dormant and 'unrealized' and remain as potential without its fuel and trigger.

It is important to state that the SMA Angular Fuels are not the only way to ignite an Angle within an individual. Rather, we see them as a highly personal and direct path of doing so. Working with the Fuels in the manner described below has been utilized in over 200 private counseling sessions to effective results: the accurate laying-out for an individual of the way(s) they are most meant to self-realize their Angular energy.

THE METHOD

As you may have guessed, the location of each Angle on the chart correlates with the sign, planet and house there. So, AC and Aries, DC and Libra, MC and Capricorn, and IC and Cancer. This method takes full advantage of these inherent relationships or 'pre-wirings' existing within the structure of the human psyche. The Fuels emanate from the planet most associated with the quality of each Angle. The one exception to this loose rule is that for the Midheaven. If we look at the chart, the Midheaven begins the 10th house which would connect it to Capricorn and Saturn. However, the nature of the Midheaven and its functioning is more aligned to the quality of the Sun, in that the Sun is how we are seen and known by others and how we present ourselves within a larger group. We have explored using Saturn as the fuel for the Midheaven, to rather pessimistic results. For us, the Sun is more aligned to the popular Midheaven. We've conjectured that the MC- ♑ - ♄ connection is in large part due to the patriarchal overlay of our current culture which sends the cultural message to 'fit into existing structure' (♄) rather than 'create who you desire to be' (☉).

1. *The 4 Fuels* – The first step in this Method is to identify the signs of natal Mars, Venus, Sun and Moon. Next, connect them to Ascendant, Descendant, Midheaven, and Lowheaven, respectively. Conceptually connect each pair just as in the 'engine and its fuel' analogy above, where the fuel feeds the engine. Here is the formula for determining each Fuel-Engine pair:

[The Sign of Mars *Fuels* the Ascendant] *or*
[The Ascendant's Fuel is the Mars sign] *or* [♂ fuels AC]

[The Sign of Venus *Fuels* the Descendant] *or*
[The Descendant's Fuel is the Venus sign] *or* [♀ fuels DC]

[The Sign of the Sun *Fuels* the Midheaven] *or*
[The Midheaven's Fuel is the Sun sign] *or* [☉ fuels MC]

[The Sign of the Moon *Fuels* the Lowheaven] *or*
[The Lowheaven's Fuel is the Moon sign] *or* [☽ fuels IC]

Diagrammatically, here's how it would look (for you visual learners):

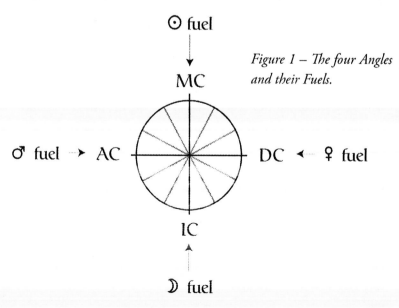

Figure 1 – The four Angles and their Fuels.

When learning this Method with charts, I strongly recommend laying out on a piece of paper each Fuel-Angle pair in the respective positions (Mars-AC on the left, Venus-DC on the right, etc.)

2. Once you have the layout, attune to each 'fuel-engine' or 'fuel-Angle' combination one at a time. Ask 'How does (the fuel sign) fuel (the Angular sign)?' This is consistent with the SMA principle of becoming intimate with each sign/planet/house energy. Here, you are opening your intuition to how one energy can support the other, within the context of the Angle's function. Practicing this will help you feel the energies in new ways. We suggest you begin with your understanding of the Angle itself and what its domain is. This will help you 'frame' how the energies work with one another. In other words, the nature of the Angle will determine 'how' the energies will speak to you through your intuition. For example: 'How does Cancer fuel Taurus?' will be *very different* if Taurus is the sign of the *Midheaven* versus the sign of the *Lowheaven* because *how* the Midheaven functions is different than the Lowheaven.

So let's more fully look at the example above: *'Cancer is fueling a Taurus IC'*. This means the IC is in the sign of Taurus. And from the formula in Step #1, we know that for a person to have a *Cancer fuel* for their IC, that means that Cancer must be the sign of their *Moon*. We can thus finalize our question with 'How does Cancer fuel a Taurus IC?' Now, we have a good starting point!

When a person shows Taurus on the IC the intent is to know oneself most intimately, deeply and on one's own terms (IC) by learning how to manage one's money, to stabilize oneself within a larger and threatening environment, to learn how to receive fully and wholeheartedly, and to be sensually grounded in one's body (all Taurus qualities). If Cancer is *the fuel* for this Taurus aspiration (IC) to be actualized, then the most meaningful and direct way for this Taurus IC person to know themselves is to *emotionally stabilize* within themselves (Cancer) regardless of other people's needs of them or the quality of their care-taking (Cancer qualities). In other words, this person's Cancer qualities are directly connected to and specifically support their sense of personal rooted-ness (Taurus IC). What a valuable piece of information to share with someone about themselves! This takes practice to learn to interpret and communicate effectively but it is very accessible once you do so.

3. Our recommendation is to begin with this basic process. Again, the sign of the fuel-planet *feeds* the sign of the Angle. Interpret this relationship or this flow from the context of the Angle and what it's function or aspiration is within the psyche.

NEXT STEPS:* For those who want to add to this basic Method, you can next include:

1. Any planets conjunct the Angle in question. In our example above, perhaps Jupiter is conjunct the Lowheaven.

2. The House of the Fuel-planet. In our example above, let's say the Moon is in the 8th house. This would add to your understanding of their natal Moon function which would certainly add to your understanding of how the Lowheaven is fueled to be actualized.

3. Any aspects the Fuel-planet is involved in.

But again, we recommend not making this more complex for yourself too soon. The three additional factors mentioned above will hinder your effectiveness with this Method if you are not firmly grounded in the basics of Angular dynamics first.

VI
MANIFESTATION: THE DANCE OF THE SUN AND THE MOON

Together the astrological Sun and Moon form the structural core of a Soul's incarnational Identity (yet they do *not* include that Soul's prior, karmic Identity nor its future Identity to be). With the Moon as the inner stability of self and the Sun as the outer radiance of self, the Self-Identity can be identified and illuminated by the astrologer.

If we were to return to the time of our birth, identify where the Sun and the Moon were, and then calculate the distance between them, we would be taking the first step towards determining our *personal new and full moon times.*

Let's say your calculations produce a distance of 123° of arc, stating that at the time you were born the Moon and the Sun were 123° from each other. From this, you would know that each month when the Sun and the Moon reached this degree of distance, you would be experiencing your personal new moon, or the seeding time of your intentions, prayers and manifestation intents. From this, you could then calculate when your *personal full moon* timings would occur. To do this, simply add 180° to the birth elongation. In our example, this produces 303°. Each month, the Sun and the Moon will also reach this distance, which would mark your own full moon time.

But what does this mean? What's behind this? The Sun and the Moon together indicate our personal fertility cycle which imprinted us at birth. The moment we take our first breath, we are the most open, innocent, undifferentiated, and in a sense fertile with life potential. Each subsequent month's repeat of that Sun-Moon spatial relationship aligns with our natal imprint, releasing the potential for manifestation into opportunities for us. You might imagine that if we were to plant our intentions during our new moon times, the natural alignment between our birth Sun-Moon dance and the current Sun-Moon dance would produce fruit far more efficiently, quickly and powerfully. Wouldn't we rather throw our seeds into fertile soil than desert dust?

So why the Sun and the Moon specifically? Let's look at each individually and then at their union.

THE MOON

As the Moon is our current-life ego identity and methodology for structuring ourselves as an independent self, the Moon provides the first of the three necessary ingredients for this manifestation alchemy to work. The Moon provides a container or a context from which intentions are focalized and within which manifestation can occur through. So the Moon can be seen as our *Soil For Growing*.

THE SUN

The astrological Sun signifies the specific quality or range of energetic frequencies which run through our body-mind, animate it and produce our 'aliveness.' It is the quality of current or light which we bring everything to (because it is in everything we are!) It juices our actions, or our ACT-SUNs! It determines how others see us because it is the most visible part of us, just like the Sun in our solar system. So the Sun can be seen as our *Light Energy For Growing*, the second ingredient.

THE THIRD INGREDIENT

What's missing from our formula for manifestation is *Our Intention*, what we want to attract to ourselves and to create. Many of us think we know what we want, but more often we remain fixed in the wanting itself. In other words, we don't look under the surface of our desires and ask questions like, 'Who's the one doing the wanting here?' or 'Do I really want that?' One very good way to clarify our desires and intentions is to come to understand our Sun and our Moon energies more deeply. This requires going beyond mainstream and Sun-sign astrology meanings of the signs and houses. It means delving into the energies and being honest with ourselves. As many have discovered, often it is not our prayers which are the reason for our intentions not manifesting, but our insufficient self-awareness which sends 'weak signals' out to the universe in the form of our prayers and intentions. And Loving Universe needs a clear message so it knows what to send back and how to support us. So we often need to strengthen ourselves, as transmitters of intent. The combination of strengthening our Sun sign energy and deepening into our Moon sign energy can create this result. When worked with together, the Sun and the Moon create a type of unification which produces a personal engine for manifestation. Thus if we can introduce an *empowered and aligned third ingredient* – a prayer or prayers made by someone who is deeply in alignment with their own, authentic nature – then Loving Universe has what She needs to start sending it our way! Life becomes fun. We become powerful creators.

The monthly re-occurrence of our natal Sun-Moon relationship re-energizes our birth-state's deep connection with the fecundity of life. A mini-portal opens in which the context of who we are becoming in this life can be consciously accessed and empowered. We can then plant our intents (seeds) into this *personal soil* through dreams, sacred altars, ceremonies, prayers, affirmations, etc. Plus, physically observing the Sun and Moon in the sky at these times further empowers the results.

For further detail about each month's *personal new and full moon periods,* look to those signs, houses and aspected planets which the Sun and the Moon each experience. Though you may have been born with Sun in Taurus and Moon in Sagittarius 123° apart, each month when this distance is repeated, the Sun and the Moon will be in different signs, houses, and aspects to different planets. Remember, it is the spatial distance – the relationship – between them that is the key for your monthly manifestation times, not the signs and houses. Once you find next month's timing (new or full moon) for yourself, you can allow a one-day window on either end of that point. So if your next personal new moon occurs at 3pm on a Monday, then from Sunday at 3pm to Tuesday at 3pm is a 'portal' in which you are ripe for making your prayers or intentions. Finally, I will always suggest to my clients working with their personal Sun-Moon Dance to create and maintain an altar of some kind at home to build momentum month to month. *Enjoy your manifestations!*

† *Many thanks to astrologer Carolyn Brent for first introducing this core concept to me.*

VII
CHIRON: THE MYTHIC & MUNDANE REALITY OF THE SACRED WOUND

Between the orbits of Saturn and Uranus – between the realms of the known and the unknown – lies a large asteroid (a 'planetoid') – called Chiron. After the main ten planets used in astrology, the most popular asteroid used in natal and transit work is Chiron. The reasons for its popularity are many as evidenced by the thousands of pages written about it since its discovery in 1977. Actually, for 90% of its orbit it moves between Saturn and Uranus; the remaining 10% sees Chiron actually *inside* Saturn's orbit (closer to the Sun than Saturn) or *outside* Uranus' orbit (further from the Sun than Uranus). Chiron is a true liaison between the two.

Archetypal Chiron addresses the entire transition between memory and forgetfulness at the level of the Soul which can only be initially experienced at the level of psychology. If the Soul is the consistent consciousness transmigrating through incarnations, then Chiron signifies that Soul's sacrifice – each time it chooses an incarnation. Its inevitable forgetting of itself – which occurs each time a new incarnation begins. Traditional cultures hold that this forgetting, this *loss of knowing and of source,* is necessary and a natural part of life. In fact, they say it is crucial for maintaining the balance between this world and the *other world.* Greek myth contributes the image of the River Lethe, the river which each Soul must drink from just before entering life. Its waters cause forgetfulness to thoroughly wash through the Soul erasing any immediate knowing of its Desire, which we may call life purpose. (For more about the Soul's Desire, see Chapters 1 & 8) A piece of Jewish folklore explains the human loss of knowing self in a different way. It tells that an angel gently places one finger over the lips of the newborn just before birth as if to symbolize 'Shhhhhh' in the baby's consciousness and thus to cause it to lose its memory of itself. It's also said this is the reason for the indented cleft between the human nose and upper lip. Other mythologies echo this basic premise in a variety of ways.

Let's look at the loss of self-knowledge more closely. The phenomenal world – the world in which forms arise and disappear in our perception – which is also known as the physical world from a slightly different perspective, is run by different laws than the *other world*, the world of dreams, of ancestors, of spirits and of an altogether *other* reality. For our purposes here, this *other world* is seen to encompass both the *underworld* and the *upper world* together; we will not distinguish these two as they are both essentially *other than* this world of visible forms. While we in our lives spend exorbitant amounts of energy struggling, learning, loving, hurting, adventuring, integrating and growing while in incarnation, our actual source, that which *we actually are* – which SMA terms Self-Essence – is *energy itself*, magnetized, constellated and matrixed by an ineffable intelligence or knowing. Thus, in order for this knowing – our Soul – to enter into *this* (phenomenal) world which for it is the *other* world, there needs to occur a transduction of energy. The fact remains that the laws of this world are inherently different than those of the other. This, despite the pervasive and naïve message from some current prophecies that this too is changing[1]. It is precisely the threshold between this world and the other world, between knowing and forgetting which Chiron fully addresses[2]. The planetoid also has been examined and framed in a number of ways[3].

On the level of the psyche, Chiron signifies the causes, expressions and results of the individual's attempt to cross the threshold between the worlds... between Saturn and Uranus, *Self-Identity* and *Self-Essence*, between *Self-forgetting* and *Self-remembering*. To walk a Chironic path requires great courage as it will open the very aspects of self which have closed off to protect oneself from the harsh and intense experience of their splitting. To do so is to invite deep pain and confusion to arise from within. Let's take the idea that Chiron correlates with a deep source of pain a few steps further.

Chiron reveals our particular 'device of protection', the psychic shell or protective layer which has been pre-consciously constructed deep within the psyche the first time the infant experiences separation. This 'device' has as many forms as there are people; by 'forms' I do not suggest a physical form, but an *energetic pattern* which is consistent and always running.

THE SACRED WOUND

The most popular title Chiron has been crowned with by modern astrologers is the Wounded Healer. This image itself arises from the notion of a *sacred wound*[4], which has been connected to traditional cultures, ancient Egypt and Greece, and contemporary psychological and sociological work.

Let's look at each word of this archetype – 'sacred' and 'wound' – to understand it as a whole. In context of its connection to Chiron, a 'wound' implies something which an individual carries with him/her throughout life, something buried very deep within the self, and something which pains them greatly. A 'wound' runs deeper than a 'pain'. A wound is closer to the idea of a disability, handicap, being broken, or an insufficiently-treated disease. That each person carries a wound suggests that life will necessarily produce painful experiences, that that pain comes from within, and that a portion of one's life should focus on contacting, learning and incorporating its 'lesson' for us; in other words, *doing something about it*.

The term 'sacred' in this context implies something set apart from normal conditions, something rendered divine or holy or special. It suggests something *from the other world* which is recognized *in this world* as such. The word-vibration 'sacred' has its ancient roots in the notion of being set apart or *separated* from mundane life. This should give the reader interested in the Chiron's dynamic a jolt of recognition: it is precisely the issue of separateness as well as the experience of being separated which lies at the heart of the *sacred wound* implied by Chiron's presence in the psyche.

THE CAUSE OF THE WOUND

Psychologists have theorized that an individual's initial wounding experience occurs very early in life at ages 9-10 months[5]. Their suggestion is that either at or before this age the individual will *directly experience* for the first time being separate from its source. The experience may be overtly hurtful, such as abuse of any kind, but it need not be. Before this age, the infant is in a pre-conscious state and has neither capacity nor need of knowing itself to be separate or different than what surrounds it.

The infant's first experience of separateness produces both an explicit and an implicit result. Explicitly, the child will naturally develop a behavior strategy to protect itself from continuing to *feel acutely* without *what it needs*. This has been too loosely coined by previous writers as the child 'wanting love.' More accurately, it should be thought of as the strategy the child develops to pacify the overwhelming threat it experiences on every level of its being. At its level, the infant of course isn't conscious of this dynamic nor is s/he able to identify the threat it experiences as that of the cessation of its life, or death. Rather, the pre-conscious infant is for the first time experiencing self-difference or separateness which it instantaneously equates to (what we call) death. If for example the child learns that only loud screaming will bring the breast or the bottle or the warm hug, then perhaps a core pattern of acting-out may be seeded. Or if the child is hit when it cries very loudly, then quiet or silence becomes the strategy. Deep emotional patterns are formed from these early experiences. Yet the evolutionary impulse – to protect itself against threat – develops into explicit, recognizable behavior patterns in direct reaction to the child's relationship with its (newly perceived) external source of comfort and need-fulfillment. At this point in the development, there is no difference between the external and the internal. They are the same, until the wounding experience rends them apart.

The implicit effect is even deeper; it is also quite beautiful. Within consciousness itself irrespective of the child's individual qualities, these first experiences of separation actually catalyze the formation of a preliminary structure within the pre-conscious soup of the child's consciousness. This 'structure' can also be seen as an opening, a splitting or a new space forming. It forces the creation of individual components or parts, just as when a large bowl of water is divided into many individual cups of water. When what was contiguously One becomes individually many, there can be said to be a 'relationship' formed between all the parts as they share a common origin. What was whole and uninterrupted is now split and fleeting, which has disastrous effects on the infants' psychic reality. The child now enters a world of perceived self-lack, self-limitation, and external need-fulfillment. The opening or rift occurs at a precise 'place' which later is to be known as the sacred wound, or *the seat of one's Chironic wisdom.*[6]

However, this initial split is also the birth of self-consciousness, or the ability to sense self *as a distinct self.* The implicit result is also the catalyst for the later development of one's ego, an absolutely crucial (though some would argue cursed) stage in human development. The astrological natal chart precisely reveals this exact 'place' within an individual by indicating which archetypal energies are being protected against. There also seems to be, perhaps unsurprisingly, the potential for a consistent physiologic location of the wound as well.[7] From this we can see that the natural evolution of a human being will include the psychoid (psychic + physical) split or wounding and is not in any way an abnormality or tragedy, so often argued in light-polarized or 'new age' literature.[8]

THE CHIRONIC EXPERIENCE

The actual 'Chironic' experience can very often manifest as a *profound and unavoidable emotional breakdown*. When it occurs, it cellularly triggers the early-life protection patterns (formed in infancy). It is as if the original pre-conscious separation is psychologically repeated. It is analogous to the body's formation of a scab to protect the healing process occurring underneath. In adults experiencing Chiron's influence, I've observed many 'feel like a child' or return to the childhood issues of being unloved, abandoned, and unprotectable. Chiron reveals a 'tender spot' within the self-definition, a place which cannot be strengthened through outer achievements or outside validation. Another way I describe it for clients is the raw feeling of being *too* exposed, *too* vulnerable, broken or somehow defeated.

Chiron's effect is specifically to bring about this experience from within in order to: 1. tap the individual back into the (almost always) unaddressed issues from infancy; in order 2. force a deeper opening of the heart and a greater humility. Through Chiron, this will occur through re-contacting the subconscious patterns of protection and separation. What is being suggested here is that until an individual effectively deals with what for them is their ongoing pre-conscious pattern of protecting themselves – their woundedness – by summarily suppressing any vulnerability or signs of weakness, Chiron will continue to play its wound-trigger role. There is nothing here implied that all human beings are doomed to a life of irreversible wounded misery. In fact, it might surprise many to learn that Chiron is one of the most powerful catalysts for a radiant joy, and a deeper connection and understanding of one's humanity. Which in turn fuels a greater connection and understanding of *others' humanity* as well.

> *"The only heart worth having is a broken heart."*
> – Michael Meade, storyteller, author, and scholar,
> referencing a piece of Irish folk wisdom.

THE MYTHOLOGICAL CHIRON

Let's introduce the mythological Chiron and the story of his death as a way to discuss the archetype of the Wounded Healer. This image, like many, sources in ancient Greece with the myth of the Centaur (half-man, half-horse) Chiron.

It is said Chiron was the immortal king/priest of the Centaurs, a race of beings half-man half-horse. He was born of Kronos or Saturn (son of Ouranus) and Phylria (an ocean nymph), though his 'legitimate' mother was Rhea or Cybele, the Great Mother Goddess. To mate with Phylria, Kronos had taken the form of a horse and so Chiron was born with the upper-half of man and the lower-half of horse. There is much rich meaning in this, but this paper is not the place to reiterate the work of others.[9] I suggest that the most relevant aspects to practically working with astrological Chiron is found in Chiron's 'death' which as we'll see was no normal death.

Chiron was a teacher, healer, astrologer, priest, warfare expert, musician and gymnast. Chiron was accidentally poisoned by his student Hercules (during his famous Labors) with a poisoned arrow Chiron himself had given Hercules (Chiron was Hercules' teacher among many others). Rather than fight back or take revenge, Chiron endured the pain for a very long time without dying for he was immortal. It was during this long period of personal suffering which Chiron studied and mastered the art of healing, which he later passed down to Asklepius and formed a healing temple, the Chironium.[10] He finally acquiesced to surrender his immortality on the agreement that Prometheus – the deity who had stolen fire and given it to mankind – would be released from his perpetual torture of having his liver eaten out by vultures for eternity. To do this, Chiron agreed to enter Hades (Underworld) to 'release the fire' (which Prometheus had stolen) of humanity's learning and to end Prometheus' suffering. The major variation to this tale has it that Chiron himself dropped a poisoned arrow on his own foot after seeing Prometheus' and humanity's need, setting the same results in motion.

THE WOUNDED HEALER

Chiron teaches that it is in an individual's courageous, self-responsible and honest aligning himself to his psychological (and sometimes physical) wound that determines his ability to 'bridge the worlds' of forgetfulness and remembering, between matter and spirit, between Soul and ego. This is perhaps the most powerful message in the myth for our times. Chiron *owned* his wound and ultimately devoted his life to the benefit of humanity that it should eventually learn to claim its own spiritual fire and to balance its animal and human natures. Indeed, an empowering way to frame the massive transformation of collective consciousness occurring on and in the planet now is to see all transformations as a radical attempt to *own one's own reality*; that is, to develop the energetic capacity to *include* every experience one has or has had, rather than discounting, blaming, victimizing, manipulating, or in any other way separating oneself from truth, or actual reality.

THE BEST STRATEGY

Chironic wisdom is altogether different than that gained through other outer planet initiations. It purports a strategy of complete surrender in order to most efficiently move through the experience. This will almost always produce a strong emotional component of helplessness, sorrow, sadness, and futility. This is quite difficult to accept for most western culture people as we are nearly universally addicted to *doing something* to fix the problem. Chiron suggests the opposite tack: *don't do anything*. It seems to tell us at those times, 'Only in fully giving in to the truth that your human life is predicated on separation will you find the inner clarity of how to transcend it.' Without doubt, there are those who are much more capable of moving with Chiron's effect in this way than others. For some, this will feel natural and perhaps familiar. For others, it is contrary to everything they've been taught in popular spiritual healing schools, personal growth programs, human development models, or psychological counseling. In my practice, I have witnessed clients achieve powerful and rather quick access to core wound issues using the wisdom of Chiron. With guidance, they can embrace and integrate the regained wholeness implied in their choice to incarnate.

CHIRON TIMINGS

Chiron's synodic return occurs at about age 50. Its orbit creates an exaggerated ellipse, producing a widely variable window for both Chiron squares and the Chiron opposition. Other possible triggers for the Chiron effect might be: transiting Chiron in catalyzing aspects with any natal Angle, Lunar Node, or personal planet, Pluto-Chiron or Saturn-Chiron aspects, or any involvement of a progressed planet with natal Chiron. This list is by no means exhaustive; there can be many other interactions of Chiron natally or by transit which can trigger a Chironic effect psychologically. Again, there has been much good statistical analysis of both natal and transiting Chiron's effect by astrologers for 20 years.

NOTES:

[1] Many see the current goal of human evolution to be the bridging of the worlds, the ushering of a new age which will require a radical purifying of this world's fallacious structures – both inner and outer. But this notion does not and should not support the summary homogenizing of 'realities' or worlds. We mustn't make the mistake of believing that an absence of diversity will produce harmony automatically. Likewise, an individual's psychic or telepathic gifts do not mean in any way they are more evolved than those without a strong 6th sense. For example, there are many individuals with great gifts at accessing other levels of reality in a variety of ways: communicating with 'the dead', shamanic (non-ordinary reality) healing, and prophetic visions. But do these gifts correlate in any direct way to the ability to be generous, to selflessly do for others, to be responsible, or to deeply receive love? We only need look back 25 years or so – to the rampant, unethical behavior in various guru-lead, spiritual communities – for an example of the potential distance between spiritual attainment and embodied maturity.

[2] Its discovery in 1977 bodes well for the collective consciousness bringing more awareness – more *knowing* – to how the Soul makes its inter-world transition. And for the last 28 years, many astrologers and others have done just that.

[3] Barbara Hand Clow, *Chiron: Rainbow Bridge Between the Inner & Outer Planets*, 1987; Melanie Reinhart, *Chiron and the Healing Journey*, 1999; and others.

[4] Carolyn Myss, the well-known medical intuitive, teacher and practical mystic coined the term 'woundology' in the mid 1990s to refer specifically to the pattern of egoically identifying with, energetically investing in and melodramatically perpetuating one's pain or woundedness, be it physical or otherwise. As the reader of this paper may well be aware, Ms. Myss' term and the sacred wound are fundamentally different. Where the former is a recent development in the last hundred

years due to the spiritual destitution of western culture, the latter reaches back to the earliest sources (1500-1300 BC) and touches on an inherently human archetypal pattern, regardless of a specific culture's emotional immaturity.

[5] I'm intrigued by the equal 9-month span of a human zygote preparing to be born and the post-partum 9-month span required for the wound to first occur. I offer the hypothesis that the wounding experience is itself the birth of the infant's autonomous consciousness, just as the physical departure from the womb is the birth of the infant's autonomous physicality.

[6] On more than a few occasions while working with a client and their Chironic condition, I've found myself pointing out that this new space or opening is inversely related to the gradual closing of the infant's anterior fontanelle – the baby's 'soft spot' at the top of the skull. An intriguing correlation arises: while the infant's inner sacred wound signifies an opening of consciousness, his/her outer fontanelle is actually a congealing or closing of the physical self. For me, this is poetry, a beautiful observation of life's dynamical balance and a potent example of *hieros gamos* or the unification of diverging impulses. Anecdotally, there are in fact two fontanelles at the top of the infant's head. The main one, an anterior diamond-shape, has been observed to considerably harden after *9 months of age!* (see endnote 5)

[7] I currently consider the initial opening of the infant's pre-conscious state to become physiologically expressed just below the occipital region (upper back of the neck, below the cranium). My working hypothesis is the break in the preconscious state will physiologically constellate around the base of the brain stem. There are many theoretical explanations for this, but most tend to rely on overly-esoteric guesswork. Because I have come to see that the stem's base is the locus of the most basic level of ego identity, I suggest the anatomical integrity of the upper cervical vertebrae with/into the cranium may correlate to the 'integrity' or relative integration of the initial wounding experience within consciousness, and thus within the body. I can also report a level of confidence in the notion that a client's back and neck pain can be accurately correlated with the natal condition of Chiron. Combining this with the natal chart conditions of Aries/Mars/1st House (head) and Taurus/Venus/2nd House (cervical spine), will give an accurate picture of the physiologic tendencies of those areas relative to the more subtle-energetic condition of the sacred wound.

Here is a suggestive image for the reader to meditate on or perhaps journey into: the area of and around the base of the brain is counterbalanced by the concavity of the cervical spine below and the rigid protective bone of the skull above. Where one is flexible, the other is fixed. Where one can respond fluidly, the other protects dogmatically. Their meeting point is a place of potential weakness, mitigated only by the strange sort of sacred marriage or dualistic balance within opposition achieved by its neighbors.

[8] Hopefully, this understanding will help counter much of the light-polarized and one-sided views of a wound as something to be 'fixed' or 'returned to balance.' It seems there is a well-hidden projection buried within these notions that physical life is meant to be without pain, without hurt and without separation! If this is so, how have thousands of traditional cultures for thousands of years spiritually flourished from the opposite position – that life in the *seen world* is intended to be challenging and filled with imperfections and hurt?

There are many outright symbols of this in indigenous wisdom. For example, it is thought in some cultures that breaking a hip is a precursor to Elderhood (quoted by Michael Meade of www.mosaicvoices.org). In many of the native North American Pueblo cultures, master ceramicists and potters will follow their culture's ancient tradition of in some way *imperfecting* a pot they may have spent months or years on. The idea behind this is a powerful bit of wisdom all but lost in 'modern' cultures. It says that this world in which humans live and die is an imperfect world. In order for us to live in this world, we need to first acknowledge this as truth and then go about discovering and re-discovering how to bring more beauty into this imperfect world of ours. The Navajo Dine' people refer to this as The Beauty Way. Only the *other world* holds the potential to be perfect or, at least, closer to perfect. So, if we humans create something so perfect in every way – in shape, color, texture, proportion, spiritual alignment, and wisdom-embodiment – be it art, a relationship, or an idea – there needs to be also something included that is in fact *imperfect* in order to **keep it in this world.** For without that flaw, our 'perfect' creation will disappear from this world and enter the other world, which as I've heard a traditional Elder say, 'is a shame cuz lord knows we need more beauty in this [world]... just look around [at] what we've done to Her [the Mother Earth].'

[9] Mythological texts covering the Chiron myth abound. Any decent Greek Myth title should do the trick, though it is always important to read mythological translations with a grain of salt culled from one's own salt-mine of discernment.

[10] In dream mythology and perhaps also in dream imagery, a broken bone, a deformity, a limp, or a handicap of some kind often indicates a type of Chironic wisdom. They often suggest that their bearer carries a special wisdom, a knowing of 'the other side' from which they've returned, or that they may be a guide, an initiator, a mentor or teacher to those who've not yet discovered their own wound or are not on the same path.

CHAPTER 16

QUICK STUDY AIDS

I
ASTROLOGICAL COMPONENTS

SIGNS	Aries, Taurus, Gemini, Cancer, Leo, Virgo, Libra, Scorpio, Sagittarius, Capricorn, Aquarius, Pisces	Specific domains of divine consciousness. They are essentially unknowable in their totality. In astrology, Sign energies are seen to emanate from/through specific domains of space located along the ecliptic. Signs are different than constellations which have their own frequency of influence and reflection for us. Signs are sometimes called 'Faces of the God or Goddess' in that they emanate divine intelligence into and for all other astrological components (below). *The center of any sign system in astrology is the Earth.*

PLANETS	Sun, Mercury, Venus, Moon, (Earth), Mars, Jupiter, Saturn, Uranus, Neptune, Pluto. Also, asteroids: Chiron, Pallas Athene, Juno, Ceres, Vesta, Hathor, Eros, Psyche, among many others.	Specific functions of the human body-mind. They exist on the level of our psyche and represent individual components of our psychological makeup. Their physical presence in physical space point to their specificity within us. They are the vehicles for the Sign energies to express through/as us. Together, planets comprise the full, multidimensional blueprint or strategy for realizing our Soul's Desire. When they are placed in a sign and house and aspected by other planets, they can point to our past lives, determine our physical attributes, reveal patterns of disease or delusion, identify our values and belief systems, and define our unique individuality. *The center of any planet system is the Earth* (in geocentric astrology).
HOUSES	1st through 12th	Specific, identifiable areas of life (ie., family, children, sex, work, etc.) Houses are the fields in which the 'sign-infused planets' manifest. They are areas of our external life in which things occur and also the areas of our inner life where things occur or become lodged internally. *The center of any house system is the individual.*

ANGLES	Ascendant (AC), Descendant (DC, Midheaven (MC), Lowheaven (IC)	Angles are the deeply personal and highly individualistic inner potentials in which the resolution of the psyche's conflicts are most intimately, authentically, and meaningfully embodied and actualized. The Angles provide the human organism with a dependable and consistent 'dimensional balance' for his/her centering. Angles can also be thought of as our personal aspirations for what we are meant to become and do. This alchemy necessarily contacts and engages the Self-Essence (Soul vibration). *The center of the Angular axies (usually depicted as a cross) is the individual.*
ASPECTS	Conjunction, Trine, Opposition, Square, Sextile, Septile, Quintile, Semi-Square, Sesqui-Square, Quincunx, and others.	The spatial distance (measured in degrees° of arc) between any two points (planets, asteroids, angles, nodes, etc.) Aspects reveal the highly personalized relationship between every facet of our psyche: harmonious, conflictual, non-effecting, catalyzing, stressful, non-stressful, etc. Aspects can also be thought of as alchemical processes individualizing each person's psychic structure; each aspect represents a different alchemical process. *The center of any combination of aspected planets is the individual in general, and his/her psyche in particular.*

LUNAR NODES	NorthNode of the Moon, SouthNode of the Moon	Technically, each Lunar Node is the hypothetical point in space created from the intersection of the Moon's orbital path around the Earth with the ecliptic. The South Node represents our karmic past and the North Node represents our karmic (Soul-intended) destiny. *The center or 'midpoint' of any pair of North and South Node is without doubt the individual in general, and the individual's Soul's path of evolution in particular.*

II
SIGN GROWTH IMPULSES

SIGN	GLYPH	GROWTH IMPULSE	CONSCIOUSNESS DEVELOPMENT
ARIES	♈	to live	Engaging in life experience to discover authentic Desire.
TAURUS	♉	to entrust	Embracing physicality as inwardly and outwardly supportable and self-sustaining; stabilizing in oneself.
GEMINI	♊	to understand	Developing left-brain function to successfully participate in physical existence; exploring duality.
CANCER	♋	to feel	Forming an independent self; nurturing life; developing emotional awareness/maturity.
LEO	♌	to create	Learning and radiating self-love; developing capacity to create.
VIRGO	♍	to devote	Developing self-accuracy; devoting the self to selflessness; performing a greater function.

LIBRA	♎	to relate	Exploring 'other' as mirror/ window into the self; learning harmony/balance through exploration of extremes.
SCORPIO	♏	to empower	Effectively aligning one's will with the force of creation; developing the power to transform oneself.
SAGITTARIUS	♐	to know	Seeking and expanding into higher intelligence (spirituality); learning to connect to a greater reality.
CAPRICORN	♑	to lead	Appropriate application of wisdom/authority/ responsibility; effectively managing within the constraints of time and space.
AQUARIUS	♒	to improve	Commitment to innovating impassioned change with detachment; learning to bridge between consciousnesses.
PISCES	♓	to unify	Evolution of the personal space to empathically merge with all; developing awareness of actual reality/Truth.

III
PLANET GROWTH IMPULSES

PLANET	GLYPH	DOMAIN
SUN	☉	Persona, Personality, Life Current, Charisma, Creativity, Sexuality.
MOON	☽	Self-Identity, Ego, Nurturing, Protection, Subconscious, Personal Love, Mother, Parents.
MERCURY	☿	Cognition, Inner Reality, Left-Brain, Communication, Modes of Learning and Thinking.
VENUS	♀	Femininity, Environment-relatedness, Receptivity, Values, Instinctual Feeling, Self-Stability.
VENUS	♀	Femininity, Relatedness, Interactive Balance, Relationships.
MARS	♂	Masculinity, Desire, Willpower, Instinctual Action, Self-Assertion.
VESTA	⚶	Commitment, Self-Control, Devoted Service, Work Ethic, Sacred Space, Self-Improvement.
JUPITER	♃	Intuition, Higher Intelligence, Right-Brain, Personal Truth, Spirituality Seeking, Connection to Greater Reality.
SATURN	♄	Definability, Strength, Structuredness, Mass Consciousness, Authority, Rules, Father.

CHIRON	⚷	Wound, Medicine, Separation/Wholeness, Initiations, Healing/Teaching Service for Others.
URANUS	♅	Growth in Consciousness, Personal Unconscious, Liberation, Originality, Freedom, Inventiveness, Electricity.
NEPTUNE	♆	Union, Disillusionment, Actual Truth, Death, Collective Unconsciousness, Transmigration, Unknown.
PLUTO	♇	Soul Uniqueness, Lack, 'Shadow', Transmutation, Depths, Domain of Empowerments.

IV
SIGN/PLANET/HOUSE FORMULAE

The basic idea that each sign/planet/house combination provides the full picture of one of twelve domains of consciousness can greatly assist our astrological interpretations. Each of the twelve "formulae" lay out how to interpret a birth chart with this level of comprehensiveness for each of the twelve. In essence, we frame the entire chart to examine each domain. Let's look at an example, using the relevant formula for Aquarius/Uranus/11th House and this sample chart:

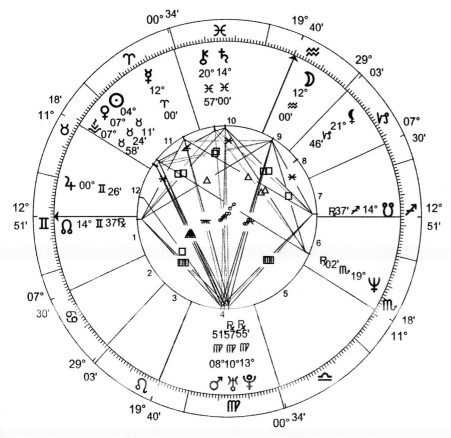

First, here's the formula*:

The sign(s) on the 11th House, its planetary ruler; the house(s) that Aquarius occupies; any planets in Aquarius or in the 11th house and their prominent aspects; and the house, sign and prominent aspects of Uranus.

Now examine our sample chart on the previous page to track along with the following identifications:.

The Sign(s) on the 11th House:	Aries and Taurus
(their) planetary ruler(s):	Mars (Ruler of Aries) in Virgo in the 4th House conjunct Uranus and Pluto, and Venus (Ruler of Tauras) in Taurus in the 11th House conjunct the Sun and Vesta;
the House(s) that Aquarius occupies:	9th and 10th;
any planets in Aquarius:	Moon;
...and their prominent aspects:	Moon sextile SouthNode and Mercury; Moon quincunx Mars, Uranus, and Pluto; and Moon square Venus and Vesta;
any planets in 11th House:	Mercury in Aries, Sun in Taurus, Venus in Taurus, and Vesta in Taurus;
...and their prominent aspects:	Mercury quincunx to Mars, Uranus and Pluto; Sun conjunct Venus and Vesta and trine Mars; Venus conjunct Vesta and trine Mars; Vesta conjunct Venus and trine Mars;

and the house and sign (of Uranus): Uranus in Virgo in 4th house,
...and prominent aspects of Uranus: Uranus conjunct Pluto and Mars,
Uranus opposite Saturn, Uranus square NorthNode, and Uranus trine Vesta, Venus and the Sun.

Theoretically, we can perform this combination-by-combination delineation of the sign, house, and aspect indicators for *all twelve* combinations when preparing a chart, but this will produce unnecessary complexity and inhibit our intuitive instincts. But using this formula as an exercise to strengthen our identification of the many different yet related factors on the birth chart is more tenable. In practice, each formula is best utilized to thoroughly illuminate one of the twelve domains of consciousness in its fullness and depth.

* For any other sign/planet/house combination, simply substitute the appropriate sign, planet and house.

SMA SIGN/PLANET/HOUSE COMBINATIONS

ARIES

Engaging in life experience to discover authentic Desire.

The signs on the 1st House, their planetary rulers; the houses that Aries occupies; any planets in Aries or in the 1st House and their prominent aspects; and the house, sign, and prominent aspects of Mars all signify our Masculine nature, how we (are meant to) act on our Soul's Desire, how we experience our own autonomous existence, and how we engage our will in the world.

TAURUS

Embracing physicality as inwardly and outwardly supportable and self-sustaining; stabilizing in oneself.

The signs on the 2nd House, their planetary rulers; the houses that Taurus occupies; any planets in Taurus or in the 2nd house and their prominent aspects; and the house, sign, and prominent aspects of Venus signify how we stabilize ourselves and interact with our physicality, what our personal values are, and the nature of our instinctual drives to perpetuate our life (procreation, survival, etc.)

GEMINI

Developing left-brain function to successfully participate in physical existence; cognitively exploring duality.

The signs on the 3rd House, their planetary rulers; the houses that Gemini occupies; any planets in Gemini or in the 3rd House and their prominent aspects; and the house, sign, and prominent aspects of Mercury signify the nature of our cognitive function – how we perceive phenomena, how we learn, and our intellectual "relationship" or level of understanding of our environment. In other words, the inner cognitive reality formed from the outer, environmental reality.

CANCER

Forming an independent self; nurturing life; developing emotional awareness/ maturity.

The signs on the 4th House, their planetary rulers; the houses that Cancer occupies; any planets in Cancer or in the 4th house and their prominent aspects; and the house, sign, and prominent aspects of the Moon signify the current life ego structure and definitions, its emotional needs and patterns, the implied relationship with our beginnings, the type and mode of ego resistance, and the level and quality of our identity-autonomy.

LEO

Learning and radiating self-love; developing the capacity to create.

The signs on the 5th House, their planetary rulers; the houses that Leo occupies; any planets in Leo or in the 5th house and their prominent aspects; and the house, sign, and prominent aspects of the Sun signify our innate sense of purpose, creative vitality and expression, how/who we desire to be seen as, and the general quality of our energy radiance (charisma) and self-love. In other words, how we are meant to realize ourselves through our creative action in the world.

VIRGO

Developing self-accuracy; devoting the self to selflessness; performing a greater function.

The signs on the 6th House, their planetary rulers; the houses that Virgo occupies; any planets in Virgo or in the 6th house and their prominent aspects; and the house, sign, and prominent aspects of Vesta and/or Mercury (depending on which you use) all signify the issues around and intensity of our critical self-awareness or analysis, our receptivity to taking criticism, our level of humility, our path toward self-accuracy, our devotion to a higher function, and ultimately our deep self-acceptance.

LIBRA

Exploring "other" as mirror/window into the self; learning harmony/balance through exploration of extremes.

The signs on the 7th House, their planetary rulers; the houses that Libra occupies; any planets in Libra or in the 7th house and their prominent aspects; and the house, sign, and prominent aspects of Venus signify how, why and with whom we engage in purposeful, contributory relationships of all kinds, how we contribute to and receive from our significant others (intimates, friends, colleagues, etc.), and the qualities we look to develop within ourselves through the archetype of relating with others.

SCORPIO

Effectively aligning one's will with the force of creation; developing the power to transform oneself.

The signs on the 8th House, their planetary rulers; the houses that Scorpio occupies; any planets in Scorpio or in the 8th house and their prominent aspects; and the house, sign, and prominent aspects of Pluto signify in general the nature of our transformational intent in the current life or, cumulatively, what our limitations are, how we are meant to transform or metamorphosize them and what wisdom is meant to be gained. And on the level of the Soul, these signatures indicate what the current life represents within the larger Soul's Desire, or the Soul's evolutionary intention larger than just the current life.

SAGITTARIUS

Seeking and expanding into higher intelligence (spirituality); learning to connect to a greater reality.

The signs on the 9th House, their planetary rulers; the houses that Sagittarius occupies; any planets in Sagittarius or in the 9th house and their prominent aspects; and the house, sign, and prominent aspects of Jupiter signify the domain in which and how we seek a personal connection to a greater reality in order to reveal our deeper truth (spiritual path), including our religious/spiritual past and present, intuitive functioning and interest in broader ideas, meanings and cultures.

CAPRICORN

Appropriate application of wisdom, authority, and responsibility; effectively managing or operating within the constraints of time and space.

The signs on the 10th House, their planetary rulers; the houses that Capricorn occupies; any planets in Capricorn or in the 10th house and their prominent aspects; and the house, sign, and prominent aspects of Saturn signify our entire participation with the explicit collective consciousness personally and socially; our current-life intent for realizing self-authority; our contribution to society through an improved inner balance of social need and personal desire; and how we manage our lives in all practical ways within the constraints of time, space, and the mortality of our body.

AQUARIUS

Commitment to innovating impassioned change with detachment; learning to bridge between consciousnesses.

The signs on the 11th House, their planetary rulers; the houses that Aquarius occupies; any planets in Aquarius or in the 11th House and their prominent aspects; and the house, sign, and prominent aspects of Uranus signify our personal unconscious; the patterns, attachments, associations, and idealisms which we strive to free ourselves from; the new visions, understandings, and social forms which we are uniquely capable of coalescing or manifesting for the collective, and those others with whom we share friendship or similar vision.

PISCES

Evolution of the personal space to empathically merge with all; developing awareness of actual reality/truth.

The signs on the 12th House, their planetary rulers; the houses that Pisces occupies; any planets in Pisces or in the 12th house and their prominent aspects; and the house, sign, and prominent aspects of Neptune signify our tie to the collective unconsciousness; where and how we intend to become more real and truthful, to enlarge our reality, and to expand into a fuller connection with all of life or consciousness.

V
ASTROLOGICAL GLYPHS

Glyphs are a fascinating subject to explore. The astrological glyphs, especially those for the Planets, are of particular interest to me because they literalize the Planet's meaning in graphical form. These icons transcend descriptions. What many people overlook in the glyphs is the language of *gematria*, the ancient, intuitive science of sacred geometry which seeks to understand cosmic principles through symbol, shape and proportion. Much can be learned about the planets, signs and aspects by intuitively opening and journeying into the innate intelligence of a glyph.

SIGN GLYPHS

In general, the glyphs used to signify the Signs are more literal than those of the planets. This is because the astrological Signs (and their glyphs) actually emanate from the earlier study of star patterns, or constellations. These pre-Greek civilizations would name each star pattern with a familiar animal. This practice got transferred to the Signs when they were conceived of by the earliest Greek astrologers.

This created a very interesting dilemma; namely, the names and glyphs for the Signs refer, not to the Signs themselves, but to their ancestors, the star patterns or constellations. While this in no way undermines the reality of the Sign energies, it does enter us into the unique situation of using ancient glyphs to refer to something today which they were not intended to refer to (because Signs had not yet been formulated). Perhaps the point can be stated like this: as long as we are aware that the Sign glyphs of astrology point to constellations and not to Signs, we can make a conscious choice whether to continue to do so or change course. I continue to hold the opinion that what we currently refer to as 'Signs' in astrology will be evolving into something new. We will see them more as ineffable Faces of

Divine Consciousness and less as being tied to the star patterns in the sky. For more about the difference between Signs and constellations, see chapter 3.

ARCHETYPE	GLYPH	CONSTELLATION REFERENCE†	POSSIBLE OCCULT MEANING ‡
ARIES	♈	Head or horns of the Ram.	The strength required for coming into life. Fully engaging in duality.
TAURUS	♉	Head and horns of the Bull.	Wide receptivity from many sources to procreate life.
GEMINI	♊	Twins or Siblings.	Through the double gate of Above-Below and Past-Future.
CANCER	♋	'Backward-moving' Crab.	Female breasts or fallopian tubes. Completing, or rounding out the development of identity. Foundations ability to cultivate.
LEO	♌	Head, mane and tail of the Lion.	Male sperm. Generating out of the vortex of oneself one's creations.
VIRGO	♍	Harvest goddess holding grain (Demeter or Ceres).	Earth's fertility (above the glyph's baseline) and the journey of the male consort or Persephone into the Underworld (below the baseline – not shown in this glyph). The fruit of self-accuracy.

LIBRA	♎	Scales measuring balance.	The Sun (light of individuality) setting below the horizon, or the Sun (light of partnership) rising out of the horizon.
SCORPIO	♏	The body and stinger of the Scorpion.	The force of transformation causing death and new life.
SAGITTARIUS	♐	The aimed bow and arrow of the Archer.	Seeking higher attainments.
CAPRICORN	♑	Mountain Goat with tail of a fish.	The stamina (goat) required to gain true wisdom (fish tail).
AQUARIUS	♒	Water flowing out of the Water-Carrier's vessel.	The unimpeded flow of information; direct knowing or clairgnosis.
PISCES	♓	Two swimming Fish connected by a cord.	The One Truth is threaded through all things.

† *These are the literal translations of each glyph. They are undisputed among astrologers and astronomers. Each refers directly to its associated constellations (star patterns).*

‡ *These meanings are speculative. They arise from within our post-modern context and thus are subjective.*

PLANET GLYPHS

Compared to the glyphs for the Signs, the planet glyphs are more esoterically oriented as they are more vibrationally aligned to the ancient *gematria* in which the symbol carried the entirety of the message. This does not go to say however that we cannot bring out our own interpretations of the Sign glyphs which transcend their usually literal references to animals (again, harkening back to the ancients labeling the star patterns as animals – ie., the glyph for Aries clearly suggests its associated constellation, the Ram). A well-developed intuition can pick up on valid and powerful esoteric or occult information from the Sign glyphs just waiting to be discovered! But if we want to tap into an ancient language of iconographic symbol – and practice our skill with *gematria* – we must look to the Planet glyphs.

COMPONENT SYMBOLS FOR PLANETARY GLYPHS

Each of the planet glyphs are created from 3 primary symbols: a Cross, a Crescent, and a Circle. These symbols are described here:

SYMBOL	NAME	MEANING
+	Cross of Matter	Earth, matter, form, identity, knowable. Creates dimensional balance.
‿	Crescent of Soul	Soul, essence, life perpetually evolving.
O	Circle of Spirit	Spirit, origin, ineffable. All That Is. Nondual source of consciousness.

One interesting note in this regard. I have observed that two different pairs of planets which are widely seen as embodying clear polarity between each other – Venus and Mars, and Jupiter and Saturn – also share the same base components in their glyphs. The glyphs for Venus and Mars are made up of only a Circle of Spirit and a Cross of Matter, while those for Jupiter and Saturn are formed from *only* a Cross of Matter and a Crescent of Soul. In both cases, the only major difference between each is that they are vertically flipped: the Mars glyph has its Cross over its Circle, while the Venus glyph has its Circle on top. And while Jupiter has its Crescent to the left and above its Cross, Saturn has its Crescent to the right and below its Cross.

GLYPH	PLANET	SYMBOLS	MEANING
☉	Sun	Circle of Spirit with centered Point of Manifestation	*[Centered dot is the human life-spark]* Current of light- or life-force moving through us which is visible by others. Vital principle of self-awareness and 'centered-in-selfness'.
☽	Moon	Crescent of Soul	Crescent represents individual identity, yet un-connected to matter or spirit, so it resides in the largely undefined waters of the subconscious.
☿	Mercury	Crescent of Soul on top of Circle of Spirit on top of Cross of Matter.	All 3 in right relationship with each other. Hermes' winged helmet atop Spirit-and-Matter in right relationship. Triumvirate of reality creation: perceiving, then processing/understanding, then communicating or expressing (creation). *NOTE: Glyphs for Venus and Moon combine to form the glyph for Mercury*
♀	Venus	Circle of Spirit on top of Cross of Matter.	Spirit pours into expression, creating beauty. Spirit-and-matter in right relationship. Crescent of Soul is missing, so Soul knowing isn't present. *Lesson:* Femininity's foundation is matter; its mastery is spirit; its action is condensing/descending/interiorizing. *Esoteric:* Galactic Core itself. This glyph was the original glyph for Isis which later became the Egyptian Ankh.

♂	Mars	*Slanted Cross of Matter* on top of Circle of Spirit.	Circle of Spirit underneath Cross of Matter (without the slant) refers to the ascension of Spirit, the highest goal and actual nature of the Masculine. The path this realization takes is seen in the slanted Cross, suggesting an energetic imbalance or incompleteness which motivates the incessant searching externally for that balance or completion. *Lesson:* Masculinity's foundation is spirit; its mastery is form; its action is expanding. *Esoteric:* pointing to/searching toward Galactic Core.
♃	Jupiter	Crescent of Soul connected onto Cross of Matter.	Unbinding the Soul from matter. Engendering Soul essence from deep within matter. Seeking what is beyond matter or the wisdom arising from the maturation of matter.
♄	Saturn	Cross of Matter on top of Crescent of Soul.	Containing the Soul in matter, or defining/expressing the Soul in form. Striving to define the Soul/essence/the timeless through an expression. The Soul seeks right manifestation of itself.

♅	Uranus	Cross of Matter in between two Crescents of Soul and on top of Circle of Spirit.	1. *Cross between two Crescents:* Manifestation into form originates from Soul intent. Identity results from essence. Essence requires matter (essence guides matter). Evolution through the vehicle of individual incarnation. *Alternate:* Matter/form/identity is formed from choice. 2. *This triad above Circle:* All Souls begin, remain, and end as spirit. Spirit foundations (Soul) evolution. Spirit sources all knowledge.
⚷	Chiron	A Centaur (half-human and half-horse); a Key; or first letter of discoverer's last name (Kowal)	The 'K' is a half Cross of Matter: wholeness cannot be attained from the visible (world of form) only. Backbone of Cross extending and disappearing into a Circle of Spirit: A 'wholed' heart requires knowledge of the invisible.
♆	Neptune	Crescent of Soul encompassing an upward-extending Cross of Matter.	Crescent facing upwards: wide receptivity to collective. Upward-extending Cross: matter seeks its origin. Crescent on top of Cross: Soul surrounds and penetrates all matter, and is not bound by it. (Origin of matter is within itself) *Esoteric:* Trinity of matter, Soul and their alchemy.

Glyph			
♇	Pluto	Crescent of Soul on top of Cross of Matter. Circle of Spirit within Crescent of Soul.	Soul dominates and interpenetrates all matter and hides spirit (All That Is) within itself.
☊	North-Node of the Moon	The exterior half of the Moon's orbit, relative to the ecliptic. *(Small circles are points of intersection.)*	Current or intended realization of Self-Identity.
☋	South-Node of the Moon	The interior half of the Moon's orbit, relative to the ecliptic. *(Small circles are points of intersection.)*	Prior karmic Self-Identity.

ASPECT GLYPHS

Aspects describe specific qualities of energetic dynamics between two or more components in relationship of any kind.

GLYPH	ASPECT	MEANINGS
☌	Conjunction (0°)	'Togetherness' or 'as one.' Implies a beginning, an alchemy, pre-conscious transformation, a conception or birth. Inward.

☍	Opposition (180°)	'Diameter.' Experience of conjunction outwardly (with 'other'). Pulling away effect to create higher/more durable balance. Dynamic tension.
□	Square (90°)	Structuring, containing, forcing definition or resolution, strengthening.
△	Trine (120°)	Duality + the magical third = harmony. Ease of action and lack of difficulty.
✱	Sextile (60°)	Diameters of a hexagon. Ease of action and lack of difficulty with less awareness than the trine.
∠	Semisquare (45°)	One-half a 90° angle.
⬚	Sesqui-square (135°)	One and one-half a 90° angle.
S	Septile (51°)	'S' for septile.
Q	Quintile (72°)	'Q' for quintile.

There are many more insights waiting to be discovered from intuitively and playfully exploring astrology's glyphs!

VI
SIGN TRIGGERS[1]

Another way to explore the sign energies is through one's right-brain, intuitive function. In the list below, the image-descriptions described after each glyph can trigger a visual, experiential journey *into* the sign energies themselves. This requires trust and an ability to follow the energetic cues of the images. There is no right and wrong with this method; there is only *your experience*.

To practice this method of attunement: sit or lay quietly and center yourself. Bring your awareness to the center of your heart and allow your breath to deepen of its own accord, gently. Once you feel ready, simply speak out loud the relevant description you've chosen to work with and allow your 'journey' to begin and lead you where it will. Allow the energetic qualities of the scenes and sensations you experience to impress into you. Allow yourself to trust what comes. It is you.

♈	Rebar unfurling to straightness
♉	The loss of time for the gain of love
♊	Laughing music is my lead dance partner
♋	Squares losing their corners
♌	Whirling sands become a crown
♍	Large tables to lay out maps
♎	A crooked dangling earring in a beautiful display

NOTES

♏   Stone breaking, then adorning a crown like jewels

♐   Pristine change of a C- to an A

♑   Returning with a wider view

♒   Groundhogs brushing each others' teeth

♓   Inside a spiraling slinky

NOTES:

[1] I was originally introduced to this way of exploring energy by Christopher Emmer or Excalibur in his work with the Mayan Sacred Calendar.

VII
GLOSSARY OF TERMS

Conscious Embodied awareness; self-awareness aligned with
cognizance.

Consciousness Total 'material' and/or context of a human being's awareness,
as distinct from the particular quality or level of an individual's
conscious-ness.

Context "Placing knowledge within a particular view of the world to release
meaning." (Michael Meade)

Dissociation The condition resulting from the Self-Identity's un-inhabiting
of specific domains of its otherwise indigenous experience, such as
emotional vulnerability, memory of its past, social notoriety, or
healthy awareness of one's physicality. Dissociation occurs entirely
within the psyche and effectively removes the ego's center of gravity
from any threatening experience. This creates a faux presence as the
majority of the individual's attention is elsewhere engaged.

Initiation A cellular-altering experience.

Integrity A substantive depth of alignment.

Objectivity (Objective Consciousness) The general impulse or function of
consciousness which initially separates the self from its direct
experience, and ultimately reunites the self with the Soul.
Objectivity is the entire context for an individual's experience
of *Self-Essence.*

Phenomena Objects that appear and can be observed by our physical
senses; or, 'things as they appear to us.' [Contrast this with *noumena*,
or *the thing itself, its essence or* de facto *existence, separate from how it
arises or is observed.*]

Sacred Marriage The unifying of opposites. 'Sacred' implies *alignment* with
larger forces including time, cosmos, and evolution, and
'Marriage' implies the *alchemical transformation* into something

'new', and not possible through a simple combining of the parts.

Self-Essence or Soul That which persist throughout incarnations, the individual spark of God-light, the deep, autonomous and identifying uniqueness or essence of a being, separate from any concept or belief *about* it. In SMA, the Soul is alternately known as *Self-Essence*. Connecting the notion of essence to the Soul is a useful tool, because the Soul is not fixed in time or to a certain incarnation. Rather, it is self-originating and self-perpetuating as it emanates throughout space-time dimensions *simultaneously*. It is pure consciousness at a specific frequency or vibration. From the standpoint of undifferentiated consciousness (God), the Soul is an individuated expression of that unity, a light traveler guided only by its growth needs which get met through the incarnational lessons. Throughout its experience in a life, the Soul retains its essential nature and oneness with God. Regardless of how much the Identity remembers of it, the Soul remains the Soul. And as all Souls are whole, they forever remain whole. They all emanate from the same source – God – and are thus synchronized in all times and dimensions with every other Soul. It can only be this way as there is nothing in existence which is not part of existence, or God.

Self-Identity or Identity The main structure within the psyche that orients and maintains subjective consciousness in order to consciously participate in its ongoing evolution. The ego, the persona, the physical body-mind, and one's Karmic patterns are components of the Self-Identity.

Social Environment Any outward, expressed context involving an Other either internally created or externally experienced in which an individual or a self operates, lives, or interacts.

Soul's Desire The evolutionary impulse. The urging of the unmanifest for manifestation. The 'intensely erotic' will within consciousness for experience of itself. That which motivates a Soul-uniqueness to reincarnate. The longing for Self. The realization of the Soul's Desire is loosely called 'life purpose' or 'personal destiny.' While these phrases are accurate, they are formulated from within a different level of self than the Soul, the Self-Identity, and thus their focus is on the individual.

Subjectivity (Subjective Consciousness) The general impulse or function within consciousness to experience self, other and the world from the singular context of the self. How we experience ourselves within a larger (different) context (i.e. other, society, world, universe, etc.) as an independent agent. Subjectivity is the entire context for an individual's *Self-Identity*.

Subconscious(ness) Domain of the psyche 'below' the level of conscious awareness and therefore not immediately accessible by the conscious awareness.

Unconscious(ness) Area of the psyche not known to exist to the self's normal awareness.

BIBLIOGRAPHY & SUGGESTED READING

Listed alphabetically by author last name.

ASTROLOGY

John Addey, *Harmonics in Astrology*, 1976.

Stephen Arroyo, *Astrology, Psychology & the Four Elements*, 1979.

Tamsyn Barton, *Ancient Astrology*, 1994.

Dr. Philip S. Berg, *Astrology, The Star Connection*, 1986.

Bernadette Brady, *Brady's Book of Fixed Stars*, 1998.

Geoffrey Cornelius, *The Moment of Astrology*, 1994.

Michaël Delmar, *Symbols of Astrology*, 2000.

Rabbi Joel C. Dobin, D.D., *Kabbalistic Astrology*, 1999.

Zipporah Dobyns, *The Node Book*, 1973.

Maurice Fernandez, *Neptune, The 12th House and Pisces*, 2004.

Steven Forrest, *Measuring the Night*, 2000.

------------------, *The Book of Pluto*, 1994.

Adam Gainsburg, *The Mars & Venus Journeys: Empowering our Collective Strength*, (forthcoming in 2006).

--------------------, *The Soul's Desire & the Evolution of Identity: Pluto & the Lunar Nodes in Sacred Marriage Astrology*, 2005.

--------------------, *Medicine-Making through Chiron: The Evolution of the Sacred Wound*, 2005.

Daniel Giamario & Carolyn Brent, *Shamanic Astrology Handbook*, 1995.

Rupert Gleadow, *The Origin of the Zodiac*, 1968.

Jeffrey Wolf Green, *Pluto, The Evolutionary Journey of the Soul (Vol. I)*, 1985.

------------------------, *Pluto, The Soul's Evolution Through Relationships (Vol. II)*, 1997.

Robert Hand, *Horoscope Symbols*, 1981.

-----------------, *Planets in Transit*, 1976.

David Hayward, *Shorthand of the Soul*, 1999.

Max Heindel, *Rosicrucian Cosmo-Conception*, 1937.

Isabel M. Hickey, *Astrology, A Cosmic Science*, 1992.

NOTES

James Hillman & Liz Green, *The Alchemical Sky*, 2005.

Ralph William Holden, *The Elements of House Division*, 1977.

Richard Houck, *The Astrology of Death*, 1994.

Bruno & Louise Huber, *The Astrological Houses*, 1978.

Hermann Hunger & David Pingree, *Astral Sciences in Mesopotamia*, 1999.

Robert Jansky, *Astrology, Nutrition & Health*, 1977.

Alan Leo, *The Complete Dictionary of Astrology*, 1983.

Kaldera, *MythAstrology*, 2004.

Dona Marie Lorenz, *Tools of Astrology: Houses*, 1973.

John Mini, *Day of Destiny*, 1998.

Eileen Nauman, *Medical Astrology*, 1982.

Linda Reid, *Crossing the Threshold*, 1997.

Dane Rudhyar, *The Astrological Houses*, 1972.

------------------, *The Astrology of Personality*, 1990.

Franco Santoro, *Astroshamanism book 1*, 2003.

------------------, *Astroshamanism book 2*, 2003.

Howard Sasportas, *The Twelve Houses*, 1985.

Martin Schulman, *Karmic Astrology – Retrogrades & Reincarnation*, 1977.

Jan Spiller, *Astrology for the Soul*, 1997.

Jan Spiller & Karen McCoy, *Spiritual Astrology*, 1990.

Erin Sullivan, *Retrograde Planets*, 2000.

Bill Tierney, *Dynamics of Aspect Analysis*, 1983.

Carol Payne Tobey, *Astrology of Inner Space*, 1973.

Noel Tyl, *Solar Arcs*, 2001.

-----------, *Astrological Timing of Critical Illness*, 1998.

ASTRONOMY

Richard Hinkley Allen, *Star Names, Their Lore and Meaning*, 1963.

Geoffrey Cornelius, *The Starlore Handbook*, 1997.

Giorgio De Santillana & Hertha Von Dechend, *Hamlet's Mill*, 1969.

Michael Gill, *The Mysterious Signs of the Zodiac*, 2002.

Hermann Hunger & David Pingree, *Astral Sciences in Mesopotamia*, 1999.

J. Norman Lockyer, *Dawn of Astronomy*, 1869?.

Joachim Schultz, *Movement and Rhythms of the Stars*, 1963.

POETRY

Robert Bly, James Hillman, Michael Meade, eds., *The Rag and Bone Shop of the*

Heart, 1992.

Coleman Barks, *The Soul of Rumi*, 2001.

Daniel Landinsky, *The Gift: Poems by Hafiz, The Great Sufi Master*, 1999.

------------------, *Drunk on the Wine of the Beloved*, 2001.

DEPTH MASCULINITY

Robert Bly, James Hillman & Michael Meade, *Men and the Life of Desire*, 1991. (audio)

Adam Gainsburg, *Bridges of Union: The Archetypes of Masculine & Feminine Transformation*, (forthcoming in 2006).

Daniel J. Levinson, *The Seasons of a Man's Life*, 1978.

Michael Meade, *Men and the Water of Life*, 1993.

------------------, *When Men Went One Way and Women Went the Other*, 1994. (audio)

Eugene Monick, *Phallos: Sacred Image of the Masculine*, 1987.

------------------, *Castration and Male Rage*, 1997.

Gregory Max Vogt, *Return to Father*, 1991.

James Hollis, *Under Saturn's Shadow*, 1994.

Graham Jackson, *The Secret Lore of Gardening*, 1991.

Deldon Anne McNeely, *Animus Aeternus*, 1991.

DEPTH FEMININITY

Joseph Campbell, *The Hero with a Thousand Faces*, 1949.

Joan Engelsman, *The Feminine Dimension of the Divine*, 1979.

Adam Gainsburg, *Bridges of Union: The Archetypes of Masculine & Feminine Transformation*, (forthcoming in 2006).

Daniel J. Levinson, *The Seasons of a Woman's Life*, 1996.

Michael Meade, *When Men Went One Way and Women Went the Other*, 1994. (audio)

Betty de Shong Meador, *Inanna, Lady of the Largest Heart*, 2001.

Maureen Murdock, *The Heroine's Journey*, 1991.

Sylvia Perera, *Descent to the Goddess*, 1981.

Nancy Qualls-Corbett, *The Sacred Prostitute*, 1988.

Cynthia Eller, *The Myth of Matriarchal Prehistory*, 2000.

PSYCHOLOGY

Aldo Carotenuto, *Eros and Pathos*, 1989.

NOTES

John P. Dourley, *Love, Celibacy and the Inner Marriage*, 1987.

Thom F. Cavalli, Ph.D., *Alchemical Psychology*, 2002.

Edward Edinger, *Anatomy of the Psyche*, 1994.

James Hillman, *Dream & the Underworld*, 1997.

James Hollis, *The Eden Project*, 1998.

ALCHEMY

Thom F. Cavalli, Ph.D., *Alchemical Psychology*, 2002.

Mantak Chia & Michael Winn, *Taoist Secrets of Love*, 1984.

Harriett Augusta Curtiss & F. Homer Curtiss, *Key of Destiny*, 1919.

Edward Edinger, *Anatomy of the Psyche*, 1994.

Carl Jung, *Psychology & Alchemy*, 1968.

Tom Kenyon, *Mind Thieves*, 2001.

-----------------, *The Magdalen Manuscript*, 2004.

Adam McLean, *http://levity.com/alchemy/*.

Jay Weidner and Vincent Bridges, *Monument to the End of Time*, 1999.

OTHER

Manly P. Hall, *The Secret Teachings of All Ages*, 1988.

Don Handelman & David Shulman, *God Inside Out: Siva's Game of Dice*, 1997.

Dr. Ernest Klein, *Klein's Comprehensive Etymological Dictionary of the English Language*, 1971.

Robert Lawlor, *Sacred Geometry Philosophy & Practice*, 1982.

James M. Robinson (ed.), *The Nag Hammadi Library*, 1978.

Robert Ullman & Judyth Reichenberg-Ullman, *Mystics, Masters, Saints, and Sages*, 2001.

SMA Areas of Exploration

To explore any class or title below, visit www.SacredMarriageAstrology.com

SUBJECT	TITLE	NOTES
Sacred Marriage Astrology	"Journey through the Wheel of Consciousness: Signs, Planets, Houses, & Angles in SMA" (classes, CDs)	
	The Soul's Desire & the Evolution of Identity: Pluto & the Lunar Nodes in Sacred Marriage Astrology (book)	
	"Medicine-Making Through Chiron: The Evolution of the Sacred Wound" (book, classes, CDs)	
	"The Two Modes of Identity" (class)	
	The Mars & Venus Journeys: Empowering Our Collective Strength (forthcoming book)	
	"Complete LifeCycle Ephemeris" (pamphlet, software)	
	"Mars & Venus Journey Ephemeredes" (pamphlet, software)	

NOTES

"A Case for Clockwise Houses"
(essay)

"The Rules of this Game: The Astrological
Mandala as the Medicine Wheel of Life"
(essay)

** Other courses, classes and workshops are
offered periodically.*

Masculinity & Femininity

"The Archetypes of Masculine
& Feminine Transformation"
(workshop)

*Bridges of Union: The Archetypes
Masculine & Feminine Transformation*
(forthcoming book)

"Plumbing the Depths, Soaring the Heights:
The Transforming Feminine & Masculine"
(class, CDs)

"An Emerging Myth of the Masculine"
(storytelling) (CD)

The Mars & Venus Journeys
(book)

The Sacred Marriage

"Renewing Our Vows:
The Timeless Sacred Marriage"
(essay)

"The Sacred Marriage Alchemy Meditation"
(guided meditation CD)

About Sacred Marriage Astrology

The name 'Sacred Marriage' derives from the ancient ritual of annually renewing the human connection to the Divine. This was done through re-enactments of the symbolic Marriage of the Goddess with the God, which was believed to ensure a greater wholeness within individuals and a greater bond with the forces of creation.

Sacred Marriage Astrology is an open integration of the astrological mysteries, ancient wisdom traditions, depth psychology and evocative mythology. SMA's intent is to counsel, educate and promote the transfer of unconscious and unrealized energy into valid pathways of self-discovery and alignment.

Sacred Marriage Astrology is one of four components currently offered within the broader initiative of Sacred Marriage Alchemy which was founded to explore the inter-relationship between expressed dualities such as masculine-feminine, self-other, right-wrong, light-dark, etc. Sacred Marriage Astrology investigates this inter-relationship through astrological observation, interpretation and counseling.

Sacred Marriage Astrology utilizes a Soul-focused approach to the horoscope. Therefore, personal traits, old patterns, great abilities and challenges all are seen from within this Soul-level context. Healing techniques, visualization and journey work, meditation, body and energy development are utilized to assist the individual in embodying their Soul or Self-Essence vibration.

Sacred Marriage Astrology is taught at three levels. The first two levels are presented in class and workshop formats both in-person and over the phone. The first level of learning occurs in the Journey Through the Wheel of Consciousness and the Astro-Energetics courses.

Both of these courses are presented in a 3-day workshop intensive, and a 7-class phone intensive. The second level is made up of the following courses: The Soul's Desire: Interpreting the Soul and Reaching Higher, the Intermediate Course. These courses are presented both in-person and by phone as well. The third level of learning occurs through a variety of advanced work with astrology, energetic alchemy, and multi-dimensional communication. In addition to these stages of learning, there are additional courses offered periodically which address specific astrological or spiritual subjects in greater depth, such as Medicine-Making Through Chiron and Pluto: The Issue of Lack. For information about any course and an upcoming schedule, visit *www.SacredMarriageAstrology.com*.

Sacred Marriage Astrology was founded by Adam Gainsburg, an intuitive guide, healer, and teacher to meet the widening and deepening needs of clients looking for transformational support, beyond the accepted paradigm of mainstream astrology.

A list of current and forthcoming book titles from SMA Communications:

- *Sacred Marriage Astrology: The Soul's Desire for Wholeness* (2005)
- *The Soul's Desire & The Evolution of Identity* (2005)
- *Medicine-Making through Chiron: The Evolution of the Sacred Wound* (2006)
- *Bridges of Union: The Archetypes of Masculine & Feminine Transformation* (2006).
- *The Mars & Venus Journeys: Empowering Our Collective Strength* (2006).

Web site: www.SacredMarriageAstrology.com
Email: info@SacredMarriageAstrology.com
Phone: 323.761.6449

For more information about Adam's other work,
visit www.adamgainsburg.com.

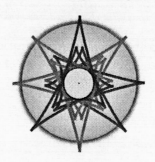

Printed in the United States
48285LVS00004B/67-104

9 781583 850367